PHOTOJOURNALIST
The Life Story of Ara Guler

Biography

Nezih Tavlas

D1719759

"The person running towards an explosion is a photojournal- ist, the one running away from it is a photographer."

Ara Guler

Nezih Tavlas took up photography when he was a student at the Faculty of Journalism in the 1980s. As a reporter, his news photos have been published in both national and international magazines & newspapers. His 18-year journalism career took him to war zones such as Iraq and Somalia. Since ending his career as a journalist, he continues to take documentary photos from street and daily life.

*Dedicated to
my wife Umran & my son Mehmet,
the reasons for my existence.*

Contents

Preface. 10

At Beyoglu Talimhane, in the summer of 1928, 18:00 o'clock..... 13

Mihitaryan Monastery School...15

The Family's New Name..16

The Child Touring Behind Ataturk...17

The War Years..17

Blackout Nights..18

Days of Hardship. 19

The Convict 20

Getronagan Armenian High School..20

Cinema Dream..21

A Studio fire. 22

Cinema Projectionist License. 23

Theater Stage Experience. 25

World Story Competition. 26

The First Camera. 28

Spirits That Provoked the Fishermen..28

First Step into Journalism..29

The Eyuboglu Factor...31

Orhan Veli-Sait Faik. 32

Orhan Kemal...34

Nazi Fan Newspaper Boss. 35

Enrolling in the Institute of Journalism.. 37

Kemal Tahir. 37

The Photos of Nazim Hikmet that He Burned............................38

I'm in the Army Now...39

Tennessee Williams on the Heated Marble Slab. 41

Hello to Turkish Life...43

Argentine Generals. 45

The Istanbul Pogrom of 6/7 September.....................................46

Woman and Allah. 48

Time-Life. 49

The Nurtured Press. 51

The Horse Cart and the Tramway...51

Cannes Film Festival 52

Debauchery in Paris..53

Indigence in Poland. 54

Intervention with the Gallows. 54

The Bloody Price of a Passion for Imagination. 55

In Asik Veysel's Village. 56

Le Tumulus de Nemroud-Dagh. 57

The Uskudar Disaster. 59

Going Places. 60

Fikret Mualla. 61

The Anatolia We Do Not Know. 64

Egg by God. 65

The Discovery of Aphrodisias. 66

Explosion on Babiali Hill. 68

A Star is Born. 68

Riboud Flown From a Truck. 69

Chasing Noah's Ark. 70

In Sophia Loren's Bedroom.. 73

The Onassis Yacht of Celebrities. 74

In The Shanties of Taslitarla. 75

Tunes of the Unplayed Kemencha. 76

Hospitalization in a Mental Hospital 78

Military Coup Days. 79

Farewell to Turkish Life. 82

Master of Leica. 83

Magnum Gang. 85

A Film Proposition to the Spy of the Century. 87

A Fragrant Film.. 89

The Cyprus Crisis. 90

Solitary Wheel Rolling on Its Own. 92

Chasing the Pope. 93

In the Family Homeland. 95

The Greasy Notebook. 97

With Philosopher Bertrand Russell 98

Historian Arnold Toynbee. 101

A Life and Death Situation. 101

15 Vodkas, 4 Cameras. 103

Here It Is, Istanbul Bashing. 104

An Old Friend in Paris. 105

Standing Guard at Charlie Chaplin's Door. 107

A Photojournalist Carries Scissors in his Pocket 108

Mister Shah. 109

In The Palestine Guerilla Camps. 110

Ataturk Culture Center Fire. 111

The Fisherman of Halicarnassus. 111

Picasso. 114

Chagall from Buyukada. 119

Salvador Dali 122

Pitch Black. 127

Control Officer Perihan. 128

Creative Americans. 130

A Serious Business. 136

William Saroyan from Bitlis. 137

A Modicum of Marriage. 138

The Censored Yavuz Documentary. 140

When Europe Meets Asia. 143

Psychic Surgery. 144

Inside Wars. 145

When His Mother Meets his Father. 147

In The Homeland of the Turks. 148

The Woman of His Life. 151

Aragon 152

His Uncle's Separated Legs. 153

Exhibition at the CIA Venue. 154

Bounty Hunters 156

The Crime of Desecrating a Film.. 158

A Market Vendor Punching Salgado. 159

Doctor of Photography 160

5 Kilograms of Ara Guler Photos. 164

Awards and Honors (1961-2008) 195

Books (1960-2008) 196

Exhibitions (1965-2008) 198

Dissertations (1984-1999) 201

Bibliography. 202

Index. 2188

Preface

As the pages of this book turn, narrating the life of the legendary name in photography Ara Guler, you will experience the underlying 80-year history of Turkey in these passages.

You will hold your breath as you read the incredible tales that Ara Guler encountered throughout his life, as he ran after wars, coups, civilizations, disasters and people who changed the fate of the world.

These pages bear witness to the efforts and the price Master Ara Guler ended up paying to be able to be in the right place at the right time. Following Alfred Stieglitz, Ansel Adams, Edward Weston, Henri Cartier-Bresson and Paul Strand, the representatives of the realism movement in photography in the world, Ara Guler, who was raised on the soil of Turkey, claimed his rightful place among these legendary names. His photo-interviews were a cause célèbre because he focused his lens on the individual and photographed the individual without eliminating reality, yet managed to include a similar proportion of aesthetics in his work.

The Editor-in-Chief of Magnum Agency, James A. Fox, described Ara Guler as, "Above all else he is a generous, elegant and witty man. He is one of the best storytellers I know. His life like the lives of many well-known photojournalists is full of anecdotes. These are the living memories of this century which are never reflected on film and only partially caught on camera".

It is evident from the words of Ugur Mumcu, the master of investigative journalism in Turkey, how accurate the name of Nezih Tavlas was in rounding up the *living memories* of a giant such as Ara Guler. While writing about his life Mumcu said, "The number of those involved in investigative journalism in Turkey can be counted on the fingers of one hand. Underdevelopment is rife in this area as well. Nezih Tavlas is one of these few journalists".

Nezih succeeded after arduous labor.

I introduced Ara to Nezih. Perhaps it was because both were journalists, their frequency synced right away. Although Ara was known by all as a rough rider, an he did something he had never done with anyone else before, he opened his heart and his archive to him. He gave his letters, his works, his notebooks, everything that he had never shared with anyone to Nezih. I enjoyed watching their debates based on an immediate mutual trust which was often accompanied with laughter.

Do not think this process was simple; there is no such thing as "Ara narrated and Nezih wrote". I have personally witnessed Nezih working for days and hours in the National Library, the Library of the Turkish Historical Society over a single word uttered by Ara. When you look at the reference section at the end of the book you will understand his diligence.

They did not have the opportunity to meet whenever they wanted because they lived in different cities. Nezih used his weekends and annual leave to meet at every opportunity, and when that was not possible, he took advantage of telephone calls which lasted for hours. However, he always did his homework regarding the era they were working on; he put newspaper clippings from the relevant times, tickets, carnets, photographs, whatever he could lay his hands on to facilitate Ara's memory, and put them in his case. Like a detective, he asked hundreds of questions to uncover the tiniest issue. Although Ara could get frustrated at times with this method, Nezih was able to shed light on many issues and put them in chronological order. In fact, this was instrumental in supplementing Ara's archive with works and news items that were not available. During the interviews which lasted for days and hours and which I observed with interest, I frequently heard Ara's surprised exclamation of "how do you know that?" Or "who told you?" There were issues that Nezih inquired about for which Ara would say "Don't write that," and he would respect it.

Nezih, who Ara would introduce everywhere we went as "My biographer", is one of those people who are not keen on having their names and personalities exposed to the public which is why he delegated the writing of the preface to me and asked me to extend his appreciation for all those who were involved in the book.

I am thrilled to have brought to you the life of a legend such as Ara Guler, whom I have had the honor of working with for 10 years.

With every page you turn, you will feel that terrific sense of humor Master Ara has in his outlook on life, and you will appreciate that the unforgettable images which have been embedded in our minds were not generated merely as a result of chance or coincidence.

Hasan Senyuksel
Istanbul

At Beyoglu Talimhane, in the summer of 1928, 18:00 o'clock …

Hot days in August of 1928...

The Republic of Turkey to which Mustafa Kemal Ataturk had dedicated his life was about to deliver a new baby, and with the excitement of the delivery Mustafa Kemal had not slept all night.

On the ninth of August 1928, a Thursday evening, Ataturk shared this joyous news with the public in Istanbul's Gulhane Park:

"Comrades: we have created new letters to express our beautiful language."

The excitement of the birth as experienced in the delivery of a new alphabet to the Republic was transported to the home of the Derderyan family in Taksim Talihane on the sixteenth of August exactly one week later.

In the evening hours at 16 minutes past 6, after a hot day when the sun had gradually retreated, a new member joined the family.

The baby, who was a home birth with the help of a midwife, was named Ara.

Ara Geghetsik who the baby was named after is the unfortunate king of Ararat also known as "Handsome Ara" in history.

The baby's middle name was given after his grandfather Migirdic in Sebinkarahisar.

Ara Geghetsik who was coveted by the lascivious queen of Babylon Semiramis, regardless of the fact that he was married and had children, rejected her offer and paid for it with his life

Ara's father Dacat, had been sent to Istanbul to study when he was only 6 years old with his mother Maryam with their pockets stuffed with fruit, from the village of Sebinkarahisar Yayci where he was born in 1896. He was the single Kesisogullari who had survived.

When the Derderyan family, which means *son of a monk*, was deported from Sebinkarahisar which was one the cornerstones of rebellion and conflict within the scope of the Armenian Deportation in 1915, Dacat was 19 years old and he never heard from his family again.

Since he had been the lone resident in Ortakoy Tarkamcas boarding school for years, Dacat felt no adversity in walking alone for the subsequent episode of his life. Tarkamcas was the first official Armenian school to be opened in 1875 by Eginli Sinork Migirdic Amira Miricanyan in Istanbul, with the official permission of the state.

As well as going to school Dacat also joined the Kusan Choir of composer priest Gomidas Sogomonyan from Kutahya, comprised of 300 members.

With the help of the parish of the Yerevman Holy Cross Armenian Church, who listened to the recitals of the choir on Sundays with rapture, he finished his schooling and practiced as an apprentice and assistant master in Alalemciyan Pharmacy for a long time. On enrollment in the Darulfunun-i Ottoman Medical Pharmacology School he had realized his biggest dream.

Dacat's closest friend in the Pharmacy School was Suleyman Ferit Eczacibasi. After completing his education and receiving the pharmacology certificate that resembled an order issued by the Sultan with its Ottoman tughra, he enlisted in the Dardanelles War. Dacat, who was enlisted in the medical corps, suffered a leg injury on two occasions.

"Sometimes when my father heard insinuations in the vein of 'you Armenians' he would curse and retort with pride 'while your father worked as a blacksmith I was warring in the Dardanelles.

I lost blood for this country in the Dardanelles, I am a veteran, but tell me what the heck did you do."

Ara's mother Verjin was born in 1903 to a prominent family, the Sahiyans, who moved from Egypt to Istanbul. Araksi, the youngest member of the family who spent summers in Istanbul and winters in Egypt, was born on a ship during one of these passages. Verjin had two brothers named Adurjan and Nisan, and sister named Araksi. Her father Kirkor Efendi from Egypt was among the respectable wealthy in Istanbul. He owned a caulking business near Karakoy equipped with advanced technology of the times with power lathes to repair boats and ships. The employees of Kirkor Efendi who had allocated his repair shop to M.M. (Mudafaa-i Milliye / National Defense), a clandestine organization of the Turkish War of Independence were not recruited to enable the operation of the power lathes.

"That is why Armenian families would beg my grandfather to employ their children in the factory so that they would not be drafted..."

Ara's mother Verjin was kind of a woman who had never even been into the kitchen before as she had servants in the house. The family had to move to a bigger house with the birth of Ara because a nanny had to be also recruited. They moved into an apartment in Taksim, the Ankara Palas Apartment in Beyoglu Talimhane, Sehit Muhtar Bey Street, Safak Apartment, number 4.

Verjin, boasting as "I am a smart woman, I had only one child", submitted the upbringing of Ara into the hands of nanny Agavni.

"My family was a quite wealthy family. I was the only son of the owner of the pharmaceutical warehouse in Beyoglu. I had been brought up well. I was not a naughty kid."

Ara was a quiet child who played nicely in the corner with his tin soldiers.

"The first major incident I remember: We had a summer place in Yakacik or its vicinity at that time. I was hit by a bicycle and fell ill. I was around four years old or thereabouts. That was the first calamity I experienced."

The household had a white cat called Ciconi, named by young Ara. The name did not mean anything, it just sounded nice.

Ara was introduced to visual arts at an early age by his nanny.

"There used to be a cemetery from the current Divan Hotel to the current Officers' Club. It used to be an Armenian cemetery and there was also a music hall. That was the first time I saw artists such as Safiye Ayla. But I was just a kid at that time. So why was I taken there? I had a nanny whose brother worked in the music hall as a waiter. She took me there so she could talk with her brother. That was how I got to listen to the famous singers like Safiye."

Ara's first experience with photography took place in a studio which specialized in taking family portraits in Beyoglu. Ever since Ara was a baby his father had had him dressed up and took him to these studios at every opportunity to have his photograph taken, sometimes with his nanny and sometimes alone. This family tradition continued until Ara reached a mature age.

14

Mihitaryan Monastery School

Migirdic Ara Derderyan had been raised with "nannies, servants, in cotton wool and silks" until he was sent off to a Catholic Missionary School established by the Mihitaryan Monastery in 1825 publicly recognised as Pangalti High school. Although the family was Gregorian they preferred the Catholic Mihitryan Monastery School to ensure that their child received a good education.

"On the way to Pangalti High School, I remember that I used to pass by tram in front of a low wall. Sometimes I would hang onto the end of the tramway but it was a bit scary..."

Since its establishment it was a tradition that thePrinciple's seat of this popular minorities school in Istanbul was always filled by a Mekhitarist priest. It was Ara's luck that with the establishment of the Republic, this tradition changed and the Principle's seat was passed onto modern teachers. "

When Ara started school at Karabat Kurkciyanwas the Principle who was also teaching chemistry at Galatasaray High SchoolThe other teachers in the school were also teaching at Robert College. The legendary name of the school came from the strict teachers and difficult education because the ones who could graduate were easily accepted by the universities. Almost all of his classmates who graduated went to the USA, found jobs and already settled in.. Most of the graduates went to be doctors and engineers. Parents who sent their children to this school paid a high fee for this privilege.

"Rich kids studied here, middle class kids could not attend, do you understand? Lots of money was paid and people would boast as 'my child is a student there'."

The school, which was managed with strict rules, accepted only male students. Although the students lived in Istanbul they were not allowed to set foot outside the school until Saturday at noon, because it was a boarding school.

The curriculum was in French and the students were offered violin, flute and piano lessons. These lessons were not optional. It was out of question that any student failing in these subjects would pass the year.

As a result of these mandatory music lessons, Ara learned a lot and developed his ear for music he watched his mother Verjin play the piano at home with interest.

"Would you believe me if I said that I never opened a book while I was a student... how could that be?
I was already a smart kid. I passed all my classes. My less strong grades were in music because I did not practice. I was a brilliant student but I did not cram to be the best."

Dacat, who owned one of the eight pharmacies in Beyoglu, operated a pharmacy in partnership with his colleague Panosyan at number 16 Hacopulo Han in Beyoglu. This establishment was associated with major well-known brands such as Kanzuk and Rebul. The Silva brand colognes manufactured in Dacat's pharmacy were famous. He would prepare a box containing the lemon cologne and give it to his son Ara to take to his classmate Ferit Eczacibasi. In response, Ferit Eczacibasi would send his own creation of cologne called "Gold Drop" to Dacat...

> "These men were very successful chemists. Currently pharmacies know nothing about chemistry, they sell drugs like a store, they have price tags. Formerly pharmacists used to prepare medicines, they knew how to do that to the last milligram. The doctors would write the milligram of the drug on the prescription, the pharmacist would know what to do and prepared it in a mortar and mixed it with a pestle. The customers would collect the medicine in the late afternoon."

The Family's New Name

Pharmacist Dacat had "Kesisogullari" deleted from the "family name, in other words moniker and title" section of the birth certificate and had it replaced with Guler after the enactment of the Surname Law in 1934. The letterheads titled "Panosyan & D. Derderyan Pharmaceutical Warehouse" and the business cards with Dacat Derderyan were put away.

Small Ara who helped his father every now and then at the pharmacy was also affected by this change. His school records and the report cards he brought home were written as Migirdic Ara Guler. The family spent the winter months in the house in Beyoglu and the summers in the house that they rented from the reeve of Suadiye , Hilmi Bey the permanent member of CHP (social-democratic, The Republican People's Party), . Almost the whole neighborhood was comprised of dignitaries of the Peoples' Party, members of parliament and ministers. Ara's family was also a supporter of CHP.

During the summer when he turned 8, he and his cousin Sona ran away from their grandfather's house in Kadikoy.

> "We went as far as we could go. We went all the way from the Altiyol junction to beyond Kiziltoprak! How far! And on foot...Then we got scared and turned back. Turning back was harder. I don't know why we went, I can't remember. We left with the intention of not returning."

He believes he had an uneventful childhood but I think his mother's opinion on the issue should be sought:

> "I would lie down on the railroad rails in front of the house in Suadiye because I wanted to see how the train's switches operated as it put on the brake. Usually the Ankara Express would pass at 7.15 o'clock... I was curious to see how the brakes operated, how the brake pads clamped. I had to see from close range... Once I was sitting on the rail waiting for the train to come, another train came on the rails that I was sitting on! I was trapped between the two lines. I hit the ground immediately. One train was passing on my left and another on my right. At that moment my mother was looking out of the window, saw me and fainted right away."

This incident did not only frighten his mother it frightened Ara as well. During that time, he developed erysipelas from a skin infection beneath his chin by coincidence and it was tied to this incident to make Ara be scared and settle down.

> "After the incident was I scared or what... I got erysipelas. I wasn't aware of being frightened. They took me to a doctor. My chin was swollen. They dissected me here. See! The scar remains underneath my beard."

The Child Touring Behind Ataturk

When Ara was in third grade, Turkey lost Mustafa Kemal Ataturk, the founder of the Republic, on the 10th of November 1938.

Dacat took his 10-year-old son Ara to Dolmabahce Palace where the body of Ataturk was resting:

"I remember him, my father took me. Soldiers were passing, everybody was weeping, you know. We were standing in silence, paying homage. There were torches burning in Taksim, a ceremony was carried out but the principal issue was who would take Ataturk's place..."

Small Ara knew Ataturk from Florya.

In the summer months, the family would go to Kalitarya (which is currently known as Senlikkoy) to go swimming. After a walk through the woods to reach Florya beach, you could see Deniz Mansion commissioned for Ataturk

A pavilion was planned here because Ataturk had gone swimming a few times and liked the beach. According to the project the railway would be taken further back, the pavilion would be built on a hill at the end of the beach and a *bath venue* would be prepared below.

However, Ataturk said that he did not want to segregate himself from the people by saying, 'In Ankara I live on a mountain, in Istanbul I am imprisoned in the Palace; here let me see those who come and go, at least let me hear the train'.

"The other part of the beach was reserved for families. We always went swimming there. Ataturk would row in a small square stern canoe. There are photographs of children hanging around Ataturk, perhaps I was one of them, I could have been, I don't know. I had seen Ataturk many times because he would sit there in his striped bathing suit and there were no barriers. "

The War Years

Not even one year had passed since Turkey lost the founder of the Republic, Mustafa Kemal Ataturk, when Germany attacked Poland and the threat of war was manifest. 11-year-old Ara was sitting in a mulberry tree when the Second World War broke.

Dacat had settled himself in a deck chair in the garden of the wooden 10-room mansion that they rented in Bostanci. It was right behind the station with 360 fruit trees, and he was trying to read the news about the war. When Ara dropped the mulberries off he tree onto the newspaper, he shouted at the top of his voice, "Son, a war is starting, you have no idea".

"So, a war had begun, and I did not actually even know what a war was..."

During the war Dacat would listen to the speeches of Adolf Hitler, uncertain of where he would attack next, and news in the evenings on his Atwaterkent brand radio. These radio broadcasts - which reached Turkey from Berlin - were the fruit of the devilish tactics of the Nazi Propaganda Minister, Joseph Goebbels. He planned these broadcasts to be made on five separate continents, in 53 different languages. Moreover, in addition to enabling the delivery of news before it was published the next day in the newspapers, the radio was free of the censorship that was applied on newspapers after the declaration of martial law in Istanbul immediately after the start of the war.

The text, pictures and drawings of the newspapers were scrutinized to shreds and whatever remained had to be printed as a single column and the headlines could not exceed twenty-four font size regardless of how striking they might be. This is why the newspapers were printed as two sheets.

During one of those days while the war raged with all its violence, Charlie Chaplin, whose every film Ara had watched with great admiration, was a guest on the Turkish broadcast of Voice of America.

The famous artist, whose film the *The Great Dictator* in which the Chaplin character makes fun of Hitler, was on everybody's agenda. On the broadcast, he said 'I want to tell you a story. It is the best and most pleasant story I have heard in all my life. This is a story by Nasreddin Hodja "and he tells the Hodja's story where he replies with the famous joke punchline, "Are you going to believe me or the donkey?"

The program ended with Chaplin's words: 'Yes my dear listeners. Today the whole world is occupied with the same question: Shall we believe the people or the donkey?" When Vatan newspaper published this dialogue of the artist in which he replaced Hitler with a 'donkey' the newspaper was shut down for two months.

Blackout Nights

The Inonu administration, concerned that the German army might attack Thrace and Istanbul at any moment, established the Cakmak Line comprised of barbed wire and barriers from the Black Sea to the Marmara. Their purpose was to stop German units, and blackout measures were implemented at night - in cities where martial law had been declared – to protect against possible air strikes.

Ara was afraid of these blackout nights.

During blackout evenings, the street lamps were put out and black curtains, which prevented any seepage of light, were hung on every window of every house. Night watchmen sounded warnings and sometimes late at night they would sound the war sirens and fire blank anti-aircraft rockets one after the other to familiarize the people with the sounds.

Dacat fitted the windows of the house with iron shutters to prevent light from seeping out.

"There was a blackout. One day we went to visit my aunt in Buyukdere. We were woken up at 2.00 am by a lot of noise. We looked across the water at the Anatolian side where lights were burning. A German airplane was in the sky and our anti-aircraft operators were trying to shoot it down with the aid of projectiles. It was downed on the other side. After this event, we made airplane noises with our mouths at school to scare each other. "

Ara even built himself a bunker.

"It was the era of the Nazis... We kept seeing the propaganda journals perpetuated by Goebbels. I was only 12-13 years old but I followed them all."

Perhaps that is why Ara, who learned to use a weapon at an early age and who was often taken hunting by his uncles, had a Winchester rifle. One day when he was practicing shooting cans that he had placed in a row, he shot his uncle who was passing behind the row of cans in the shoulder. When the building on Tosbaga Street in Beyoglu became insufficient for Dacat, he started construction on the adjacent plot that he owned. He couldn't expand in the building he was in because the lower floor was leased to ironmonger Recep Usta and the ice seller Aleko, and the top floors had been leased to the white Russians working in Rejans.

"Of course, the cement ran out halfway through the work. Who in their right mind started to build in the middle of a war? The Germans are entering Poland and what were they doing!"

In those days, everyone was on pins and needles in Turkey on account of the war.

The letter presented by German Ambassador Franz von Papen at the beginning of 1941 to Inonu was not enough to alleviate the people's concerns.

Hitler guaranteed President Ismet Inonu that German troops would stop 50 km from the Turkish borders, but on the other hand allied states were trying to pull Ankara into the war.

Days of Hardship

Turkey did not enter the war; however, the impact of the war was felt in the four corners of the country. The war brought on a myriad of problems: sickness, rising cost of living, widespread black-marketing, price hike of bread, increase in lung diseases such as tuberculosis due to malnutrition and lack of medicine, people trying to sweeten their tea with raisins, people eating kochia seeds, people seeking food in garbage cans, even begging for bread. These had become familiar problems.

Due to the solid economic status of his family, Ara was not very much affected by those years of hardship. The days of the Second World War were memorable to him for the blackout nights and the ration cards for bread which the public held onto until the last day.

"Bread was rationed. Officers would write on the pages of the population identity booklet if someone bought rice. My family was quite wealthy so we did not feel the impact so much."

President Ismet Inonu managed to avoid getting Turkey involved in the Second World War with maneuvers like, "The children are without bread but let us not deprive them of their fathers".

"I remember very well, a propaganda journal named Signal was being published by the Germans in every language and it was delivered to Turkey. I now remember that this journal printed beautiful photographs of the war. When I became a photojournalist, I looked up to that journal, in fact I have a copy of this journal that was printed subsequently."

The war affected everything including Ara's education. After the Nazis lost the war, all the German teachers in the school were collected and deported to Kutahya.

"The lessons continued in French, so what, it was not so difficult..."

He was familiar with French already. In fact, he had even studied in Galatasaray High School for a short time. One of the teacher friends of his father who was a mathematician in Galatasaray High School said to his father, "You live here and send your child to Pangalti, is it not a pity, why do you not enroll him here?" Subsequently Dacat asked his influential friends to intervene and enrolled his son Ara into Galatasaray High School. It did not seem strange to him that he went to boarding school only 25 meters from his home because he was used to the disciplined schooling of the Catholics.

"I continued there for a while. Subsequently, my father's obstinacy manifested again and he enrolled me in an Armenian school."

The Convict

Ara was an avid reader who read everything that he could lay his hands on and he also wrote stories in his own right. He sent a short story 'The Convict' to *Haber Aksam Postasi (Evening News Post)* newspaper's children's page.

His story, which was published in May of 1946, manifested an imagination and logical reasoning that is rarely found in a senior student in secondary school.

The Convict

Darkness had pervaded the very depths of his soul. Light entering through a small hole up above as if through a thin reed formed a point of white light in a dark corner. The dark had extinguished his heart and soul. Remembering the past was like a killer blow for him. Silence... from time to time those who are subjected to torture scream painfully sounding no different from owls. In the dark his eyes resemble the eyes of an owl which have lost their light.

The iron door of his cell creaked open. The rusty iron door opened with a lot of noise revealing a strange face which declared its fondness for inflicting torture.

The convict put his hands on his knees to gather strength to get up and started walking from the narrow and lengthy cell without even looking at the three armed guards who were watching him.

Strange faces were watching along the small holes on the other iron doors along the corridor as they wanted to be in his place, as if they rejoiced in this situation he was in. These were criminals with life sentences. A guillotine had been prepared outside. The director of the prison and a few persons were waiting for the ceremony to start and be over with as soon as possible. The priest finished his prayer and walked the convict calmly to the gallows surrounded by bayonets.

His gaze was far away. He was thinking about his mother, the mother of whose only child he was. Without a glance at the prepared guillotine he took a piece of folded paper and a watch from his pocket and extended them to the priest saying;

'This paper is for you and I request that you hand this watch to my mother' and started to ascend the steps slowly to the gallows. Everyone was quiet. Suddenly this silence was broken by clanging of iron on iron, the director and the others returned to their places, the sentence had been executed.

The paper handed to the priest contained a sad song composed by the convict.

Pangalti High School, 8th grader Ara Guler.

Getronagan Armenian High School

After completing Secondary School at Pangalti High School Ara enrolled in Getronagan Armenian High School. Even though the status did not quite match the school he had finished, the foundations of this school had been laid by Patrik Nerses Varjabedyan and was a prominent educational institute providing services since 1886. The curriculum consisted of lessons such as Armenian, Ottoman, Farsi, arithmetic, industrial chemistry, accounting, law, stenography, and metallurgy. More importantly there were girls in the classes. After the strict rules and discipline of the Catholic School, he was so relieved that he did not even bother getting schoolbooks for the new school.

> "I went to a very tough school. The school was much tougher than any college. One school was top notch, the other school was regular... and I was full of mischief of all sorts. Every weekend we would party with girls."

He did not neglect horseback riding during the time after school.

> "There used to be a manege next to Sipahi Ocagi (Ottoman Cavalry Corps) that is currently Harbiye Officers' Club. We would go horseback riding there. The horse I leased was Inonu's former horse. I would lease it the most and they would let me have him."

The days had come when he would pound the pavement on the streets of Istanbul with girls sitting in front of his balloon-tired Raleigh bicycle. He would skip school and drag his feet on the pavement from the tramway. He followed fashion from the *Perde-Sahne (Stage-Curtain)* journal and consequently he and his friends bought Borsalino style hats from the stores in Pera and roamed Beyoglu with panache:

> "Everyone had Borsalino hats, a man without a hat was not even considered a man."

Dacat, who had separated ways with his partner and changed the signboard over the shop to "Dacat Guler Pharmacy Warehouse", noticed these changes in Ara and started to look for remedies to prevent his son from being a 'layabout' because he did not display a voluntary willingness for learning. It was clear that Ara had no intention of becoming a doctor or pharmacist as his family wished.

Cinema Dream

Ihsan Ipekci, the father of Ismail Cem and owner of Ipek Film Company, was one of Pharmacist Dacat's best customers. He sold chemicals used in the development of film, acetone and adthesives to Monsieur Franco, owner of Saray Cinema who was Ipekci's partner. Ipekci had shot *Ankara Postasi*, the first film they shot together with Muhsin Ertugrul, who was continuously supplied with makeup materials and creams by Dacat. Dacat requested his friend, the owner of Ipekci studios, to engage his son Ara as an 'apprentice'.

As Ara started to frequent the studios he became passionate about films. He never missed any films that were shown in the cinema, and he started to watch them with interest over and over again.

Dacat, who noticed his son's interest in the cinema, bought him a 35 mm Ernemann Kinox III brand film projector as a new year's gift. The Ernemann, manufactured by the German Krupp company, was one of the top models in cinema of the era and was a very expensive gift.

Ara was so delighted with the film projector that he took it to school and family gatherings and started showing films.

Ara went to Ipek Film every Saturday to collect a suitcase full of films which he got for free. All that came out of his pocket was the tip he paid to the porter who carried the huge film spools with 301 meters of film each.

"I took extinct films from Ipekci's man that they did not know what to do with for 3,5 lira. Stacks of film for 3,5 lira... Of course the boss had told the man, 'Give films to Dacat's son every Saturday'. So, I would go and give the man a tip with the money of that era and collect ten rolls of film and play them. If I kept them, I would be the owner of the richest film library in the world. What films there were... I played them. When I got bored with them, I went to get the new ones."

The films were of major interest but something was missing because they were silent.

"When I was a kid I was like an inventor, I would mix everything and try things. I could connect batteries in parallel, make panels and try to invent something like remote control."

In his own way, Ara put his name to various inventions; he worked with the idea of an exciter lamp for days to transform his silent film projector into one with sound and finally he succeeded in his endeavors to add sound to the films he played.

Ara's favorite film was Mahser (Apocalypse). It was not on the market. He bought it from Ipek Film with his own pocket money . It depicted the collapse of the world.

"I turned the ground floor of the mansion with the garden in Bostanci into a cinema. My friends would come over and we would play films. In winter, we would play them at our house. I would pretend to leave the house to deceive my mother and sneak back in and we would watch movies in the back room with friends."

However, he overdid the film playing bit.

"I was absent from school and flunked for three years to play films. My family thought I went to school but I went elsewhere and played films. My family must have known, they went and paid the school for one more year."

Film playing did not only disrupt Ara's schooling, it became an obsession:

"Film posters would be hung on the walls of the Armenian Cemetery stretching from the current Divan Hotel to Harbiye Sipahi Ocagi. I would take down those posters. The ones that were newly adhered were easy to remove. I made a poster collection with them."

Ara's adventure in the film industry ended with an incident that made everyone feel their heartbeat in their throats...

A Studio Fire

It was during the days when he frequented the Dogan Film Studio.

At that time cinema halls were glutted with an influx of Arab films. Dogan Film Studio was prepared to dub the films of Yusuf Vehbi, Abdulvahap and Ummu Gulsum, which filled the cinema halls, in Turkish. Young Ara was among great names such as Cahide Sonku, Ferdi Tayfur and his sister Adalet Cimcoz, Safiye Ayla, Cem Karaca's father Mehmet Karaca and Mahmut

Morali. Ara admired the skills of Joachim Filmerides who worked as a sound technician in the studio:

> "This Greek of Turkish origin was the great technician of that time. The man re-made the machine from scratch. Never mind repairing it, he re-invented it you know. They were weird men."

While one of the films of Egyptian Yusuf Vehbi was being voice overed in the studio, one of the technicians came and said "I prepared a new trailer, come and see, I think it is a bit long," and called everyone to the small studio in the back. They watched the trailer and went back to work, but the technician forgot to turn off the exciter lamp reflecting sound and it ignited and started burning. Ara, who was unaware of the fire but was curious as to why the temperature in the studio has suddenly increased, opened the door and encountered flames. The flames ignited the sack material that had been used to cover the walls for soundproofing.

> 'Damn we are burning!' I say. Just as we were exiting I remembered my coat was inside! I went back. I went to get my coat. I was going to save myself from the fire but a man was running in front of me and closing every door he goes through to shut the fire out and delay it reaching him. But I am right behind and he did not notice me. All around the fireburning. I stuck my foot in every door because the studio doors are one sided, and if they are closed then I am trapped inside. Thus, I managed to throw myself out of the studio and the man in front of me did not have a clue. I moved onto the roof, and there was no other place for me to go, and stayed there. I watched the fire. If the roof started burning I would have jumped onto the adjacent roof."

The fire brigade arrived in time and Ara descended with the ladder that was extended to him. He was the last man to be saved from the fire.

His father watched the fire and his son on the roof a few meters away from his pharmacy in terror:

> "I was the last person to get on the roof. I was also the last to get rescued from the roof because the fireman saw me last. My father was watching the fire. After that day, my mother was afflicted with diabetes because of the fire and the injuries I sustained. My father said 'no more studios for you, your filmmaking days are over. No more going into studios for you'."

After that event, Ara who was also very frightened by the fire, never set foot inside a studio again.

Cinema Projectionist License

Everything progressed just as depicted in the film *Cinema Paradiso* by Italian director Giuseppe Tornatore. Ara was Salvotore (Toto) the kid who was passionate about cinema in the film, and Nubar Usta, the machine operator who taught Ara all the tips of the trade, was Alfredo. The studio burned just like the cinema that was incinerated as a result of films being ignited by an overheated lamp.

> "The famous Cinema Paradiso depicts my life exactly, it is as if I am acting there..."

Furthermore, this incident completely annulled the tolerance his father had for Ara flunking his classes, and he was given a tough ultimatum to make up for the three-year loss immediately so that he could graduate sooner than later.

"My father kept me out of studios. So this time I became a projectionist, but I only did it during summers."

When Nubar Usta, the projectionist of Yildiz Cinema would sneak off to visit his lady friend, the projection booth of Yildiz Cinema would be left with Ara who managed it very well. However, in those days it was necessary to acquire a projectionist's license to play the films which were very flammable and could ignite like gasoline at the slightest heat.

There was even a law about how to carry out this hazardous work in the line of 'measures that have to be taken inside a projection booth'. Ara applied to the Department of Public Works and Engineering of the Municipality which was the office responsible to grant this license. He sat the exam together with Orhan Aksoy, who would then become a director, making 91 films and writing 43 scenarios.

"Well, I have spent my whole life with cinema films, I know all the maneuverings involved in synchronization, montage, film processing, all about voice over techniques and yet everyone in the country has become a filmmaker except me..."

However, the certificate which carried the title "Istanbul Municipality Department of Public Works and Engineering Cinema Projectionist License" signed by Mr. Ali, a friend of his father and projectionist of Ar cinema, could not prevent the second accident.

From every film that he liked, Ara cut frames and established a small cinema library for himself. In fact, he expanded the activity to create films of his own. For every roll of film, which were meters long, a spare length of 1 meter of empty film would be allocated to wrap in the next film spool. Ara would collect these empty white frames, draw figures of Mickey Mouse with drawing ink and subsequently present them to his viewers.

After returning from the beach with his cousins Mayda and Sona to their summer house in Suadiye, , at one of the displays of the films in Ara's collection (which was the only form of entertainment), a lit match caused the films to ignite.

The ensuing fire caused his aunt's hand and half of the house to burn.

This time Dacat sent his son Ara to the radio factory of the Geseryanlar in Beyoglu, who were the distributors of His Master's Voice Company in Turkey, to keep him out of mischief. At that time, the venue which was called a factory was actually a modest assembly workshop where radio parts of the German brand Blaupunkt were put together. The owner was Aram Geseryan, a friend of Dacat. His son, who was Ara's classmate, had a shop near Tunel called Bazar Du Levant which sold bags, suitcases, giftware and luxury consumables. The Geseryans from Kayseri whose distributorship was carried out by Vehbi Koc in Ankara, was the wealthiest family in Turkey. Ara enjoyed going to the Geseryan workshop where wood cased radios with lamps were assembled. He had the opportunity to use his skills in invention and also receive an allowance, albeit small

"I had technical sickness! At that time, there were these big lamps, I knew them all. I could tell the lamp number from the way I felt it in my hand, I knew by rote where it would go."

Ara's filmmaking was cut off by his father so he steered towards the theater which was one of the professions on his maternal side. The fact that one of the grandmothers in the family had been an actress with the Minakyan Theater, also known as Ottoman Drama Company, had always attracted him from when he was small. It steered him to a new world, the theater, which would shape his life.

Theater Stage Experience

The pharmacy was a haunt by actors and actresses because his father manufactured makeup materials, too.

"The theater people who performed at Tepebasi Theater visited my father's pharmacy for sure. Behzat Butak, Huseyin Kemal Gurmen, Talat Artemel were all friends of my father. They used to have their morning coffees at my father's pharmacy and then went to rehearsals."

Muhsin Ertugrul, Behzat Butak, Muammer Karaca, Resit Gurzap, Vasfi Riza Zobu, and Bedia Muvahhit would all come and get the special creams manufactured by Dacat.

Dacat had named one of these special creams he manufactured with the AR of Ara and DA of Dacat as AR-DA. The flyers printed for ARDA cream in Turkish and French said "(ARDA) creams, manufactured according to scientific basis and most recent applications is made exclusively from healthy and beneficial contents, a true companion of youth and beauty has just been released on the market".

Another very popular product manufactured by Dacat was his bitter almond cream, BIRI-CIK.

"He was a kind of man who invent creams, powders. My father's best product was Biricik bitter almond cream. There used to be advertisements on the Water Administration building in Taksim. One of these advertisements was for my father's Biricik bitter almond creams."

One of the faithful customers of the creams and makeup materials manufactured by his father was Muhsin Ertugrul, the founder of modern Turkish theater. He was a close friend of his father and they met frequently. Although Muhsin Ertugrul was a very strict man, he had said nothing to Ara running around backstage when he was 7-8 years old.

"I grew up in the theater. The theater was my second school, my home. I would roam about backstage, in the actors' makeup rooms, on set. I would watch actors apply makeup and wait for their turn, I was mesmerized. My love for the theater and art establishments hails from that time. I always wanted to be a playwright, stage manager."

Ara observed Huseyin Kemal Gurmen and Vasfi Riza Zobu on stage, watched the plays of Necip Fazil Kisakurek, Nazim Hikmet, Vedat Nedim Tor, Resat Nuri Guntekin and Mahmut Ekrem for 25 times on average without getting bored. When he started acting lessons at the Theater School established by Muhsin Ertugrul there was no conservatory in Turkey. Mucap Ofluoglu, Berc Fazli, Hamit Akinli, Ismet Ay, and Gulriz Sururi were his classmates. Ara, who was very excited by the courses he attended, had different expectations. He did not want to be an actor like the others, he wanted to live and breathe theater. He enjoyed and comprehended the most when he watched the theater from backstage. He wanted to be the man that prepared that world...

For that he had to see the world.

"The sons of the Movado watch seller across the British Consulate and Ananya restaurant in Tepebasi were my friends. He had a car, we got money from our fathers and got in the car. We went abroad. We went to many places; Italy, Switzerland, France, Spain, all the way to Portugal.... We arranged staying withacquaintances and sometimes we stayed at hotels."

In 1948 Ara witnessed a fire at the Academy of Fine Arts that his relative Osgan Efendi had established together with Osman Hamdi. In addition to 12,000 books that were in the library, the fire destroyed two giant compositions on both sides of the great hall by Velazquez and Goya. Priceless paintings, statues, crystal chandeliers, massive carpets were turned to ashes.

"We were living in Talimhane at that time, I saw the sky had turned crimson. There were not too many apartments on the hill at that time. The fire continued all night until morning. There were some original paintings among them, you know there were paintings by Rafaello that Osman Hamdi had brought at a time, and books were destroyed."

World Story Competition

When he was 20 years old he wrote a one act play "A Strange New Year's Eve". This was the ninth play he wrote.
"I tore them uplater. Everyone scribbles poetry and stuff when they are young... That is what those plays were. I wrote them because I loved theater."

He became involved in the theater troupe of Pangalti High School Graduates Association/Alumni and set up a cast that would turn professionals green with envy. They staged Eugene O'Neill's *Anna Christie* as well as other plays.

The contribution of having read nearly all the 496 literary classics that the legendary Minister of Education of the times, Hasan Âli Yucel, had introduced into Turkish language cannot be minimized.

You could easily notice the impact of John Steinbeck and Jack London in his initial work of Ara's:

"You are right. How do you imagine we learned them all by rote, you would be amazed! Today nobody knows a literary work as well as we did. I am telling you, by the time I finished high school, I had pretty much read all the world classics. "

In July 1950 when he saw the story competition announcement in *Yeni Istanbul* newspaper accompanied with the slogans "Looking for the best story in the world" and "First prize 5,000 dollars", he sent his work 'A Strange New Year's Eve' that he had turned into a narration to the World Story Competition. The competition was organized jointly by *Yeni Istanbul and NewYork Herald Tribune* newspapers.

After thorough scrutiny by a jury consisting of names such as Orhan Veli, Ahmet Hamdi Tanpinar, Memduh Sevket Esendal, Sabahattin Eyuboglu and Refik Halid Karay, Ara's 'A Strange New Year's Eve' was one of the 30 works amongst 422 stories that the jury found worth publishing. First prize went to 'Uncle Sam' by Samim Kocagoz, second place went to Orhan Kemal's "Father", and third place was given to 'A Compassionate Woman' by Necdet Okmen. Works by Orhan Hancerlioglu and Vus'at O. Bener were also among ranking stories.

The newspaper started to present the stories that were found worth publishing and which had been awarded 30 liras to readers, accompanied by the signatures of the authors. When it was the turn of 'A Strange New Year's Eve' it was noted that this work was not signed. There was not sufficient space to print the continuation of the unclaimed story and it was announced that it would be published the next day. Ara had entered the competition with the pseudonym Ali Ihsan Aygun.

"I changed my name when I entered the competition, I thought they would not award me if they knew I was Armenian. After the awards were announced I went and told them my name is Ara Guler."

The next day the story in the newspaper was accompanied with the signature of Ara Guler but with the following note:

"The story 'A Strange New Year's Eve' was submitted to the competition under the pseudonym Ali Ihsan Aygun and the second copy which had to be in a closed envelope did not have the real author's name written in it. Last night after the page was set the author informed our administration of his real name and proved that he was the author of the story. Therefore, only the last part of the story could be published with the real name of the author."

When 'A Strange New Year's Eve' was published in Armenian in parish newspapers *Marmara* and *Jamanak,* he lost himself in the magic of writing and his writing being admired. Stories that he wrote "Return of the Crow", "The Bass", "The Man Who Ascended from the Hill", "The Flies in the Foam", and "Some Strange Strikes" were published by *Hantes Misaguyti,* a publishing organ of Getronagan School Graduates Association, San, a publishing organ of Mihitaryan School Graduates Association, and *Surp Pirgic* published by the Yedikule Surp Pirgic Armenian Hospital. His stories written in Armenian were published by the weekly *Carakayt* newspaper published by Turcologist Hacik Bedros Amiryan. He also wrote for the same newspapers as a cinema critic; it would be rather difficult for them to find anyone else who watched so many films.

Ara was obliged to sit for the Maturity Examination to start at the university because Dacat did not consider these jobs as a profession.

He stood before a Delegation of Examiners comprised of teachers from various schools in Istanbul Erkek Lisesi, which used to be the Public Debts building at one time.

"Can it be said that I did not intend to study, but I was sort of forced. My father wanted me to be a doctor because he had the pharmacy, who else was he going to leave it to, me being an only child? Anyway, at that time I became interested in journalism."

The First Camera

He was 22 years old when he bought his first camera with the money given by his father. It was a Rolleicord II from the shop of Monsieur Kalimeros who sold photography materials in the Tunnel. At that time, all journalists in Cagaloglu used this camera. It was one of the good cameras.

He started to take photographs of everything in front of him, everything he saw. This caught the attention of those around. One of the neighbors could bear it any longer and asked one day:

"My son, do you always take pictures like this?"

"Yes uncle, I always take pictures like this. I am getting accustomed to it."

"In other words, I was taking photographs, taking pictures. Of course, these cannot be really considered photographs. For instance, I remember shooting a reflection in water, I shot stuff like that like amateurs do now."

He was dying of curiosity how the photographs would turn out after they had been taken. However, processing the photographs and printing them was rather costly.

"There was a shop in Kurtulus Han at the corner of Tosbaga Street. It belonged to a Jew named Judas Salti. He had a dark room whereas I didn't. He was a street photographer. He knew nothing but he had the processing material, the dark room. I'd go there to process some film and he used to charge me five photographs for one because I was a rich kid!"

Under these circumstances, he was obliged to take over the section above his father's pharmacy used as a warehouse and transform it into a dark room.

"In my childhood when we spent summers on the island, we had a joint boat with friends that we called Pirasa (Leek). We would mostly take the boat and go to the coast on the other side of the island. We would take a short cut through the potato field of the horse-cart owner's wife, a Greek lady of Turkish origin, go to a high place and wait for the sunset, and catch the moment when the crimson of the sun touched the sea. I would take artistic photographs like that. Whereas the sun has been setting for 400 million years and there I am making art. The approach in terms of photography in Turkey has remained caught between my boat called Pirasa, the lady's potato field, and romantic sunsets."

Ara found his rising passion for journalism by having his stories printed in the parish newspapers published in Istanbul. He worked with all the Armenian newspapers published by his father's friends. He was involved in art events. However, among them all *Jamanak* was different. *Jamanak* was one of the oldest newspapers which was printed immediately after the declaration of the Second Constitutional Era in 1908, and it was also the first newspaper to publish the photographs taken by Ara Guler.

Spirits That Provoked the Fishermen

He chose Kumkapi fishermen as a subject for his first interview:

"I like taking photographs of fishermen very much. I enjoy sitting with them, drinking tea together, chatting. Fishermen are very decent people. However, the work they do is hard, it is a tricky business. After all they are combating nature. Still they live a sweet life."

The 4x5 inch Speed Graphic camera was equipped with a flash bulb that he used during his first years as a photojournalist.

He set sail with the fishermen and photographed every moment of their work for days.

"I took the famous photograph from the Kumkapi fishermen's interview 'Return to port in the morning light' on that trip. With the mosque in the background, it is morning..."

He almost managed to make the new Rolleicord II camera talk for the Kumkapi interview he prepared for *Jamanak,* but already during his first interview he got himself into trouble.

During the hardship of the war days, habitual drinkers had a hard time affording raki so they started drinking methylated alcohol. The production of raki had decreased whereas 'methylated spirit' was booming. Even if the country's economy was picking up slightly, those with a low-income level kept on with this dangerous habit due to economic reasons. Ara wrote in the interview for *Jamanak* that the Kumkapi fishermen were drinking spirits. As soon as the newspaper was out, fishermen stormed the paper saying that all fishermen had been presented to the public like 'alcoholics'.

"I wrote that they drank spirits for the hell of it, and the blighters stormed the paper."

Neither the Editor in Chief of *Jamanak* Ara Kocunyan, nor Ara could forget the hours they spent trying to appease the angry fishermen. Ara was quite frightened of the reaction that he got with his first interview at the very beginning of this profession.

First Step into Journalism

Parish newspapers were alright but Ara wanted to work with newspapers with a wider clientele and share his photographs with a wider audience.

Ara liked the most ostentatious newspaper of the time *Yeni Istanbul* very much

The tenants living upstairs and his father's poker pal, Lawyer Abdulkadir Ozgen, had a good relationship with the newspaper's management. On account of his intervention Ara started working as a reporter at the *Yeni Istanbul* newspaper, which had published his story when he was a young writer. He was assigned to cover art events but because he owned a camera, the editorial department sent him everywhere. He attended exhibition galas as well as the arrival of the American fleet. Covering murders like a police reporter, as well as sitting behind the goalposts like a sports reporter, taught him a lot.

"Working as a sportscaster you learn to catch the moment behind the goal post. I enjoyed trying to capture the moment. Everyone was pleased. There! Just as the man is reaching for the ball you catch him in midair... In crime reporting you do not just catch the moment, you live the excitement of delivery on time. These two combinations add a lot of input to journalism. One teaches you about the action whereas the other teaches you about time. That is what journalism is about. Time is of essence to a journalist. A photograph may become useless within half an hour. I learned all this gradually."

Since he was just starting his career, he stayed at the paper until late hours. During that era, nobody went home before 2 am so the restaurants in Sirkeci would stay open late and wait for the journalists to come.

"I took a lot of photographs, really a lot. While everybody else was shooting one roll of film per day I was using five... They tried to fire me from the newspaper. The Administration manager said 'you spend too much' and I said 'I am paying for this film out of my pocket, so whose business is it?'"

Fikret Adil was responsible for the preparation of the art pages of the newspaper. He was assisted by Azra Erhat in the following art events.

"Every evening we would gather at Fikret Adil's house in Taksim. With names such as Yildiz Kenter, Nihat Akcan, Suavi Tedu, and Husamettin Bozok etc..."

The inclusion of art events by the newspapers was a sort of revolution.

"In that era, young writers did not intermingle with newspapers as they do today. Although there may be exceptions, usually journalists were political individuals. They gave the appearance of being interested in literature, but they were primarily involved in politics. They did not care about art. Furthermore, in those days an art exhibition was not open every weekend nor was a novel or book criticized to high heaven. The first columns to deal with theater criticism started much later. Photography, which is considered an art today, was not even mentioned. When I started this journalism business, newspaper writers were the big names, such as Huseyin Cahit Yalcin, Falih Rifki Atay, Refik Halid Karay, and Necmettin Sadak. The one closest to art among them was Sedat Simavi. Before Hurriyet, he published Yedi Gun. However, just like the others, his paper did not allocate any pages to literature or art."

Editing department managers from the young generation started to publish news, albeit small, about theater critique and, on rare occasions, art exhibitions.

"In short, in the old days, there was no room for art events or artists in journalism. Although he was from the old school, Refii Cevat Ulunay, and subsequently Fikret Adil with the signature 'FA' as art chronicler, Sabri Esat Siyavusgil, Vedat Nedim Tor, Va-Nû (Vala Nurettin), Zahir Guvemli, Osman Karaca, Adnan Benk, and Tunc Yalman from the younger generation pioneered attaching importance to the world of art and its inclusion in the newspaper columns."

Fikret Adil introduced Ara to Husamettin Bozok, who gathered all young journalists around him with the literary journal *Yeditepe* that he was publishing. At that time, there were two journals; one was *Yeditepe* published by Bozok and the other was *Varlik* published by Yasar Nabi Nayir.

Yeditepe, on the second floor of Yeni Han on Nuruosmaniye Street, was an initiation for Ara. Having a piece of one's work published by *Yeditepe* was equal to having a confirmed dissertation for assistant professorship for a budding writer.

Yeditepe was the meeting place of the writers of the era and included names such as: Fikret Adil, Eflatun Cem Guney, Ilhan Tarus, Orhan Kemal, Yasar Kemal, Samim Kocagoz, Muzaffer Buyrukcu, Nevzat Ustun, Melih Cevdet Anday, Oktay Rifat, Salah Birsel, Edip Cansever, Cemal Sureya, Kemal Ozer, Adnan Ozyalciner and Sait Faik.

This venue witnessed tea and coffee drinking from morning to night, reciprocal smoking of cigarettes and a myriad variety of debates. Sometimes Husamettin Bozok would be chasing somebody with a chair to crash it over his head, sometimes Yasar Kemal would try to throw a colleague out of a window.

In the evenings, the same society would gather at the home of Fikret Adil to have literature sessions.

Ara would buy *Camera* and *Leica Photography,* the main journals at that time from the Bookstore Isvec. He would read between the lines of the interviews to develop his journalism skills.

"I was always waiting *Camera* like waiting for the Bible. I followed it with such anticipation. The number of copies sold in Turkey was perhaps eight or five."

He believed he could only shoot the photographs of his dreams with a *Leica* because all the masters were using *Leicas*. The most prominent name in the Republican Era Photography was Selahattin Giz and he also had a Leica. The most famous war photographer in the world, Robert Capa, had also one.

I used to look at photography books all the time. I always had an eye on international work. I did not turn a blind eye like so many photojournalists. Not only Selahattin Giz operated a *Leica* but also Namik worked with it. I said to myself I am going to work with a Leica, too. I went and bought one. It was my first Leica with the following information on: *Leica IIIb, number 382418 and white, 1938 model etc.*

The family was not happy about their one and only son choosing journalism as a profession. His mother Verjin complained for years to those around her: " *What can become of journalism, is it even a profession?".*

"Can you imagine what it meant to them, to my father a profession was being a doctor, pharmacist and the ones alike..."

Even though his mother never approved, owing to journalism, Ara had the chance to offer biggest insights in his life. He got the opportunity to meet some of the major names in Turkey and the world.

The Eyuboglu Factor

Sabahattin Eyuboglu, who revolutionized the Enlightenment in Turkey with his works, had a significant contribution in *Ara* becoming *Ara Guler.*

"Sabahattin Eyuboglu is one of the men who nurtured me. I learned a lot from his writings and talks."

Bronz Apartment, the home of Sabahattin Eyuboglu on Bronz Sokak, was like a second home for Ara.

Sabahattin was an art historian who had been one of the bright students sent to Europe for education on Ataturk's orders.

"People would go to Sabahattin's house to learn, to consult and get advices about something. Most probably because of this crowd, his living and working schedule became so irregular that he started to hold plenary meetings just on Mondays. The main subjects which were literature and art changed form after a while. Talking was replaced with projection, slide shows, images shot during trips and the debates that they generated. In other words, literature was gradually replaced with images. At one point, maybe with a bit of my influence, the teacher realized that an image serves an advanced reality than narration. This also means that it would remain more "as is" in the future. His interest of visual started to be seen also in his art history lessons at university. He started giving his lessons aided by visual material. I did my best to help the teacher with this for many years. I prepared classical painting reproductions from books and lesson slides for days. The teacher prepared classics, impressionists, transitioned into the modern era, modern art with great diligence for student expositions. I must admit that while I was doing all this, owing to him, my insight in art improved a lot. I can say that thanks to him I found a new world."

Sabahattin Eyuboglu, who Ara consulted at every opportunity, was like a lighthouse spreading light around him and, as happens to all intellectuals, he got his part of what was coming:

"Sabahattin was the man who brought the atmosphere of the western world to us. He reflected the mirror of the west on our generation. First the Babeuf case, then the accusations in the last years came. He stood up to everything with patience despite not knowing the reason. Perhaps he tried to understand but could not. None of all this matched his world anyway. In a way, it was resentment to life, he kept it all to himself and did not speak anymore. He could not say what he was going to say, could not reach the necessary conclusions and could not speak out his last words. Perhaps he was going to propagate the most valuable result to the world of art of the current society, his students. More is the pity what subsequently happened to him and the bitter end that prevented this."

The heart of Sabahattin Eyuboglu, who had a major share in the enlightenment of Turkey, could not bear the accusations of establishing a clandestine organization.

"One day Sabahattin had a heart attack. He was supposed to stay in bed without moving. He was even forbidden to talk. When I entered his room, he was lying in the bed in the corner. I talked, he listened. I was about to leave when he leaned over to hand over a square piece of cardboard from the table. He wrote something with the colorful flomaster pens lying around and gave it to me. I still have it. He wrote HELLO in three colors on the cardboard. I accepted his greetings and left his flat in Bronz Apartment number 1. Now I think that Sabahattin died in resentment to Turkey. The illiteracy in Turkey was to be blamed for the death of a man like Sabahattin Eyuboglu."

Orhan Veli-Sait Faik

Being introduced to and becoming friends with great names in Turkish literature as Sait Faik Abasiyanik and Orhan Veli Kanik contributed a lot to Ara.

"The Orhan Velis, Sait Faiks... all of them. They are the people who widened my horizons. I remember all of them as true brothers. Writers have been my network. Because I live here, these men come to visit Cicek Pasaji (Cité de Péra)."

He has never forgotten the day he met Orhan Veli.

"I was having an interview with Bedri. I had gone to the shop to take photographs of the paintings. It was around noon. When I entered, Bedri Rahmi was sitting in front of an old-fashioned window with a tall, thin friend. I was going to shoot over twenty pictures so I wanted to get started without delay. They were talking among themselves, but I did not get the opportunity to eavesdrop. Suddenly Bedri turned towards me and asked: 'Tell me the name of a poet you like. One of the new ones, who do you know for example from new poetry?' 'I know almost all of them,' I said. 'Tell me who is the most interesting for you,' he said."

The question did not challenge Ara. Without pausing he said *"Orhan Veli Kanik"*.

"They both looked at each other. Then Bedri turned to me and said: 'Do you know Orhan Veli in person?' 'No.' 'Now you do,' he said. 'This is Orhan Veli!' This tall man was Orhan Veli. He was standing right in front of the window. For some reason, I have always imagined him in such a background. Whatever the object which is captured by light in photography is the same light that Orhan gives to the words in his poems. They are the ones behind the truth. That is how I got to know Orhan Veli."

They helped Orhan Veli with the *Yaprak* journal he was publishing.

"Every time Orhan Veli's sister Furuzan went out, she would distribute 10-20 copies of this journal to newspaper vendors in Taksim, Harbiye, and Şisli. Orhan would do the same in Karakoy, Cagaloglu and second hand bookstores. I made both ends meet. I shouldered journals and distributed them. I would leave journals with distributor Kemal on the Bridge at the Island boat pier. Bridge Kemal made the best sales. Everyone who went to the islands stopped by Kemal."

Orhan Veli passed away in a most unfortunate way during his most productive era.

"He fell into a ditch in Ankara and died within a few days after he was brought to Istanbul. His funeral was held here. I attended the funeral; he was laid to rest in Asiyan Cemetery in Bebek. His statue along the roadside sitting at Rumelihisari is listening to Istanbul with his eye shut.."

An interesting surprise was waiting for him when he went to offer his condolences to Orhan Veli's sister.

"We went to the sister Furuzan's house with Husamettin Bozok, owner of *Yeditepe* journal. At that time, she was working in Yapi Kredi Bank. We found three unpublished poems. We used them in the journal. Also, we found an unfinished poem in his handwriting..."

Abasiyanik, whose real name was Mehmet Sait, was different from his literary network in means of his education as well as the wealth of his family.

"I knew Sait Faik, I had read him, been reading him but I knew Sait only from his books; I met Sait himself for the first time in Agop Arad's office. This turned out to be Sait Faik, the insignificant looking man with an upturned collar and alight beige trench coat I saw frequently on the side streets of Beyoglu in the evening, and in Cagaloglu during daytime. Wherever I went I saw him,. He lived on Burgazada. He enjoyed eating and drinking. He generally became grumpy when he drank. His mother rented him a flat to sleepover in Buyukparmakkapi in case Sait misses the last ferry being drunk.

After Sait Faik learned that he was suffering from cirrhosis he retired in his own shell and took a break from writing.

"In the beginning of his sickness, he used to come to my father's pharmacy to get injections from our assistant. However, Sait did not know it was my my father's pharmacy and I never told him. It was a summer day, Sait had been hospitalised for treatment. It was Marmara Clinic. I entered his room on the second floor fearfully. Above all, I did not want him to see the camera. He was weak, he was lying down. He looked at us but did not speak much, he tried. For a moment Sait's eyes rested on me and he saw the camera next to me. 'Damn, did you come to take my picture because I am dying?' he said. Of course, I could not take a picture that day. I remember now, it was a completely white room painted with oil paint. That was the last time I saw him."

Ara could neither take photographs of Orhan Veli nor Sait Faik after his heart's content, yet they appeared to have found a formula of their own:

"Both Orhan and Sait would flee from everyone they did not know well or were close. Both were shy creatures. They used to be here all day from morning until night in Beyoglu. One day both of them said to eachother 'Let us leave a mark in the world' while nobody pays attention. Huseyin Cahit Yalcin, Yakup Kadri, who are really great men, got all the attention while nobody cares about these two. They were invited nowhere. They could not even enter the newspaper building, the doorman would not let them in. So, they walked down from Mecidiyekoy and went into every photographer's shop on the way and had their photographs taken. As they were drunk, they did not get their photographs from the shops. Let us hope that they surface someday."

Ara tried so hard to find these pictures but could never find them.

Orhan Kemal

Ara was very much impressed when he read the book "The Idle Years" written by Orhan Kemal, published by Varlik Publications.

"This book introduced a whole new world to me. The writer lived in Adana. He had previously published the book: "My Father's House". I found and read it immediately. This is how we met; He had come from Adana. We went to Guney Park Music Hall together with Husamettin Bozok, Agop Arad, painter Fethi Karakas, poet Zahrad, Kemal Sulker, Mehmed Kemal, and Salih Tozan. That was our first "Hello" with Orhan Kemal. His real name was Mehmet Rasit Ogutcu. In later times, Orhan Kemal moved to Istanbul. "

Ara became friends with Orhan Kemal after he moved to Istanbul.

"After Orhan Kemal moved to Istanbul, anyone could see him anywhere, anytime. During the day, he would take notes for his novels at the cafes in Cagaloglu. Most of the nights he would be at Cumhuriyet Restaurant in Beyoglu Balik Pazari after spending some time at Lambo's Pub. If he had more cash in his pocket, he would be at Cicek Pasaji. Since I lived in Galatasaray in a central location, sometimes they used to wait for eac other at my place."

Because of his father's political party, Orhan Kemal had to drop his school off and had to flee to Syria. The family was in exile for some time. He was still carrying the traces of those bitter times. In addition, he had been imprisoned for five years convicted of 'instigating propaganda in favor of foreign regimes and rebellion'.

"He harbored anger for political events from the time of his father. He would tell me things as we walked but I cannot remember what they were. I think his father fled to Aleppo or something, I do not know."

Ara felt deep fondness for Orhan Kemal both because of his experiences as well as his personality.

"When I think in terms of photography for me Orhan Kemal was like a movie hero always wearing a Borsalino hat, white shirt and dark suit. He resembled 1935-40 model movie peers. He wore the same hat also in winter but with a coat on him. He always looked official. If I were a director, I would think which film I could cast him in."

On the day that they decided to take photographs together they met in front of the Ziraat Bank at the foot of Galata Bridge.

"As we were walking I was thinking of the background to put him in. At first I wanted to place him among people working the side streets between Sishane and Karakoy who resembled the people in his novels. Then we went to a cafe in Cibali where he lived. I took pictures of him and his friends there. We went to his house. I took photographs of him while working, with his children. I wanted to make a scenario of my primary star with his Borsalino hat, white shirt and tie with Istanbul in the background. As I kept photographing I asked him: 'Do you pass this street often? In which corner of the cafe do you prefer to sit? Where do you get on the dolmus?' All this resulted in the photographs that I managed to take. As I was taking the photographs, I saw all these separately; Rasit Ogutcu from Adana, Orhan Kemal trying to write his novel in Meserret café, Orhan Kemal hunching over a draft correcting it in the dim light of a cafe in Cagaloglu, Orhan Kemal between Recep Bilginer and Agop Arad exiting from a pub in Kumkapi and walking downhill in a background of fog."

The health status of Orhan Kemal, who had worked in all sorts of jobs from the cotton mills of Adana as a laborer, to clerking, from warehouse clerk to printing press laborer, was not good when he was arrested. Based on information that he was involved in 'cell work and communism propaganda', he was dispatched to Sultanahmet Prison. He passed away at the hospital in Sofia where he was being treated at the invitation of the Bulgarian Writers Union.

"One day the devil must have poked me and I went to my office in Galatasaray earlier than usual. I had this strange feeling. At 10:30 a.m. the doorbell rang. Orhan Kemal was standing at the door, 'What's up?' he said. He came in and sat at my desk. I normally saw members of this crew in the evening around six or seven. Orhan lit a cigarette and said 'I am going to Sofia. I do not have any proper photographs so take one before I die and keep it'. I did as he said. That was the last photograph I took of him. "

Nazi Fan Newspaper Boss

The owner of the blue heading newspaper *Yeni Istanbul* that Ara had started to work for was an interesting individual. The owner of the newspaper, Habip Edip Torehan, was a wealthy businessman steering the chromium trade between Turkey and Germany. He was closely associated with the Nazis. No one could fathom why Torehan had established a large printing press. He entered the market one year after Sedat Simavi had established *Hurriyet,* and was known as 'the man who changed the capital structure of Babiali'. He did this by importing offset printing machines a short while before Turkey transposed the multi-party system. He had transferred major names such as Yakup Kadri Karaosmanoglu, Bedii Faik, and Sevket Evliyagil to his newspaper.

"Habip Edip Torehan the owner of *Yeni Istanbul* was a very wealthy man, millionaire Simavi is a novice compared to him. He was Hitler's friend; his wife was German or something."

After the Germans were defeated, Torehan 'fled' to Switzerland and directed his newspaper from his villa in Nyon city near Lake Geneva. Torehan had houses in all over the world and he was also the owner of Sottens Radio in Switzerland.

Torehan's wealth was also reflected in the promotions carried out by his newspaper. The full-page advertisement carrying the heading that "*Yeni Istanbul* is distributing gifts worth 75.000 lira" was almost a mirror image of Torehan's wealth:

"A list of some of our major gifts
MERCEDES-BENZ automobile
2 (JAWA) and (CZ) brand motorcycles
SWISSAIR flight Istanbul-Zurich and 15 day stay
1 refrigerator

1 BEAUTT brand washing machine
4 (SCHAUB) brand radios
2 (Minerva) hand and foot operated sewing machines
1 (Marchin 40) outboard engine
1 600 square meter corner plot for a villa in Altinsehir
2 Opema and Flexaret brand cameras
2 (HOOVER) brand vacuum cleaners
3 accident liability insurances worth ten thousand lira each
3 Family Registry Booklets with 100 lira bonus each
3 (STOK) store printed fabric coupons
5 advanced model electric irons
5 bonds worth fifty lira each"

Babiali had not seen such a promotion campaign in all its history.

Yeni Istanbul newspaper, which prioritized economy and foreign news, started to penetrate the Turkish political life in a very short time.

The full page that it allocated to art and culture events, out of a total of eight pages, was a major innovation for Babiali.

During the same period, there was another novelty in Turkey; Adnan Menderes' Democrat Party had won in the multi-party elections.

Yeni Istanbul, the newspaper that Ara worked for, was outspoken in its publications, but also admitted the 'objectivity' of both the brand new Prime Minister Menderes as well as that of Inonu who had lost his seat.

As a family tradition, Ara was a supporter of the CHP (The Republican People's Party) and he was unable to be objective to the Menderes government. Furthermore, the first thing that the new government took up was the conscription issue which was of great interest to Ara. With the doctrine of the US administration to have a strong military presence in the region, Parliament was debating the immediate conscription of high school graduates and revoking their right of fulfilling their military service as non-commissioned officers.

Enrolling in the Institute of Journalism

Ara found out that the first Institute of Journalism in Turkey had been established under the Department of Economics at Istanbul University.

"High school graduates were being conscripted immediately. As I was trying to find a university in order to postpone military service, I learnt that the Academy had already closed its enrollment. Only two universities were left which accepted students without sitting exams. So, I chose the School of Economics."

The school had only been active for one year but already presented some very interesting subjects: law, history of journalism, archiving, file preparation, and ethics of journalism, newspaper photography and economics.

The Istanbul Society of Journalists initiated the opening of the Institute of Journalism. The Founder of the Society, President Sedat Simavi, applied with a letter to Istanbul University Rector Ord. Prof. Dr. Siddik Sami Onar, requesting to establish an institute of higher education to teach journalism. The Istanbul University Senate agreed with the application and opened a two-year Journalism Institute.

Students who wanted to enroll in the Journalism Institute needed to be high school graduates and have passed the Turkish composition examination which Ara complied with.

"After the opening of Institute of Journalism, a trend started that all journalists should hold a diploma of Journalism. For example, Cemal Isin, and Vasfiye Ozkocak. We were already journalists. I was attending the Institute of Journalism and my student number was 87, I remember it very well."

He enrolled in the first school of journalism in Turkey to postpone his military service, but he was unable to attend the lessons because he was too busy being a journalist.

Kemal Tahir

In those days, he met writer Kemal Tahir who had been released on account of the amnesty granted by the Democrat Party government. Tahir was charged alongside Nazim Hikmet for "inciting military rebellion" and had been convicted and imprisoned for 12 years.

While in prison, Tahir wrote novels at the request of Sedat Simavi and after being released he returned to Istanbul. He wrote serials, scenarios, love and adventure novels for newspapers under pseudonyms such as Korduman, Bedri Eser, Samim Askin, Nurettin Demir, and Ali Gicirli.

"I have been familiar with Kemal Tahir since my childhood years. Subsequently his name was often mentioned in Babiali. During those years, I started taking photographs of artistic people. One day my artist friend Firuz Askin, who knew this, wanted to take me to see Kemal Tahir. It was a Saturday. We went to a house in Kadikoy. I cannot remember the date. We stayed there for a few hours with Kemal Tahir. He was good for a chat, the time passed well. In the meantime, I took pictures of Kemal Tahir along or with his spouse, I took various portraits. Many things were talked about, narrated; most of them were funny memories. I had taken numerous pictures but I felt a strange dissatisfaction. I had failed to put Kemal Tahir into a mood. Actually, the setup was not appropriate. The background consisted only of the single room. Perhaps I should have gone out with him, toured, sat in cafes, been a part of his life. That is what I believe a photograph should be today."

As Kemal Tahir was endeavoring to establish an idiosyncratic left wing tendency for Turkey, he was chastigated by intellectuals. Yet there were those who loved him, who were proud of him.

"I was sitting in a cafe along the Montparnasse in Paris, I had a date with Ionesco in one hour. I was passing the time. In front of me a man had opened the double pages of a newspaper and was reading. I had nothing to do so I tried to read the large print of the papers from the distance. While I was perusing the paper, the headline on the right page caught my attention. Something from the back of the man's neck. I cannot fully recall now, something like 'Village Bossure'or 'Village de Bossure'. At first, I did not get the meaning but then I understood. Yes, "Hunchback of the Village", it was the name of Kemal Tahir's novel. I was curious, had a Frenchman written a novel called 'Hunchback of the Village' or written an article? I got up to look closer at the newspaper. The author's name was under the title: Kemal Tahir. "Hunchback of the Village" had been translated into French and was serialized. I felt proud. There the Frenchmen read, and this was a

Turkish novel! When a person is abroad it is natural to feel a bit more nationalistic, especially in France in the world of arrogance."

Finally, Ara went to see Kemal Tahir together with Pars Tuglaci. He was preparing an encyclopedia.

"I took a colored photograph of him. I remember it was early evening. This time he was living near Goztepe. We sat for a while. Pars was taking biographical notes. I took a lot of pictures. But something was missing. The photographs I had taken remained photographs. As we were leaving we said things like 'we'll come again, of course we will stop by...' but unfortunately this was the last time we saw him. I took many photographs of Kemal Tahir but I failed to enter his world. A photograph cannot be ordered, it cannot be taken like a task. In the way that I understand photography, a photograph should portray the world of the individual I am photographing. This was just exactly what did not happen when I was taking photographs of Kemal Tahir. The photographs were like a visiting guest. Now that I think of it this is something that has remained incomplete for me. A man like Kemal Tahir, a great writer and I failed to capture his world. Yes, I may have taken his picture but not of his world. One of the creative individuals that I could not photograph the way I wanted to is Kemal Tahir."

Ara could have never imagined that one day he would lose the negatives of the photographs of Kemal Tahir.

"Some time went by I guess. I was looking for something in my laboratory archive in Galatasaray. One of the boxes was slightly damp. I opened it and saw that everything inside had stuck together. They had been dampened either by the rain or something wet had put on, it got damp. Whereas I believed that I kept everything very well. I opened the box and most of the negatives inside had stuck to each other. They had become almost rock-like.
I was mortified. I was angry at myself, swore some. I didn't know what to do with the negatives. I put them in water so that they would be separated but most of them melted away.
I saved what I could. I was afraid even to touch them before they were dry. We did not have any covers or separators then, photographs would start clinging to one another after a while, there was nothing to protect them. Unfortunately, the photographs I had taken the first time I went to Kemal Tahir's house were among them. If I had not been looking for something and noticed the box everything would have been ruined. Evidently such things are in the fate of photographers."

The Photos of Nazim Hikmet That He Burned

On one of those days that Ara was running from morning till night from one news story to another, the editor tasked him with an interview with Nazim Hikmet. Hikmet had benefited from the amnesty granted by the Democrat Party administration and been released from prison. Because of his years in prison, Nazim Hikmet was unable to find work so Ipekci family took him under their wing. Ihsan Ipekci was shooting a film in Topkapi Palace, the *Lale Devri* and hired Nazim Hikmet to work there. The film was directed by Baha Gelenbevi.

"He was hired as historian to prevent historical errors as an excuse to pay him a salary. I went there and Gelenbevi told me to introduce Nazim to me. I shook Nazim Hikmet's hand, I took a few frames. I did not stay there long because being a photojournalist I could easily tell that there were undercover police around. I knew them all so after a few pleasantries and photographs I skedaddled. Those days it was considered a crime even to read Nazim Hikmet."

These photographs that young reporter Ara submitted to the editing department were never published. Ara was too scared for years to mention that he had taken photographs of Nazim

Hikmet. Upon release from prison, Nazim Hikmet's health was not good. The administration was adamant about conscripting Nazim, who had been labeled 'traitor', and this meant 'death' for him. Refik Erduran, who was married to Nazim Hikmet's sister and doing his military service, found a speedboat. He took Nazim from Tarabya crossing the Bosphorus into the Black Sea and helped him board a Romanian vessel and escape abroad. After the event became known, the citizenship of NazimHikmet was revoked. Anyone who had had anything to do with him, who had even greeted him, was investigated.

Those were the days when 'witch hunts' started by US senator McCarthy wreaked havoc on the world, when everyone was accused of being a communist or spying for trivial reasons and even executed like the Rosenbergs. Ara was going to do his military service at a time when those whose objective was to be "Little America" were in power. He was obliged to burn the photographs of Nazim Hikmet that he had. He told those who knew that he had gone to interview him that he had lost the copies of his photographs:

"When I went to be a reserve officer, I burned all Nazim Hikmet's left-wing books in the stove. Turkey has gone through such weird eras."

Turkey was truly going through a strange period. In 1951 the Democrat Party, which patterned itself exactly according to the US Administration, started a 'communist hunt' to ingratiate themselves to the US Administration, get financial aid and get into NATO. During this carnage carried out by the Democrat Party in power, hundreds of left wing intellectuals were arrested and detained in prisons, from novelist Vedat Turkali to poet Enver Gokce, from sociologist Mubeccel Kiray to opera singer Ruhi Su.

Years later, fate brought Ara and Nazim Hikmet together again when Ara went to France on duty.

Artist Abidin Dino was prosecuted for his political views and sent into exile in Adana. Once his sentence was completed he left the country and settled in France. Ara, who had met Abidin Dino through the artist Agop Arad, was visiting Dino while attending the Cannes film festival. Dino said that Nazim Hikmet was also in Paris and offered him to come and take his photograph and took him to his hotel.

"Now Abidin was a member of the Communist Party, and it was a major crime even to greet a communist. I am a journalist, everybody knew me, I didn't care about such things. I was not a communist but I was a sympathizer, I was a left-wing supporter. I was going to Abidin with ease. Nazim was at the hotel. I took his photograph but I always concealed the fact that I took Nazim's photograph. Just in case."

The military service for which Ara had burned the pictures of Nazim 'just in case' was hanging over his head like the sword of Damocles. Even if he did not attend the Institute of Journalism, he had obtained a deferral certificate attesting that as long as he was enrolled there his military service was postponed, but sooner or later there was no escape from conscription.

I'm in the Army Now

As soon as Menderes government gained power, they dispatched a brigade of troops to combat under US orders in South Korea without even consulting with Turkish Grand National Assembly (GNAT). They also put the issue of troops always on the negotiation table to ingratiate themselves with the US. These were real concerns for Ara. Furthermore, the duration of military service was a constant issue of debate in GNAT in association with issues such as enhancing the current army.

On one of these days when Ara and his friends Meftun Olgac and Samet Kocyigit spent all day calculating the duration of military service for reserve officers, a rumor broke out. They heard that the military service duration would be extended. As they heard this, they immediately looked for a way to be conscripted before the reserve officer rights extended to high school graduates were revoked.

Their friend Mehmet Cemal from Galatasaray rushed to their aid.

Mehmet Cemal, who was the grandchild of Former Minister of Admiralty Cemal Pasa, relied on the multiple acquaintances he had in the military and said 'we shall be conscripted together' and tore up Ara's deferral certificate.

"Mehmet was my best friend. We were together every day in Galatasaray. He was the grandchild of one of the three generals of the Union and Progress, and they were cousins with Hasan Cemal. We grew up under a portrait of Cemal Pasa, we used to play poker every night, womanizing as in our youth, and things like that. Hasan Cemal was young, and he used to hang around and ask us to buy cigarettes".

He did not care about school, he was not attending anyway. They went to the Military Recruitment Office and got their consigments. After a training lasting six months in Ankara Reserve Officers Infantry School, they graduated from the 37th term and drew lots.

"I drew the lot and got Corlu, the need for clout was not necessary any more. Mehmet Cemal drew Sarikamis. After that he was bumped up to cavalry and came to Selimiye Barracks."

By sheer luck Ara was dispatched to Corlu which was very near Istanbul, and when he started in the 3rd Armored Motorized Infantry Brigade Battalion, 5th Brigade with the position of Lieutenant, there was not a happier man alive. At weekends, he could come home and to Beyoglu. He did not even have to dispose of his mustache; he would swagger around in his uniform.

"Do you know we used to have orderlies? For example, I had one."

During his duty as Derekoy border commander, he read more books than during any other time in his life. He finished most of the publications by Varlik Publications that time. There were two things that prevented him from sleeping during this military service, one was the frost in Corlu and the second was the military trucks that were registered to him. He would throw himself out of bed at 2 am to check the warehouses one-by-one and then go back to bed.

"Bro, it was a huge motorized unit, there were military vehicles, their spare parts, every military vehicle had 11 tires, and there was a black market for tires, so I had nightmares about them, and would check the warehouses in my dreams every night."

During the Thrace maneuvers his unit was transferred to Davutpasa Barracks. He did an additional 15 days of military service because the man to replace him failed to show up. When he was discharged, he did not relinquish the uniform that he had worn so proudly and kept it as a memento.

Tennessee Williams on the Heated Marble Slab

After completing his military service, he started to work at *Hurriyet* newspaper through his friend Teoman Orberk.

The first assignment he did for *Hurriyet* involved the underground caves and tunnels of İstanbul. He was assigned as the reporter in Beyoglu because of his language skills. All foreigners coming to Istanbul would stay at the hotels in Beyoglu and its vicinity. His beat, similar to current tabloid reporting, included visiting all hotels one-by-one and perusing the guest book to hunt down celebrities.

One summer evening in 1954 he went to the Hilton hotel to get material for the newspaper and while he was examining the list of new arriving customers he saw the name of Tennessee Williams. His work *A Streetcar Named Desire* had recently been staged by Istanbul City Theater. Furthermore, it was a play he liked very much. He said to his colleague, "*Look, apparently Tennessee Williams is here. Let's go interview.*" His colleague replied, "*Forget it. Let's look at other stuff*". This was actually a signal that his newspaper would not be interested.

He asked the reception clerk for the room number of Tennessee Williams: which was 512. His English language was not fluent at the time. He dialed the telephone and said, "*Tennessee Williams?*" to which the party replied "*Yes?*"

What followed was that he perfunctorily tried to explain that he was a journalist and that he wanted to take his photograph. Williams started to laugh and expressed his happiness that a journalist in Turkey recognized him.

"I went upstairs in the elevator and knocked on the door of room 512. The door opened. A man in a white shirt, crumpled trousers, bare feet stood in front of me. 'Journalist' I said. 'Photograph...' He asked me in to get rid of me as soon as possible. I took many photographs of him, I told him in my scrappy English with great difficulty that I had seen *A Streetcar Named Desire*, that I liked the theater and therefore he was important for me and that I wanted to introduce him to the leading actors of the play as well as the art critics."

Williams said that he would be in Istanbul for 10 more days.

He had the most significant theater writer in the world standing in front of him but this was not an article his newspaper would be interested in. He believed that he had to do something.

"Then I said 'Can I make phone call?' I made the call. Guess who I called? Fikret Adil, the art news writer of *Yeni Istanbul* newspaper. 'I am at the Hilton. Tennessee Williams is here. I am sitting next to him as I make this call' I said. 'No way?!' he exclaimed. *A Streetcar Named Desire* had just been played. 'Can you bring him to us immediately, will he come?' he said. 'Gee, let's see, I don't know but I guess he will' I said. The man has nothing to do, he has just come to visit, he does not know anybody. 'What are you going to do now?' I asked. 'Don't know, probably to get something to eat somewhere' he said."

Ara had a hard time convincing Fikret Adil that he was with Williams. He swore until he was blue in the face; "*I swear the man is here sitting in the hotel, if you want I can bring him* over". Fikret Adil was convinced and he telephoned Suavi Tedu who had undertaken the leading role in *A Streetcar Named Desire* played by Istanbul City Theater, and they decided to host the American writer at Guney Park, the flashiest music hall of the era.

"Tennessee Williams accepted our proposal without much enthusiasm. Guney Park was a music hall frequented by the public. He seemed to like it. In addition to us the table was graced by Suavi Tedu, Fikret Adil, Samim Kocagoz, Nevzat Ustun, Ayfer Feray, Cahit Albayrak and Husamettin Bozok. After hitting the booze in Guney Park, we went to Fikret Adil's house in Taksim. Our guest was interested in the paintings in Fikret Adil's house. He had loosened up, it was clear he felt himself at home."

The raki consumed by Williams made him insist "*Take me to the hamam (a Turkish bath)*" at that hour of the night. Ara remembered Cagaloglu Hamam, he knew the owner on account of an interview he had done. They got into Nevzat Ustun's Buick.

"Can you imagine I was going to photograph Tennessee Williams in the hamam? However, I did not know the telephone number of the hamam. 'Let's go, let's knock on the door, if they open, fine, if not what can we do' I said. I went and knocked on the door, knock knock. It was 01.00 am at night. I woke the hamam officer up, 'what is going on' he said. The hamam was starting to cool down. Anyway, we put the man in the hamam, 'he wanted a hamam, it's a hamam' we said. He washed in lukewarm water."

After a lengthy period of indecision, the American writer, whose original name was Thomas Lanier Williams, admitted he was gay, and then changed his name to Tennessee Williams.

"Even then he was gay. The greatest writer on earth. Can anything bigger be propositioned to a photojournalist? Naked in the hamam, on the heated bathstone."

Shortly after the visit to Istanbul, Ara visited Tennessee Williams at his home in Rome facing the river Tiber.

"It was a two floor house within a garden. There were scrub grapevines in the garden. An elderly lady dressed in black approached the door of the house. I asked about Tennessee Williams. 'He is upstairs writing' she said. I could hear the typewriter banging away, Williams was upstairs writing a play. 'Sit' he said, 'Let me finish this sentence.' As he continued to write I studied the surroundings. In the meantime, I took many photographs. Finally, he took a break from his writing. It was one o'clock. Williams would start writing every day as soon as he woke up and continued to work until one o'clock. He shut himself in his room, paced, roamed, smoked, wrote something down, tore it up, wrote again. After one o'clock his private life started. That was the second face of Williams... I asked the name of the play he was writing that day. *'Cat on a Hot Tin Roof'* he said."

The note that Tennessee Williams made about Ara's visit in his diary is very interesting:

"I woke up in the morning with diarrhea and pains. I was told that a Turkish photographer I met in Istanbul was at the door. He had brought an album of the photographs he had taken, how ugly, fat and stunted I turned out. He stayed and stayed, I could not work at all."

When Ara's newspaper was not interested, he gave the photographs he took to Husamettin Bozok's *Yeditepe* journal. Ara was not happy with *Hurriyet* newspaper anyway, he was looking for a place which would appreciate the photographs he took.

Hello to Turkish Life

Ara heard that the owner of Yapi Kredi Bank, Kazim Taskent, intended to launch an initiation for the monthly *Resimli Hayat* journal published by Dogan Kardes Publications. It was established to commemorate his son Dogan who died in an avalanche in Switzerland and he intended to publish it every week.

Taskent, who was a former General Director of the Sugar Factory, had entered politics at the recommendation of Adnan Menderes and subsequently resigned from the position of Member of Parliament of the Democrat Party as a result of disappointment. The journal that Taskent had in his mind was a Turkish version of *Life* magazine published in America with plenty of photographs.

Taskent was planning on importing unprecedented photogravure printing machines to Turkey, to give photographs their due. In the days when the proofing of *Hayat* journal was being carried out and the copy prepared by the editing staff, the journal was placed on the desk of the boss and then Taskent's reaction of "*There is still too much to read. Put emphasis on photographs, vacate the contents, lighten it up! In this state, it is too overwhelming for the readers*", heralded a breakthrough in Ara's life.

He was invited to *Hayat* journal through Vedat Nedim Tor.

"I started working for *Hayat*. It was a monthly magazine; the printing quality was poor. Then there was *Aile Journal* published by Vedat Nedim Tor. There was Orhan Veli. He was with *Dogan Kardes*. Ruhi Su would notate oriental music for Dogan *Kardes*. But when his work was published they refrained from mentioning Ruhi Su by name, can you imagine? Kazim Taskent feared the name Ruhi Su because he was a communist."

Taskent had deputized Vedat Nedim Tor who had been the Culture and Art Consultant of Yapi ve Kredi Bank for a long time with the establishment of a cadre for the journal. A major task fell on the photojournalists in creating a 'storm in photojournalism' which the journal planned to do by harmonizing local conservatism with American values. As the focus in the journal was on aesthetic and high quality photographs which were not a priority in newspaper photography, the first person to be transferred was the legendary photojournalist Hilmi Şahenk, a dappy dresser from Babiali.

He was followed by the others; Hikmet Feridun Es, Ara Guler, Sukru Enis Regu, Ozkan Sahin, Afif Yesari, Nezihe Araz, Muserref Hekimoglu, Bulent Giz, Suavi Sonar and Yahya Kemal Beyatli who dropped by once in a while. Rakim Calapala was the editor. The cadre of *Hayat* which gathered in the large hall above the printing shop of Klodfarer Street 7 of Babiali Hill was just fine, but problems often emerged because Vedat Nedim Tor was of literary origin. Hilmi Sahenk, the chief of photography of the journal, was fired when he threw a Rolleiflex camera at Tor's head and he was replaced with Ara Guler. Kazim Taskent who had been observing the events from a distance till that time had to lend a hand.

"One day Vedat Nedim went to see his own play Kor in Germany. His wife is German. Right before our eyes Kazim Taskent put another person into Vedat Nedim's position. Kazim Taskent used to join us every Thursday for meetings. It was after 5 pm. After all we were the press ... he prioritized us, he looked out for us. Such a busy man, but he came anyway! Muserref was the talkative one at these meetings. At that time Sevket Rado used to praise Taskent in Aksam newspaper. They took advantage of Nedim's departure and brought in Sevket Rado. When Vedat Nedim returned; he saw he had no place! I was happy with this situation because Rado was a journalist, whereas Vedat Nedim was a man of letters."

The moment everybody was waiting for was here; the printing machines ordered from Germany have arrived.

"The Germans arrived. They were setting up the photogravure printing equipment. I was supervising them carefully. I could even remember them putting the screws in. I observed how the machine operated... how it distinguished colors.."

With the establishment of the printing machines the *Hayat* journal, which was published monthly, started to be printed as a weekly journal so the anticipated initiative took its place. The family journal *Hayat* tripled the circulation of newspapers in a very short time. It was no surprise because with its best quality photographs people felt as if they visited the places they have never seen in their lives, particularly at a time when television was still non-existent. While *Hurriyet* newspaper was selling 70,000 to 80,000 copies *Hayat* journal was getting connected with 150,000 to 200,000 readers. This worked very much in favor of Ara because he was released from doing interviews such as 'happy marriages' and 'the life of football player Metin' for *Resimli Hayat* which were a source of total boredom for him.

"What stupid interviews I have done."

They set off with Nezihe Araz for her first interview "The Mansion with Forty Windows: the Yuruks".

"*Hayat* magazine was going to be issued on a weekly basis. Our first interview. How should it start? I was sent to Anatolia with Nezihe. We toured. Seven provinces. We left Konya to do that interview; the first place we visited was Degle village of Kilbasan. It was above the Taurus Mountains. Nezihe got sick and could not come. The Governor of Konya provided a vehicle, but there was no proper road. A man called Emin was sent to accompany me. He was riding so fast and he was not even aware that I was not as fast as him. At night, we stayed at villages. Then we were ambushed by the Gendarmerie."

Ara was very happy to be touring all over Anatolia. The owner of the journal, Kazim Taskent, donated 500,000 lira to the Democrat Party to keep relations hot with current Menderes Government, and in a way it became the official journal of the power. In line with this publishing policy, Ara was constantly tasked with attending the meetings and inaugurations held by Prime Minister Menderes.

"That was my job. Menderes' man Ahmet Salih Korur was an Undersecretary of the Prime Ministry. He would come to collect me and we would go. I worked like a photographer for Menderes. I was doing the work in Istanbul that Mehmet Surenkok did in Ankara."

There was another task that the young reporter Ara did with pleasure; collecting the writings of Halide Edip Adivar, novelist and leader of the Turkish women's movement, from her home.

"When I was working in *Hayat* journal, her most recent book was serialized. I used to collect the sections written in her handwriting and deliver them to the printing shop. Vedat Gunyol took me to Halide Edip for the first time. She liked me very much. She would sit me across her and talk about stuff. I remember that she smoked a lot. She smoked so much that one had to drive a path into the smoke to get to her. I used to drop by at weekends and collect the sections that she had written. That was when I photographed her. I took a lot of pictures but Sevket Rado seized half of them to keep them in the archives. Luckily, I had made copies of them for myself. It is a good thing I did, otherwise we would have had no photographs. Somehow those archives disappeared."

Argentine Generals

In February of 1955, as they were mulling over '*what should we interview*' with Nezihe Araz, it occurred to Ara to make an interview about *simit* (Turkish bagel).

Old-young, famous, infamous - everybody was eating simit. They held street interviews and took pictures and then set off for the biggest seat in the city, the Governorate of Istanbul.

"Even the governor eats simit. We bought simit and set off to the Governor's Office."

There was an unusual flurry of activity and excitement at the governor's office. Furthermore, photojournalists had arrived which was not a good sign for Ara.

"There were other photojournalists, there was a crowd; 'something was going on,' I said. I looked and Adnan Menderes had arrived with some others. Various men were putting on medals. I was just watching not knowing what was going on, but then I said to myself I should take photographs not to miss this thinking that it could be something important. I took the pictures and they left."

Ara did not bother asking who the uniformed men with mustaches were, who the Prime Minister awarded with medals. After the ceremony, he went to the office of Governor Fahrettin Kerim Gokay holding his simits.

"I made the governor eat the simit, it was gone, and I was back at the paper."

Ara submitted the films he shot for processing in the dark room and after a while Hikmet Feridun called for him.

"Hikmet Feridun had the photographs and he said 'what are these?'. I kept looking at them but recalled nothing. I fabricated by saying 'They are Argentine generals, Adnan Menderes was awarding medals to Argentine generals'. 'Ok' he said and I left."

The next day Hikmet Feridun called Ara again. He was slightly off color.

"'Come here, the Argentine generals are waiting for you' he says. Do you know who the men actually are who you believed to be Argentine generals? They were firemen being awarded for valor in the Kapalicarsi fire."

The Istanbul Pogrom of 6/7 September

In the summer of 1955 the waters of the Mediterranean were starting to simmer. The Greeks of Turkish origin had started to kill Turks through an armed resistance against the British Colonial administration in Cyprus. They had established the terror organization, EOKA, which was armed with the support of Greece.

Ankara issued a diplomatic note to the United Kingdom informing that Turkey could not remain passive against the bloody events. With the call of the United Kingdom which was contemplating withdrawing from the island on account of the gradually escalating terror attacks, the Ministers for Foreign Affairs of the three countries Anthony Eden, Stephanos Stephanopoulos and Fatin Rustu Zorlu, convened at a conference in London.

Turks and Greeks of Turkish origin had gathered and were demonstrating outside the hall where the negotiations continued grimly. As tension was escalating, Fatin Rustu Zorlu sent a telegraph to Prime Minister Menderes saying that 'Turkey needs to assert its determination in taking ownership of Cyprus'.

The meaning of this telegraph was understood on the 6th of September towards noon. After a news broadcast on the radio by Anadolu Agency that Ataturk's house in Thessaloniki had been bombed, the editor of *Istanbul Ekspres* newspaper, Goksin Sipahioglu, halted the paper which was being printed to change the headlines. New information was added and printing resumed.

A short while later, children selling newspapers on the street were hawking 'hear the news, a bomb was thrown at Ata's house, hear the news' and one of the most embarrassing events plotted by the Democrat Party government and applied by party members blew up.

> "I met Orhan Kemal on the street, we walked together to Harbiye. We thought about what we should do. Mehmet Cemal and I arrived at the 'Folklore Extension and Sustenance Society' financed by Yapi Kredi and established by Vedat Nedim, which was going to have a show at the Open-Air Theater that day. I was deputized to take photographs. There was no time to get there. A demolition of Eftalupos Cafe across Taksim cinema had commenced. It was frequented for betting horse races. We were taking photographs as we approached and suddenly Beyoglu Street was in a state of chaos. Was it absolutely necessary to go to the folklore display? Here chaos was going on. We used our common sense and decided that this event was more important and started to take photographs."

The bomb placed into Ataturk's house in Thessaloniki blew up a few hours later in Istanbul. Everything for this organization was actually planned by the government to 'display that the Turkish people were riled about Cyprus'. Rabble and riffraff brought under the leadership of members of the Democrat Party from surrounding provinces by trucks to Istanbul marched towards Taksim and started to attack stores owned by Greeks of Turkish origin.

As the crowd grew larger by the moment, they started to attack homes and places of business which had been marked prior, and security forces had been instructed to observe the events. Then the attacks shed their political skin and transformed into 'hostility towards property' and the homes and shops of other minorities and even wealthy Turks were targeted.

> "Mehmet Cemal next to me was saying 'Damn, I wonder what is happening at our shop?'. Mehmet's mother had a shop named Gilda which sold jewelry and ornaments. We went there and saw that she was trying to stop them by saying 'this is Cemal Pasa's shop'. They continued to

demolish the shop saying 'what does Gilda mean? Gilda is not Turkish'. If Turkey had the same mindset today, everything would be demolished in regard to a lot of foreign names of the shops."

Yeni Sabah reporter Orhan Kologlu and his football player brother Dogan, together with Galatasaray football team manager Arslan Barutcuoglu, were standing in front of Mehmet Cemal's mother Kamran's shop and telling everyone 'I swear this is a Turkish establishment' and kissed and embraced everyone to calm them down but those who were riled were hard to convince.

"It was a Japanese store. There was a grand piano on the first floor. The display window glass had been broken and this man was trying to shove it out of the window but the front legs of the piano got stuck in something and prevented it from falling. I was waiting downstairs. If he threw the piano out, I would take a photograph. I told the men 'wait, I'm not ready, I need to adjust my camera'. Then I said 'I am ready, throw it out if you like'. They pushed and pushed and finally the piano was in the air and I took my shot. Events like that happened."

Among all this Ara realised his father's shop.

"We proceeded immediately to my father's shop. It had transformed into a first aid center, people with cuts were being treated. Those who had gotten injured when they were breaking windows with sticks and stones also rushed to our pharmacy for first aid. My father's shop was the only venue in Beyoglu that eas not demolished."

Although it was some consolation that no harm had occurred to his father's pharmacy, he had witnessed with his own eye what such a furious crowd was capable of. Istiklal Street was covered with household goods, layers of fabrics, underwear, furs, carpets.

"It was not just one group, one came, the other went. It was not only in Beyoglu, it was in Buyukada, Karakoy, everywhere. Actually, they were coming for robbing, for instance; they were changing their clothes with the new ones from the shop and leave. One man had swollen up like a balloon because he had worn six overcoats one on top of the other."

The incidents, which started on the 6th of September at noon and continued until the morning of 7th September, destroyed 73 churches, seven holy springs, two monasteries, one factory and damaged 5,538 properties. The looters were instructed not to make attempts against life but still three people had been killed and tens were injured. The minimum loss of life was mainly due to the common sense of many Turkish citizens who saved their Greek neighbors from the flood of fury.

The army intervened and Martial Law was declared.

"If the army had not intervened that first night, a massacre would have occured. The next day started a search all over, our neighborhood was full of troops, they made house to house searches. There was a military mess next to our house where the troops had their meals, they deployed here and I took their photographs. They stayed for a few days. "

After these events many people left Istanbul, even Turkey.

"Pastellas used to be here in a corner shop in Galatasaray; he carried those famous blue British plates, antique plates. Pastellas was the distributor of that organization. He was also a friend and one of the partners of Eczacibasi, a chemist. 'Goodbye' he said. 'I am going, you can keep the factory'. They owned a ceramic factory on Mumhane Street jointly with Nejat. That factory progressed and went on to become Vitra today."

The Menderes government blamed this disgrace on the communists as usual.

"They arrested writer Aziz Nesin etc. This event had nothing to do with the communists, it was organized by the Adnan Menderes government. Then we took a photograph of Celal Bayar looking at the street saying, 'Whoa', 'Is this possible?' He was astonished, he has a photograph displaying his astonishment. Those people did not think things through. The story was that Fatin Rustu Zorlu was in London in a meeting and he said that something should be done in Istanbul to be a reason for me to talk here. So, they organized this event, they intended to damage a few properties but then things got out of hand. What happened was they collected indigent groups from Gebze with a truck and brought them here, Menderes government was the responsible one."

Hayat journal for which Ara was working for could not even publish the photographs depicting the gravity of the event. Menderes had used the events of 6-7 September to justify the implementation of restrictions to the laws governing the press and assembly to control the opposition and the press.

Woman and Allah

Ara Guler was sent by *Hayat* journal to cover the Kirkpinar wrestling event in Edirne in 1956. The worldwide famous photograph he took there named *Woman and Allah* served as a business card for him and eventually was exhibited at museums in the four corners of the world and entered private collections.

"I went to take a picture of the writing 'Allah' on the external wall of the mosque. As I was adjusting my camera two women in burkas passed by. There are two steps there, they stepped on the first one immediately below the writing. They opened their bundles and started to eat. I looked at the sight, pitch black writing, pitch black women, the contrast was very good as was the perspective. I started shooting, one shot, two shots, three shots etc. The women noticed me and got up, they collected their bundles and left but I had already taken 8-9 frames."

After processing the film that he had shot with the Rolleicord II and seeing the contact prints he was demoralized to observe that the women had cut off the letter 'vav' on the wall of the Old Mosque which symbolizes the word Vahid meaning "Allah is one" but then he saw that at least one frame had the composition that he was aiming for.

"In all of them Vav is adjacent, one is separate and we used that one. The photograph was published in *Hayat* magazine with the title *Woman and Allah*. Under the size of Allah the two women appeared to be very striking. I like this picture. This photograph was initially published in the National Geographic in America. They had prepared an issue dedicated to the World of Islam. All the photographs of this interview had been taken by Magnum users. Subsequently a letter came from a publisher in Pantheon France who wanted the photograph, it had been observed on the cover of a book about Islam. It has been used widely, perhaps one thousand times, I have lost count. It has been used as a poster."

The same year Ara opened his first solo exhibition in Maya Art Gallery, owned by Adalet Cimcoz, whom he knew from the voice over studios. The exhibition was a rarely-encountered "avant-garde" exhibition in which his photographs merged with the poems of his poet friend Nevzat Ustun.

"I was writing the poetry of Nevzat Ustun on tracing paper with own my hand writing. I put it here and pressed a photograph; it became a photograph accompanied by a poem. Subsequently Nevzat removed them, he also has passed away."

Time-Life

Towards the year end, Ara heard that *Time* magazine had opened an office in Istanbul. *Time* magazine, owned by anti-communist media giant Henry Luce, nicknamed *Emperor* because he was powerful enough to be able to determine who was going to be the US President, was under the same roof as influential media organs such as *Fortune, Life,* and *Sports Illustrated,* with wide circulations.

"Henry Luce was an important journalist. 20-30 books have been written about Luce. He is among the royalty in terms of the world press. For example, he can refer to Kennedy and say 'ok he can be it' and make him the President of the United States and he comes to thank Henry Luce. 'Ara, you are a young kid, you look like a good kid, it is a good thing that our President is young. I must go now, you can talk to them' and indicates his men.

Rome Office Chief Bob Neville was appointed to head the representation of *Time* magazine in Istanbul.

"Bob Neville was living in Rome. He was a good friend of the Pope. Bob was also very wealthy, he had oil wells in Texas. As you know, upper crust Americans live in Europe. He was doing this job as a hobby, he was playing. The American Ambassador in Rome would change, a new ambassador would be appointed. Bob Neville was anticipating this appointment. However, the wife of Henry Luce was appointed ambassador; Claire Booth Luce. Bob got angry, 'How can they choose that woman over me'. Of course, they had an argument with Henry Luce and he came here to establish an Office. That is why he came to Turkey, if it had not been for the appointment perhaps he would not have come here."

After losing the position of US Ambassador in Rome to the wife of his boss, the first thing Bob Neville did was leasing two flats across Macka Park, , as soon as he arrived in Istanbul. He was going to use the top floor as an office and the one below as a residence. After renting the flats, he started looking for someone who spoke English and found Editor Nuyan Yigit of *Cumhuriyet* newspaper who was a graduate of Robert College. He also found Ara...

"He engaged Nuyan as a translator to translate the newspapers every day. Nuyan was also my friend. Nuyan's father Ibrahim Sureyya Yigit was a comrade in arms of Mustafa Kemal. They needed to find photojournalists, you know for a magazine with photographs. 'I need a photojournalist, who is the best photojournalist here' he asks and Nuyan recommended me. Then they invited me to talk to Bob Neville, Bob engaged me for interviews. They paid well."

Ara, who was working for *Hayat* magazine on one hand and *Time* magazine on the other, was trying to get acquainted with his new boss.

"The man was strange. He did not write sitting down. He made a weird desk for himself where he wrote standing up. He placed typewriters all over the office. Whenever something was passing through his mind, he wrote it down with the nearest typewriter and when he remembered something relevant he returned to that typewriter and continued writing. After that the papers were collected by Nuyan. The man was both writing and farting simultaneously."

Bob Neville made a big impression on Ara, not only with his weird habits, but his journalism and form of administration as well.

"I learned a lot about journalism from Bob Neville. We learned European style journalism from these men. A journalist should consider what is and what is not together. Neville taught me how to do this. A journalist should have a head for organization. Neville was a great organizer. We felt empowered."

Neville had attested to his skills as a 'great organizer' with the way he handled the events he had encountered in the past.

"Bob Neville, Bureau Chief in Rome. He received news that the Pope was going to die. He thought; what happens if the Pope dies? There is a window in the Vatican. When the Pope dies, that window will be covered with a black curtain. Opposite that window is a building. What was the photograph to be taken, a curtain will be closed and that is what will be shot. Men manned with Leicas equipped with tele-objectives were waiting night and day. He thought, if the Pope dies, who will replace him. Who were the cardinals, they were 22 people. He dispatched a photojournalist and a reporter to the various parts of the world where these individuals were located. If the Pope dies, what will the people of the Vatican do? He collected all the reporters in Europe and sent them to mingle among the population there. He took his measures, he did not leave anything to chance!
After this preparation do you know what happened? The Pope did not die, he recovered. Thousands of dollars was wasted. But you know what? They gave Bob Neville a bonus of 50,000 dollars because he took good measures. That was what *Life* was about."

Their operation systems were very different from the operation system of the Turkish press. The fact that 40,000 dollars had been blocked in the Central Bank for the usage of Time Istanbul office, which was enough to cover the establishment capital of a newspaper in those days, had a significant contribution in making them 'feel empowered'. The Near East Office of *Time* in Istanbul was equipped with the most recent technical features. It was initially responsible for Turkey, then covered other countries in the region such as Egypt, Syria, Iran and Iraq.

"Our task was to cover the events here. We carried out a lot of interviews. One of the first ones we did was to cover the Kirkpinar wrestling event. You do the interviews as if they are going to be published the soonest like a daily newspaper but nothing happens! But that was the system, am I making myself clear?"

Ara became friend with the legendary boss of *Time*, Henry Luce, who rarely got to meet the people he employed.

"Even the most important reporters of *Life* never saw Luce's face. He came here with his wife. I reserved a suite for them. We toured all Istanbul with them for one week. I became pals with Henry Luce. I took his wife on a tour of Istanbul to Sultanahmet, the Hagia Sophia. They were here for one week, what can I say."

The Nurtured Press

The brilliant years of the Democrat Party government was drawing to an end. The Party blamed the press for the failure of its policies in the political and economic area. The government had forsaken its planned economy and lost control of the economy due to continuous foreign debt. When the press started to criticize the government and reflected the hardship on the people with news about the black market and queues, like all powers, Menderes decided that he needed to control the press.

On one hand, the government was applying censorship to the press as well as economic pressure. The paper used for newspapers was 'allocated' by the state and the allocation for newspapers which criticized the power was restricted to the point that it did not cover circulation. Newspapers that were pro-government received a surplus of paper. The government gave all official notices and advertising to pro-Democrat Party newspapers. These newspapers would sell the surplus paper they got on the black-market. The press that benefited from these privileges were named the 'nurtured press'.

"After the 11th edition we ran out of paper, and *Hayat* magazine stopped. There was no paper. We were importing paper from Hungary. We had started flirting with the government but it was not official yet, we were eyeing each other coyly. We had been assigned a day's worth of paper from the paper factory in Izmit because we needed a special absorbent paper for the photogravure printing machines which was not available in Turkey. We got the paper and in return we had to flatter the guys. We had mutual interest so I was tasked with following Adnan Menderes wherever he went and interview him. We printed the picture of all inaugurations like a party paper."

Kazim Taskent, whose *Hayat* magazine had to suspend publishing for 6 months 13 days because it ran out of paper, had other businesses in addition to journal publication. He was not going to infuriate the government and endanger those businesses.

"There are other stories. Yapi Kredi imported tractors from abroad. Caterpillar, John Deere etc. Promotional meetings were organized for them which I covered. Yapi Kredi's tractors were our business. Then there were the famous lotteries."

The Horse cart and the Tramway

Hayat magazine was being published again and Ara was busy again...

Sevket Rado's assignment for a news item that would capture the essence of the winter of 1957 was instrumental in the shooting of the well-known photograph of *The Horse Cart and the Tramway* by Ara Guler.

Ara hits the shutter button of his Leica as the route of tramway number 26, with its green and white signboard along line 37 between Edirnekapi-Bahcekapi going to Sirkeci under snow, intersects with a horse cart.

There was a note attached to the lower right hand corner of the frame, the horse with sacks tied to its hooves so it would not slip in the snow and the cartman:

"Horse with galoshes- various hardships and problems are generated also for non-motorized vehicles on the streets of Istanbul in winter. Is this horse with sackcloth tied to its hooves to enable its progress pulling the cart along the steep streets of Istanbul a typical example of this?"

"Winter was here but there was no photograph of winter on the back cover of the magazine and I was told to get a picture of winter so I went to Karakoy, there was so much snow that I took a picture in Sirkeci. The original of that tramway picture got lost. Two years ago, I washed the film because it was dusty and it dissolved in the water, I wish I had not touched it. I swore I would never handle film again. I guess I put it into acid or processing fluid or something that softened it and the negative disappeared before my eyes. Thankfully very good prints are available."

Cannes Film Festival

He was over the moon when asked whether he had covered the Cannes Film Festival for *Yeni Istanbul* newspaper, where he started his profession, since he worked for an international broadcasting organization and spoke languages. Suavi Sonar was monitoring the Cannes festival for the magazine. The approach of the Turkish press to Cannes was evident. While Ara viewed the Cannes Film Festival as a platform for world renowned actors and directors to meet, Suavi Sonar, who worked for the same magazine, had a different approach. Sonar took pictures of beautiful women wrapped in cobras in Cannes and published them under the title 'the last nudes in Cannes'.

"Suavi Sonar is involved in fashion business because he has a boutique and he is also a good friend of mine. He was preparing the page and grabbed a camera. As he is a womanizer this was a great opportunity to flirt with the ladies."

In the summer issues of *Hayat* magazine in 1957 there is a photograph of Suavi Sonar trying to reveal more of the cleavage of a starlet who has come to Cannes with the hope of becoming a star with the title 'This is how cleavage is shot in Cannes'.

"Suavi Sonar who returned from Cannes a few days before the end of the festival basking underneath the warm and sunny Mediterranean narrated what happened after the Festival. This starlet owes our photojournalist Suavi Sonar the crowd of photographers surrounding her. Naturally the efforts made by the girl herself have some impact. How is that? She revealed some more cleavage as recommended by Suavi. After that everything was easy. They went to the beach, started to take pictures..."

"Now lots of men go there and shoot the artists for their bodies. Do you understand? Our editors do it too because the philosophy is 'Women are portrayed at the Cannes festival'. There are also other things in Cannes. Our men are not interested in that. Really well known personalities come there. For example, I saw Orson Welles, Alberto Moravia, the best screen writer Cesar Zavatini, Alberto Lattuada and Vittorio De Sica, Jean Marais, and Jean Cocteau; I befriended these men."

As well as great names of notoriety, fame excited the journalists...

"We photojournalists were at the festival taking pictures of the famous at the palace gate. All the stars were accompanied with elegant companions. Suddenly a major commotion incurred. Everybody toppled over from the pushing and the wave of crowd movement, lamps were overturned, screams were heard. In all my life, I have never seen photojournalists get so excited. It was infectious, I got very excited too. Somebody was coming but who? A frail, small man looking like a villager was approaching; it was Picasso. Even the Queen of England could not have caused such excitement. In all that commotion, I was able to take only a few pictures."

Cannes was an opportunity for new initiatives for Ara. That is how he made contact with *Paris-Match*, one of the most influential magazines in France.

"We were in Cannes. There were personnel from *Paris-Match*. We were peers so we talked and they say; 'You work for *Time*; would you also work for us and send us current news from Turkey?' Would I not, man? At that time, Andrea Lakaz was the editor of *Paris-Match*. Subsequently he quit journalism and became a novelist. I said yes but I had to check etc. I asked the Americans, they didn't care, they said 'go ahead our market is different'. The text of the interviews I made for *Paris-Match* were written directly in French together with Abdi Ipekci. I would dictate and he would write. After that I visited Paris often... I would drop by *Paris-Match*. During my first visits I stayed at a small bed & breakfast for 16 franks. In St. Michel, a street near Rue des Ecoles..."

Debauchery in Paris

After the Cannes Festival was over Ara went to Paris and, while he was staying with his Ethnologist friend Alain Gherbrandt, he fell in love with a French girl. He was really smitten, blind to all else.

"I fell in love with a girl; 'Stay here, don't go' she said. I made a telephone call to Istanbul and said; 'I am not coming, I shall stay in Paris'. Without thinking. I am not going back. I want to stay in Paris. They don't fire me. I told Editor Yilmaz Polda on the telephone 'make me a reporter in Paris for the paper so I can stay here with my woman.' I had very limited money left. Without thinking. Yilmaz says, 'Habip Edip wants to see you, go to the Plaza Athénée Hotel and find him'. I couldn't refuse to go."

It would be unseemly to disregard the summons of the wealthy boss of *Yeni Istanbul* newspaper, Habip Edip Torehan, being Ara's old friend. Torehan, who had houses on the four corners of the world, stayed in the Plaza Athénée which was the best hotel in Paris at that time. Torehan had a permanent suite in this luxury hotel.

"I went to the hotel and called him from reception. 'Come on up,' he said. 'Our people are going to organize a Press Publication Turkish Night in the Bagatelle Rose Garden. They will introduce Turkish fashion. Models will be attending from Olgunlasma Institute and I want you to interview them,' he said, but there was 20 days to go. 'Stay until then, organize this business, I will also attend.'"

Torehan had perceived that Ara had a problem. Just as he was leaving, he called out from the other end of the room the size of a small apartment with its cream color wallpaper and rare ornaments: 'I bet you don't have any money either.'

"I said 'I have money from my father'. He waved his hand toward the fireplace and said 'there is money over there, take it so you have money with you'. I went and looked, there were thousand frank notes, I took two, it was enough. 'No no take more' he sayid. I took one more. 'Look I'm telling you to take it, take it all' so I did. I swear there were hundreds of thousands of franks there. I took it all and spent it with the woman. It was a very large amount in those days. One month later I had a hard time getting enough money together for plane fare and returned to Istanbul. We toured, enjoyed, spent that money."

Indigence in Poland

In 1957 Ara was in Poland to cover a game to be played between the Turkish National Football Team with Poland in Warsaw, for the *Yeni Istanbul* newspaper. It was Turkey's National Youth and Sports Day being celebrated all over the country. Santral Stadium in the capital was covered in ice and filled with 60,000 sports fans, including the Prime Minister of Poland and his ministers. The Turkish National Football team to play the game directed by Australian referee Grinn, was comprised of Captain Turgay Seren manning the goalpost, Ahmet Berman, Basri Dirimlili, Mustafa Ertan, Ergun Ercins, Nejat Kucuksorgunlu, Isfendiyar Aciksoz, Mehmet Ali Has, Metin Oktay, Kadri Aytac and Lefter Kucukandonyadis.

The game was competitive and the Turkish National Team managed to win 1-0 against Poland, recognized as one of the giants of European football. The winning goal scored by Mehmet Ali Has during the 43rd minute of the game.

When the money that the newspaper promised to dispatch through the Central Bank did not come through, Ara who was monitoring the game, was held as collateral by the hotel. Ara's passport was seized and he spent difficult days in his hotel room waiting three weeks for the money to arrive.

"I had no food. When I got hungry I drank water from the tap. "

Ara lost all hope in the newspaper and he contacted his father to save him from this nightmare.

"My father intervened and I was rescued. He gave money to a Jew over there and I collected the money from a Jew here and I was saved. Wherever I went with a lot of money it was always my father's money. What the paper paid me was not enough for anything, it was not enough. I would be held like this in many places and my father would send money to rescue me. I did significant work, but unfortunately the management was not even aware."

Intervention with the Gallows

The court case of the 'Sariyer Monster' named so because he raped and killed a small girl in Sariyer and disposed her body in the river, had concluded. The perpetrator had been sentenced to the gallows. Ara heard about the execution and thought that it would interest *Time*.

In those days, executions would be carried out on Sultanahmet Square for all to see. Ever since the Ottoman era, the state had used the branches of the centenarian maple tree for hanging and this tradition continued in the same venue.

The people of Istanbul would gather before the gallows which was established in the area, currently occupied by benches in a row between the Hagia Sophia and the Sultanahmet Mosque. They would sit with each other a few meters from the man to be executed, eating doner kebap, meat patties, simit and drinking sherbet (frozen fruit juice) and watch the convicts dangling at the end of noose. That day the place was like a fair ground, everyone was waiting for the execution but it kept being postponed.

"We waited until dawn every day at Sultanahmet Square for the execution which was kept postponing and on top, they did not tell us when the execution would take place."

After days of waiting, just as the crowd was about to lose its patience, restlessness started in the square.

"The gallows were set up, the convict was delivered in the prison vehicle. Of course, we were looking from a distance, there was a distance of 25-30 meters between us, the executioner and the prosecutor stepped forward and the convict was executed. After the execution was completed, I wanted to take photographs. However, the man hanging kept turning around. I could not photograph him from where I was because the man kept turning his back our way. I wanted to shoot the man so that I could get the placard on his chest holding the numbers of the law but I could not. I went and turned the body around. Why should I be scared! The convict started to rotate slowly and everybody took photographs. I had two cameras, one color and one black and white. I withdrew slightly. The night was dark, it was necessary to use a flash."

Executions have their own rules.

"A man cannot be hung during the daytime. If you are convicted to be executed it is your right to live only until 12 o'clock at night. The convict must not see the sun rise the next morning, That is the procedure."

The Bloody Price of a Passion for Imagination

The biggest train accident in Turkey happened in October 1957. 36 km from Istanbul between the stations of Ispartakule and Yarimburgaz. Europe Express train number 8, on its way towards Edirne, and a motor train going in the Sirkeci direction collided. At 22:16 a deafening noise was heard when the express train was coming full speed downhill in the region and collided with the motor train coming from the opposite direction. The head-on crash killed 95 people and 150 were injured.

"A news item was delivered that the Orient Express had collided near Catalca and many were dead. Painter Firuz Askin had a car, I said 'Take me there'. We got in the car and went to the accident area, ambulances had arrived, etc. We saw the train downhill, wagons had overturned, had climbed on top of each other. What a sight. We went down. He said 'I don't want to come'. 'Why not?' 'Such events frighten me' he said. I said 'what kind of journalist are you bla bla'. He was holding his stomach, and vomited. Whatever, I let him vomit. I left him there and went down; the situation was very bad."

Everyone was bewildered because they had never encountered such a disaster before. The fact that it rained all night made it harder to facilitate rescue search activities. All the ambulances in Istanbul had been dispatched to the incident area, the accident site was in a state of chaos.

"They were removing the dead and placing them in a row near the train, 10 here, 15 there, 20 over yonder. I took photographs and decided to enter a wagon that was in a vertical position thinking there might have been something extraordinary within. Taking magazine photographs is something else. The job was not finished after pictures of collided trains have been taken. Details are necessary. Symbolic details. I could not show the bodies in the foreground. I needed to be imaginative."

Ara dived into the overturned wagons in search of the 'imagination' in his mind.

"I entered a wagon, the compartment was crooked but it was still possible to walk inside. I saw a hand and an emergency brake perhaps two handbreadths from one another. I played a composition in my head, if this hand was sightly further as if it had been reaching for the emergency handle; would that not make a more dramatic picture? I was pulling the man's hand, that is the body's, but it wouldn't budge. I tried pushing his body, it was stuck, it was not moving, I pulled and the balance was interrupted and all the blood that had accumulated underneath the man poured down over my head. I was covered in blood from head to foot. I was unable to hold the man's hand so I departed covered in blood. I took some pictures with the Orient Express and the casualties with the train wreck in the background which made the full page in Paris-Match."

In Asik Veysel's Village

Toward the end of 1957, Ara accompanied Ethnologist Alain Gherbrandt to the Selcuklu monuments around Sivas to shoot a culture documentary for French television.

"For four or five months, we criss-crossed throughout Anatolia. When we got to Sivas we immediately found minstrel Âsik Veysel. I met him for the first time in Sabahattin Eyuboglu's house. Alain also knew him from Sabahattin's house. The next day we went to Yildizeli together and from there to Sivrialan village of Sarikisla. It was the first time I went to Sivrialan, to Asik Veysel's village..."

Ara and his French friend Alain were welcomed with a lot of hospitality. They settled into Turkish minstrel Asik Veysel's house and took plenty of footage in the village.

"For days on end I photographed life in the village; from putting three flat stones on top of each other to making a coffin rest. Harvest gathering, grinding grain with a grinder which was turned by a blindfolded horse, gathering bales with a harrow; I photographed village activities. I took photographs of many faces, working girls, men, an elderly woman churning away. Subsequently I found out that they were all Veysel's grandchildren, children, daughters-in-law, and the elderly lady churning was his wife. Thus, I photographed Asik Veysel's whole extended family..."

Asik Veysel and Veysel Erkilic who was from the same village as well as his namesake travel throughout the country, they sang and played instruments and were known as "Veysel and Small Veysel".

"One early evening I brought Veysel and Small Veysel to the village agora and asked them to play their instruments. First heads appeared over rooftops, the villagers were observing us. Subsequently children drew closer. Finally, I saw the whole village gather toward the village square. They gathered around the two troubadours and listened to their music. After a while their eyes became subdued, each and every one of them had withdrawn into their internal world. The reed instrument transported them away from the village works that night."

Ara never forgot the hospitality he was extended in the Sivrialan village of Sivas province.

"In the evenings Asik Veysel would play the saz (reed instrument) for us. With Small Veysel of course... Whatever food was available in the village was brought to us. Naturally they also had raki. A raki glass is held from beneath, brought to chest level and then consumed. From time to time before Asik Veysel played the saz he would say, 'we wine and dine but the saz is starving'. Then he would pick up the saz and start playing. For days, we listened to him play and sing. We wined, dined, talked. Words alternated with the saz. The two Veysels narrated the problems, essence, past of Anatolian people with their instruments-words. Then Small Veysel died and Big Veysel was left alone. It seemed like the branch of a tree had been broken off. I never saw Asik Veysel alone. Later I heard about him. He had rejoined his friend, the black soil. Now there is a museum in his village established with my photographs and books. Salute."

Le Tumulus de Nemroud-Dagh

Hayat magazine wanted an interview about 'the famous in our museums'. Fikret Arit was writing the story, Ara was going to take photographs of artifacts such as the head of Alexander, Heracles.

The shooting started at the Istanbul Museum of Archeology.

"Technically, I was taking very difficult photographs. I was not just standing opposite the object and taking a picture; I was taking artificial shots which means that I prepare a background, prepare the lighting accordingly, work with projectors, close windows, etc. The photography is like surgery, it takes hours; another interesting thing was while I was working in the museum, a man always accompanied me, as if I was going to hoist the five-ton statue and take it away...."

Ara would be totally concentrated on his photography and he would forget the concept of time which would victimize the officers who accompanied him.

"I concentrate on my work, lunchtime comes and goes, the men go without food. After two days of working like this the men said 'Bro, you work all the time and we are hungry, can you please take a break so that we can go and eat'. 'Ok, go eat' I said and went upstairs into the library and waited. In a library what can you do? You look at the books. Suddenly I saw a book in French; Le Tumulus de Nemroud-Dagh."

Ara became intrigued by the leather covered, A4 size, two separate slim volumes in French bearing the signature of "O. Hamdy Bey". When he opened the cover, and saw the signature of his relative "Osgan Effendi" he was even more astounded. He knew the authors. One was sculptor Yervant Osgan while the other one was his close friend Osman Hamdi. The founders of Sanayi-i Nefise, in other words, the Academy of Fine Arts.

The first volume of this ancient work which carried the date MDCCCLXXXIII (meaning 1883) with yellowed pages, had been prepared in the order of a book, while the other one was like a dossier with its edges laced with brown ribbon. As Ara untied the ribbons he was flabbergasted at the sight of the sketches and photographs he saw.

"I saw some old photographs taken with primitive methods with a plan behind them. I was astonished. 'Wow' I said. I had travelled all over Turkey taking photographs but I never saw or heard of something like this. There were fabulous things on a mountain. The archeologists had taken their own photographs in front of heads of huge statues. A lot of statues. I was thinking to myself who put these statue heads larger than a man on the mountain? Where the dickens was this place? I started to look at the drawings to find out how to get there."

Ara's heart started to beat faster with excitement as he tried to determine the place that he had not heard of from the sketch that looked like a treasure map.

"I looked around and found some thin paper like tracing paper and placed it on the plan and copied it on the paper and took it with me. I also took some notes."

This book that fascinated Ara was the first work in terms of Turkish archeology and, except for a few people within the narrow world of archeology, no one was aware of this work. He pinned the sketch he had drawn with the notes with care and put them away in his drawer.

"After that day, I was constantly looking for an opportunity to go there. One day a professor came to me. He said that his permission request to go East had been rejected. He showed me a journal. It was in French. I made a reproduction of the journal with the Leica just in case. I went to compare the picture with the book in the drawer and I saw that they are about the same place. I pinned them all together and put them away again."

He had made up his mind, come hell or high water he was going to find this place and photograph it.

He got lucky five years later. He accompanied the shooting of a documentary *Color Walls* in Anatolia by a French team for which the text had been written by Sabahattin Eyuboglu for Eczacibasi Culture Films.

"I was like their art director. I toured them all over Anatolia. As the team worked they kept telling me 'is there something interesting in the vicinity, let's get it on film too'. I mentioned Nemrut Mountain to the director of the film, Pierre Biro. They had the vehicles, the materials. However, I did have one condition; no one can take photographs other than me."

The French team found this condition a bit weird but they accepted and off they went.

"They did not object too much; we set off. How do you go to Nemrut Mountain? There was no road then as there is now. First, we arrived in Adiyaman. From there we went to Kahta but the Old Kahta road was not a road for motor vehicles it was just a narrow trail. We proceeded with the car with difficulty. When we arrived at Old Kahta the trail faded away completely, there was nothing more. Well what shall we do now? We shall ride mules! A villager said 'I will take you to Horik'. It took exactly nine hours to travel from Old Kahta to Horik on mules. We got there but guess how? We proceeded along a narrow path with an abyss on one side. I looked at the animal's hooves – if it stepped just one centimeter to the side I would have been a goner. The abyss is about 600-700 meters. I couldn't talk to the men, one of them spoke Turkish but it was limited. He learned some Turkish when he was doing his military service. Anyway, we arrived safe and sound. We gaped looking out at what we did. I said 'wait' give me the cameras… you shall shoot only film and I shall only take pictures...' It's a deal..."

The team was absolutely mesmerized by the scene in front of them.

"We all worked relentlessly. They shot for television until the sun set while I took photographs. At that time one of the heads was on top of a statue. Then it was hit by lightning and rolled off. Evening came, the sunset and in half an hour it was going to be pitch black. We were on a mountain, there was no village, no light. How should we descend from the mountain? The mules were there as was the mule keeper but we were scared to get on the mules in the dark of the night. Finally, we descended with the mules walking in front and we trailed behind them. We went up in nine hours and it took us 12 hours to go down in the dark. It was not that we were afraid but we wanted to avoid accidents of course. "

After descending safe and sound from the mountain with no paths or markings, Ara processed the films and printed them on cardboard in an atmosphere of excitement as if he had discovered one of the rare treasures in the world and submitted them to the editorial department.

"I showed these photographs and my commentary to *Hayat* magazine, they did not care. They did not understand anything from the work. 'What shall we do with these, pictures of rocks and stones? Why don't you interview artists instead of rocks, take pictures of artists and we will use the photographs' they said. This work was published 137 times all over the world. The French *Paris-Match* published it under the heading 'The Discovery of our Reporter'. It was very important to be published in a major magazine like this. Whereas here when I delivered the photographs, the reaction was 'you took pictures of rocks and soil?' Thatwas the mindset, the learning..."

The Nemrut commentary that the Turkish press ignored as rocks-soil created massive interest in the world.

"This commentary was published in the UNESCO Courrier as well as many other publications. It was one of my best-sellers. When our people saw the commentary in the foreign press they lamented 'Wow, what they are capable of'.
'Damn...' I say, 'Look at the signature it is Ara Guler'.
Unfortunately, that's the way it is."

The Uskudar Disaster

In March 1958 Ara witnessed the biggest sea disaster in the history of the Republic of Turkey.

"It was a Saturday. Our caricaturist Firuz heard it on the radio and called; 'Look, something has happened in Izmit, find out will you'. I called Associated Press and asked 'What is going on?' They said, 'Man, a vessel has sunk, there are many casualties'. I immediately telephoned Sevket Rado and askedHow to get a car, how to go. Yapi Kredi has a Central Garage in Elmadag. 'I am ordering a car, you go and get it and follow the commentary' he said."

Uskudar, the old faithful ferry number 72 built in Elbing Gemany in 1927 and belonging to Sirket-i Hayriye (Maritime Authority), had been hit. Apparently it was hit by a black waterspout (a columnar vortex) which was the product of an intense storm. The storm appeared suddenly along the skyline shortly after the ferry departed from Izmit port, with its weary black trunk and tired steam engine.

As soon as the windows of the *Uskudar* shattered, the captain rang the alarm bell and called on all passengers to don life vests, after which the waterspout ripped the deckhouse apart. The ferry was left without control as the captain was thrown into the sea and the rudder was fragmented, after which the ferry overturned in Sogucak and 272 people drowned.

The ferry was known as the 'Student Ferry' because it carried students living in the area, and therefore most of the passengers that day on the *Uskudar* were students.

"Students used to get on this ferry. They were the offspring of people living in Golcuk and Degirmendere – mostly officers, returning from school. It was only a short distance, but a storm broke out, a waterspout appeared behind the bay which occurs a few times per year and sunk this vessel."

The spectators on the coast observed the life and death situation 500 meters offshore in a state of confusion and helplessness.

The first responders were rowboats and motor boats and subsequently vessels and submarines from the Golcuk Fleet arrived at the scene. The only thing that they could do was collect the bodies of those who had perished of the cold. In the disaster that only 40 people survived, some of the bodies were never even found.

"Fishermen came and went in their vessels carrying frozen bodies. The bodies were placed on the ground and I took their photographs. For example, the school bag of a student had opened and his ruler, notebook was floating on the water. I entered the water up to my waist, the bottom was marshy."

It was not an easy trauma to overcome when a coffin departed from every neighborhood in the Bay area. All of Turkey was in profound mourning. People would wait for days on end in the cold weather hoping to find a trace of the bodies of their lost loved ones. Many people living in the region stopped eating fish after the marine disaster, which was a reflexive reaction to their indescribable pain.

"Divers, etc.... The last frame I shot was the flue of the submerged vessel which had appeared above water. I took photographs and returned in the evening to process the film. The next morning, I went back to take more pictures, thus, I delivered three rounds to *Paris-Match*. *Paris-Match* allocated 10 pages to my commentary."

Going Places

Interviews in featuring the human element were followed with interest by local and foreign colleagues. The photography editor of Germany's main journal *Stern* found Ara.

"The Germans wanted me. Gunther Beukert, who was the Bureau Chief in Germany for United Press International, had become the photography editor of *Stern*. At that time, *Stern* was being published by Henry Nannen. Gunther called me and asked if I would be his reporter. But I asked *Time* first. 'I have been offered a reporting job from Germany, what do you say?' I said. They said 'We are the US, Europe is of no interest to us, do what you want'. So, I accepted the offer."

By this time, Ara was working for four different publishing organs which were leaders in their relevant areas.

"I was at a point when I went somewhere I had to distribute to four places, I used to carry four cameras. I had allocated each camera to one publishing organ. One camera had the label *Stern* while the other belonged to *Hayat*. You chose which camera to use by things the Germans were interested in, and the British were not interested. Sometimes you sent the film without developing it. The most painful part was not seeing what you had shot, without knowing what you had captured. Subsequently, the film was returned within four months regardless of whether the film was used or not. This application is something particular to Europe. In Turkey, forget it! Journalism has not started in Turkey yet, perhaps in the future in the year 3800 or maybe not before 4000."

As if this was not enough, he also rushed the orders of *Yeni Istanbul* newspaper as he had done at the beginning of his career.

"All this did not amount to a major income. If that was the case, I would be a wealthy man. You know about the men who get a 40,000 to 50,000-dollar salary in journalism, that was not the case in this world, only in their dreams they got that kind of money. Was it possible? The best of them do not get that kind of money, how much does the editor of *Time* earn, were our people more important?"

Fikret Mualla

After the Cannes Film Festival, Ara went to his beloved Paris and fabricated an interview subject to justify his stay there.

"We went to the Cannes Festival every year with *Hayat* for interviews. When the Festival was over I went to Paris. To justify an 8-10 day stay in Paris, I needed to generate a job for myself so that I could account for the stay to the magazine editors. So, I decided to carry out an interview with 'Turkish Painters in Paris'. I interviewed and photographed Abidin Dino, Selim Turan, Hakki Anli, Avni Arbas. Fikret Mualla remained. I said to Abidin Dino 'Abidin, I need to take photographs of Fikret Mualla, help me.' The reason why I could not take photographs of Fikret Mualla was he thought that everybody coming from Turkey was a police officer that he woul avoid seeing. I went to this café he frequented called Select. He did not show up if I was there."

A sad story underlies why Painter Fikret Mualla avoided everyone from Turkey because he believed them to be police officers, and why he had his irrational behavior and aggressiveness with everyone. When he was only 12 years old, he broke his leg playing football and he became disabled as a result of the bones being set incorrectly. When he was a child he lost his mother to Spanish flu and always blamed himself for his mother's death, because he was the first one in the house to get sick. When his father remarried and left home, he ended up getting treated for alcoholism at an early age. Another tragedy topped all these traumas and he left Istanbul never to return.

At the end of 1936, Fikret Mualla went to Degustasyon Restaurant at the entrance of Cicek Pasaji to have a few drinks and, as he was imbibing, his eye caught a portrait of Ataturk made by a German painter which had been distributed to all stores and offices at that time. According to Mualla's criteria, he felt that the portrait carried no value as a painting and every time he saw it he was upset. When he criticized the portrait by saying *"Why is the same poor portrait everywhere?"* his words were construed as an insult against Ataturk and he was detained and taken to Galatasaray Police Station. Fikret Mualla, who was beaten all night by police officers, was rescued by the intervention of Fikret Adil and Bedri Rahmi Eyuboglu and taken to Bakirkoy Mental Hospital. He had gone to France with the permanent scars of his days in the mental hospital and the beating he took at the police station.

"For example, while he was sitting in the café, he might have suddenly gone crazy and began swearing at De Gaulle. He was arrested for insulting the President and subsequently released because he had been certified as mentally incompetent, do you understand?"

His mother wanted a girl so she named him Mualla before he was born. He was raised like a girl, dressed in girl's clothes, and his hair was kept long. Because of this upbringing, Fikret Mualla had never been able to be with a woman in his life.

"The man was a lunatic, crazy all the way. He hated women."

Once, when he was sued for beating a girl, he defended himself by telling the French judge that *"I am a Turk, it is a tradition with us that from time to time men hit their wives. It is not considered a physical beating. We do it out of affection for those we love. We do not mean any harm".* The judge said *"I have never heard this before, bring me a document from ambassador and prove that it is a tradition in your country to beat women. Perhaps it can be presented as mitigating circumstances",* and he had no compunctions about applying to the Turkish Embassy in Paris to get such a document.

"I sent the word with Abidin 'he is not the police you can trust him' after which he came. We were sitting at the café talking when I said; 'I would like to take photographs of your paintings, while you are painting etc.' I took his photographs sitting in the café, walking along the streets but what I really wanted to see was the room he lived in. He was staying on the top floor of a hotel at the other end of Paris in the laundry room. It was actually a servant's room which he had transformed into a small atelier for himself. I took photographs while he was working there, from the opposite building. Then the hotelier lady said 'thank you very much for taking him'. She had thought that I was a relative. I said, 'I am a journalist, I am interviewing him, I am not taking him anywhere.' The woman said 'Take him away, he fights with everyone, he pisses all over the place'. He admired Germans, he thought like a Nazi, he had blown the whistle on everyone that is why the French disliked him, the woman wanted to get rid of him."

Ara's interview with Fikret Mualla lasted about one week.

"I took the photographs but frankly I did not want to get too involved in fear that I would be held responsible for him. During the shooting he talked about a lot of sympathetic things but what he talked about had no relevance for you."

Fikret Mualla, who led a miserable life, had stooped to selling the painting dedicated to him by Picasso to buy alcohol. The artist was homesick and feared that if he went to Turkey, which he missed, he would be killed.

"He drank constantly yet he had no money. A woman called Madame Angles was taking care of him because he was a talented painter, he was her protege and the paintings he did became hers. They took the pictures and gave him tips, his room is paid by Madam Angles, etc. "

Madam Fernande Angles, collector of art, was a fan of Fikret Mualla because of his genius, and she always supported him through dire straights. Madam Angles, whose compassion made Fikret Mualla feel slightly appreciated, acted like a guardian angel. She dealt with everything regarding the painter, from opening exhibitions to hospitalization, until the life of agony of the genius painter came to an end in the summer of 1967 in a hospice.

It is sheer irony that Fikret Mualla, who had received the beating of his life in a police station for supposedly insulting Ataturk, and whose life had subsequently been derailed, drew his last breath in a room where a picture of Ataturk and a Turkish flag were hanging.

Guardian Angel Madam Angles was on holiday and could not be reached and it was sheer luck that the painter was saved from being buried in potter's field. He was laid to rest in the Reillanne Village south of the Alps where he had spent his last five years, and which Madam Angles had organized for him to regain his health away from urban life.

"Mukadder Sezgin was the tourism attaché in Paris, I visited his office on a regular basis. After Fikret Mualla passed away an exhibition was opened in the tourism office on Avenue Champs-Elysées. Before the exhibition, I tracked the paintings like a police detective. I visited the framer, coffee shop owner, whoever... he drank, ran debts and donated paintings instead of money. I took photographs of the paintings that I was able to locate. Some had 40 paintings. Collectors had discovered this; for example, a collector called Ester turned out to have 80 original paintings. Madame Angles had quite a few. I located the majority of them. The coffee shop owner of the place he lived in has a tremendous collection. He used to drink there and since he had no money he would leave a painting. I had money but I felt it would be inappropriate to buy so I did not."

Ara, who set off to find Fikret Mualla's paintings, managed to locate most of them.

"I leased professional cameras, I would establish a studio where I went and employed electricians, and took the photographs that way. The camera weighs 40 kilograms. I came and went just like you do now for a year."

It offended Ara that he had to take photographs and make reproductions of work by a Turkish artist who had been scorned throughout his life and whose work had been snatched by foreigners. The reality that his final resting place was in France was totally unacceptable.

"We killed the man, starved and made him miserable. This French Madame Angles rescued him. If it had not been for her, Fikret Mualla would have perished long ago. Now we are all endeavoring to take ownership. Well it is not given any more. Madam Angles gets to keep the whole collection."

He decides that he had to do something.

"Fahri Koruturk had become president, the first lady Emel was Fikret Mualla's classmate from the Academy. I was the presidential photographer. I showed the pictures I had taken. 'Have you seen these, unfortunately he passed away. The least we can do is transport his remains here,' I said. 'That is a very good idea,' she said. She proceeded to summon Fine Arts General Director Mehmet Ozel and issue the necessary orders. He was transported. He had a will about being buried in Karacaahmet Cemetery and he got a beautiful grave. I took photographs of the grave."

In the beginning of the 80s, when Ara showed the Fikret Mualla reproductions he had prepared to his fellow townsman writer Aziz Nesin from Sebinkarahisar, he got an unexpected offer.

When Aziz Nesin saw what I had in my hand he said 'Nobody knows about these, we must make a book'. 'Who is going to do it?' I said. He immediately called the owner of Cem Publishing House, journalist Oguz Akkan. I said to Abidin, 'You write it, you knew him the best'. We worked a lot with Abidin but in terms of book printing technique the job was a disaster. The capabilities of the technical equipment of printing in those days was what it was."

The Anatolia We Do Not Know

One early evening as Ara finished his work for the day and descended down Cagaloglu hill he ran into Ali Karakurt, one of the famous police reporters of Babiali. When Karakurt, who worked for *Yeni Istanbul,* saw Ara he embraced him. Ara could tell that Karakurt had been drinking and was complaining about "*Damn do nothing in life...*", so he took him to the Gar Music hall in Sirkeci to cheer him up. They started to drink together.

"We went and settled in Sirkeci's Gar Music Hall. We watched the trains, he says 'damn all trains are going somewhere and we go nowhere'. 'Where shall we go?' I say. 'Let's just go...' he says. Well, ok, why not- but these trains go to Europe. 'Let's go to Haydarpasa and get on a train there' he says. We got up and went to Haydarpasa. Our pockets were empty..."

63

The two drunk colleagues reached the editor of *Yeni Istanbul* newspaper in the middle of the night.

"Yilmaz was on duty then in Yeni Istanbul. It was around ten, ten thirty at night that we called Yilmaz. Ali Karakurt sayid to Yilmaz: 'We are at Haydarpasa station at the moment and we are the greatest journalists in the world. We are going to carry out a major interview. Send us money!' And guess what he said?! 'OK bro...'"

This drunken conversation on the telephone was concluded with the decision that the needed funds would be collected from Mehmet Kemal, the Ankara Representative of the newspaper, and they continued their drinking on the train and arrived in Ankara.

"We used our press cards and bought tickets for 40 kurus and went to Ankara. We collected 5,000 lira from Mehmed Kemal. That was a large sum in those days. Where should we have gone from there? We went to Sivas... Why? Because we both liked cream. That was where they had the best cream. We were having cream in Sivas. What next now? We said, 'This is no way to eat cream like this. We need dessert with it! The best thing to do is to buy a kilogram of cream and go to Diyarbakir and have this cream with a dessert, that is the way it should be eaten...' We boarded the train after midnight. Wonderful! We arrived in Diyarbakir very early in the morning. We checked into a hotel. Subsequently we went to the dessert shops. We spread the cream on the them and ate..."

As the duo started to sober up from this journey where every kilometer had been accompanied with plenty of alcohol, they started to worry about bringing news.

"Now it is time that we have an interview. We went to the director of highway authority, Orhan Buyukalp. He knew journalists then. He recognized us. We said, 'We are going to carry out a major interview. Can you allocate us a vehicle and tour the area with us?' The man said, 'Of course I will take you around but I want a favor from you...' What was it? All the roads out there are going to be rebuilt according to the American plan and the man wanted us to take photographs of the roads that had been built to put in his file. Sure, why not! It's a deal. So be it! The man gave us the vehicle and we turned the place upside down. The only person to go there previously was Omer Sami Cosar. He is a writer of course. He did not take any photographs. The interview titled 'The Anatolia We Do Not Know' was published in *Yeni Istanbul* and we received a journalism award for it in 1958."

Egg by God

The two cronies making this unplanned journey into Anatolia had stayed at the State Highways guesthouse.

"When we crossed the Malabadi Bridge and arrived in Siirt it was night time. We went straight to the State Highways Directorate guesthouse just out of town. They knew we were coming so they had prepared something to eat. The man who was taking care of us was slightly overweight, of medium height, an Eastern Anatolian man with friendly eyes. He asked me: 'Sir, what would you like for breakfast?' I thought of fresh eggs. 'Soft boiled fresh eggs would be nice' I said, 'I will try to find it' he said and went.

When Ara opened his eyes in the morning his reporter friend Ali Karakurt was still sleeping.

"I looked at the clock it was 7:30. The man who was going to bring us breakfast should have been here by now so I got dressed and left the room and looked around. There was nobody in sight. After waiting a bit, I went and woke Ali up. 'The man has not come, breakfast is not ready' I said. What is more, the driver who was driving us was not around either."

After waiting for about half an hour they saw someone approaching the building.

"It is probably someone working for State Highways. When he came he said 'Osman Aga went to the market in Siirt to get you something, there was a shootout, it was a blood feud matter and they have shot Osman' he said. He died right there."

They were both in shock.

"I felt as if inadvertently I had caused a disaster; if I had not wanted eggs the man would not have gone to the market and his enemies would not have found and killed him. I was devastated. But there was nothing to do. Ali said 'Let's go and take pictures and interviews'. The man took us to the market and I took photographs of the man lying on the ground. That was the first time I was in Siirt and I always kept it in my memory like that."

Ara made a note in his head that this geography is way different than the place he was born and raised.

"There is a place called Tillo. It also hosts the tomb of Erzurumlu Ibrahim Hakki. We were told that a family had a copy of the famous *Marifetname* (encyclopedia) but that they were not showing it to anyone any more. After lengthy pleading, they brought a large bound book. I took photographs of a few pages but it was not an original, it was in English, at that time it had not been printed in Turkish."

As Ara was photographing the *Marifetname* he noticed a man sitting on a high platform watching him. So, he approached him and learned that he was a teacher.

"I am a teacher but I have no students' he said. 'Is there no school?' I asked and he said with a sardonic look, 'this is the school but the families do not send their children here, they take their children to the hodja,' and pointed out to a building across."

Ara proceeded to the indicated place and after descending a few steps he found himself in a semi-dark room.

"On entry, the room appeared to be very dim but after my eyes adjusted I could see children sitting cross-legged on the floor, and facing them I saw the hodja in his black robe and almost white beard. 'Hello' I said but he just smiled. I tried to engage with him but that did not happen because he did not speak Turkish. As the lesson continued the hodja would poke the children with a long stick from time to time. At one point he interrupted the class was and came near me. He showed me an 18x24 photograph with the most primitive frame. He was saying something in Arabic and pointed his finger at a well-dressed man in the picture and smiled. I looked harder and realized that this modern man in the picture was Democrat Party's Assembly Spokesman Refik Koraltan. The Hodja was proud and happy. I turned around and saw the teacher, an officer of the Ministry of National Education, sitting on the platform who was watching me with murky eyes."

The Discovery of Aphrodisias

In September of 1958 *Hayat* magazine received the news that the Prime Minister would be inaugurating Kemer, the largest dam in Turkey, and Ara, the reporter deputized with following Menderes and his practices, was dispatched posthaste to Aydin province. The dam inauguration had to reach the press before the weekend. As soon as Ara arrived in the city he went to the Governor's office.

"I explained the situation to the Governor. He allocated me a car and a driver. We set off for the dam. I took photographs of the dam from various angles. Then I went to the dam crest and waited for the sunset so I could photograph the whole dam with sparkles in the water. The driver was writhing down below. It was late, there was still 150 kilometers to drive. The man wanted to go home. The sunset, we finished our work but also the color film and there was only black and white film left. By the time I got off the dam crest it was dark and the driver said, 'There is an intermediate short cut. It is a mountain road but it is short. Let us go that way.' I was in no hurry. We hit the mountain road and went. We came to a place, the driver lost the road. Streams were running, the big rocks looked like the devil in the pitch-black darkness. Naturally he was demoralized. We were lost he said. 'Fine' if we were lost so be it. After all this was Turkey. We know we were in Turkey, we had not gone off to Japan. This time he said, 'I am tired. Let us spend the night here and we can continue in the morning.'"

After struggling until 11 pm to find the road they decided to give up and stay at the first village they encountered.

"We stopped at a mountain village. We entered the café. A gas light was burning. There was no electricity in the village. We greeted the villagers and told them about our plight. The Mukhtar came. A place was found for us. Something caught my attention in the café: the men were playing cards. On top of a Roman column heading! There were three marble tables like this in the café made from column headings... Then I saw a huge column in the middle; a Roman column was holding up the ceiling of the cafe! I immediately took two-three photographs then and there. But I did not think anything... The men gave us a place to sleep, we shared the room with the driver and went to bed. We did not talk; the man was mad at me. But what I had seen stuck to my mind; early in the morning I got up to tour the village. There was something here man... I looked and the place was riddled with sarcophagi. Exquisitely decorated... marble... The villagers used the sarcophagi to crush grapes! There were marble statues inside the houses... a statue held up a porch. My god... My god! The village children followed me around. They took me to a place, a huge temple; the temple of Aphrodite. There was a huge hippodrome at the other end of the village... They had turned it into a cabbage plantation; a man was plowing it... There were huge columns in the cabbage fields. There were 40 intact columns inside the forest. I took wonderful pictures but they were all black and white..."

When he returned to Istanbul he showed the photographs he had taken to Sevket Rado in a state of excitement. He was very upset when the reaction was *"Never mind these pictures of rocks and soil, did you shoot the dam, the dam?"*

I showed the pictures to Sevket. He scorned them. 'Never mind stuff like that...' etc. he said. I printed the pictures and took them to Sabahattin Eyuboglu. 'I took these photographs but what are they?' I said. He started thinking 'Rome' but which Rome?' Who knew? Nobody knew... we went to see the Director of the Archeology Museum to ask if he knew. He looked at the map, he couldn't figure it out. I was left holding the interview."

He thought about *Architectural Review*. This architectural journal which had been published in the United Kingdom since 1896 had sometimes printed photographs he had sent depicting Ottoman architecture.

"I took the map and marked the village on it. I also added a text in English and sent the interview. It turned out to be eight pages. They looked into it and found something. They had discovered that the name of the place was Aphrodisias. It was thus established that Geyre village had been established on Aphrodisias."

After this article in the *Architectural Review* a telegraph arrived.

The telegraph was from *Horizon*, one of the most important journals in America. At that time, I did not know what this journal was. I went to the American News Center and found out that *Horizon* was an amazing journal... Experts in their field contributed to the contents. Churchill, Herbert Read etc.... *Horizon* wanted color photographs of the work. I had taken black and white pictures. I replied with a telegraph: 'They will be ready within a week...' Let's go... again a flight, back to the place... This time I took Sadan Cayligil with me. Again, we went to the governor. I asked for the same driver, I said to him 'now get lost again' but he didn't, he found the place. We took the color photographs and sent them. However, this time the editor wanted a 'very well known' writer. They asked who the best candidate was for this work. We went again to the Director of Archeology, Rustem Doyuran, to ask who could write such an article. He said, 'I have a relative in America, He is a Turk but has become an American. He can write it.' He provided the name of a professor at Princeton University: Kenan Erim. We informed *Horizon*."

With the photographs that Ara had taken he had contributed to Prof. Kenan Erim taking ownership of Aphrodisias and uncovering and revealing it to mankind.

One of the greatest archeologists in the world, Professor Erim, studied the area, he brought money from many companies and families, and carried out excavations. There was nothing bigger. I did my duty, I introduced a wealth in my country to the world. So did he, he studied, researched, but Turkey demanded VAT from the man and he perished from heart attack. Indifference and the rigid attitude of bureaucracy killed Kenan Erim. It resulted in the death of a man who had been so generous with himself, done so much good and uncovered a civilization."

His initial joy and enthusiasm at the sight of Aphrodisias turned into resentment.

"The demands for Aphrodisias were endless. After my fourth, fifth visits to Geyre village it had started to disappear. The whole village had to be moved to carry out the archeological excavations. In a short time, a new Geyre village was established about two kilometers further and all traces of the old Geyre village were gone. Now the ghosts of invisible Romans, Hellens, Byzantines roam the area at night."

Explosion on Babiali Hill

In the early days of 1959, Meserret Hotel, which was located on Cagaloglu Hill at the intersection of Ankara and Ebussuud Avenues was demolished by an explosion. It had hosted Yakup Cemil, the key name of the 1913 Ottoman coup d'état (also known as the Raid on the Sublime Porte), which paved the way for Union and Progress once upon a time.

Tan Printing shop, which was immediately opposite the hotel and had been demolished by youth with sledgehammers and axes with the justification that it was a haunt for communists, also got its share from the explosion. The explosion was violent, killing 38 and injuring 160 people, and was caused by the 300 kilograms of dynamite belonging to Kumla mining company operating in Neyyir Han next door to the hotel.

Municipality bus number 28 on its route from Fatih in the direction of Besiktas during the explosion was covered by the rubble. At the moment of the explosion Ara was walking down the hill.

I was going down Babiali hill. I was at the front of Inkilap Bookstore when something went 'boom' which was followed by a massive cloud of dust over on the Sirkeci side. As I was walking in the cloud of dust and wondering what had happened, I saw that a building had gone down. Large walls were falling all over the bus, cars... People were fleeing. There were bodies! Wow. I remembered vaguely that I saw a man through the smoke, he was alive and looking at me, he had been caught between the concrete. He extended his hand toward me and I immediately took a picture and he died. Apparently, he was waiting for me to take his picture to die. Afterwards an excavator appeared. The excavator plunged into the construction and compacted it further so if there was anybody alive underneath the rubble, well I guessed they weren't any more. I remember a photograph taken by photojournalist Meftun Olgac with a body hanging out of the excavator. Ignorance kills people in this country. In the world people die as a result of coincidence, in Turkey people live as a result of coincidence."

A Star is Born

The United Kingdom held a special place among the countries where Ara delivered photographs which were becoming popular in the world media.

"I was best known in the UK and then by the US. *Observer, Sunday Times* started to print my work. There was an officer in the *Observer* by the name of Peter Keen. He was the photography editor. He had fallen from an aircraft in Africa. Half of his head was missing and he wore a turban, I thought he was a monk. All great British photographers passed through there. This man wanted photographs from me and I sent them. They were printed from time to time, perhaps eight of my photographs had been printed and I received £400. I immediately bought a tweed jacket for myself. That is why I have a lot of jackets. They have shrunk. I can't wear them anymore."

When the team of the British newspaper *Observer* transferred over to *The Times* newspaper, Ara moved with them.

"When the team transferred to *The Times* I transferred with them. All of these men were actually from journalism. When I transferred to *The Times* the guys would say 'Ara Guler came' and we immediately went somewhere to sit and drink. Imagine the bars in the UK.
As we sat we talked photography. You might have said 'you took this photograph, can I have a print'. For example, during that time Philip Jones Griffiths became a photojournalist for the *Observer*. In the beginning we never saw one another but became friends later. Another significant person there was Norman Hall. Then he became the photograph editor of *The Times* in addition to being the editor of the *British Journal of Photography*. He was also the editor of *Photography Year Book...*"

Norman Hall, who was originally from Australia and had relocated to London, was known as the greatest photograph editor of the era. The legendary Hall knew Ara from his interviews.

"Norman was the editor of *The Times*. He was the father of photographers. He selected all the interviews to be printed. The man printed one of my interviews in *The Times* which was one of the biggest newspapers in the world, he saw my work."

Toward the end of 1959 Norman Hall contacts Ara.

"One day he said to me, 'Send me lots of pictures...' Didn't ask why. I sent the pictures and observed that I had been allocated a large space and I was depicted among 'Star Photographers'. Seven star photographers had been selected in the world. One of them was me... I guess I was being noticed by that time."

The British Journal of Photography Year Book which was directed by Normal Hall was a highly prestigious album which published the work of star photojournalists every year after a diligent selection process was made among thousands of photographs.

British Journal of Photography Year Book had selected seven star photojournalists in 1960, comprised of Philip Jones Griffiths from the United Kingdom, Lennart Olson from Sweden, Giovanni Massora from Italy, Walter Wissenbach from Germany, William Klein from the US, Janine Niépce from France and Ara Guler from Turkey.

This commendation had a major contribution in spreading Ara's fame throughout the world.

"I worked there but my foreign reporting had been instrumental in introducing me to the whole world. I never worked in second-rate organizations. I worked for *Time, Observer, Stern, Paris-Match.* They were the royalty among the press."

Riboud Flown from a Truck

Ara's reputation had spread throughout the world and he was now famous. One of the young names of the legendary Magnum Agency, Marc Riboud, sought out Ara when he came to Istanbul.

"He came to Istanbul and found me at *Hayat* magazine. John Hilelson sent him, the John Hilelson in London who is the distributor of Magnum... Lots of things in my life started in the United Kingdom. John Hilelson made a recommendation to Marc. He came here to prepare a book. He came to *Hayat* magazine, I introduced him to Vedat Nedim Tor, he toured Istanbul, Anatolia. We asked him for an interview with *Hayat* magazine but naturally he rejected this. That was when he took the famous photographs of Cappadocia."

Bilge Karasu, who was an interpreter at the General Directorate of Press-Publications, acted as a guide to Riboud who joined Magnum after quitting his primary profession as an engineer. Ara recommended a subject to Riboud, who had traveled widely in Turkey.

"It was the time when Kirkpinar wrestling was taking place and I was going to attendboth for *Hayat* and *The Time.* I said; 'Let me take you there'. 'I will take you to the Hamam' I said. He took photographs of me in the Hamam. I took some good shots of him too. Then we went to Kirkpinar. As you know Kirkpinar is two kilometers away from the city. A truck was going that way so we got on. It was carrying potatoes and stuff. We were traveling on an open truck bed with laborers, packages, etc. Suddenly he said 'Great' and jumped off the moving vehicle and rolled into the stream. 'Ah' he moaned and could not move. We stopped and realized that his leg was broken. He had seen something that he wanted to photograph and jumped for that reason. For that reason we had to go to Edirne first and then the Park Hotel, Istanbul. We went to a doctor... He received the first treatment, got a bit better and then went to his own country to get the major treatment."

Chasing Noah's Ark

The editor of *Yeni Istanbul* newspaper telephoned Ara to tell him that an American looking for Noah's Ark had come to Istanbul and asked whether he could accompany him to Agri province. Ara, who was ready to go to the end of the world for news, accepted immediately.

According to widespread belief in the world, Noah's Ark went aground on Agri Mountain, which is the highest point in Turkey. In fact, during the era of Ottoman Sultan 2nd Mahmud, the mountain was climbed with the intention of finding Noah's Ark.

That is why every year Turkey hosts foreigners who search for Noah's Ark. Although Noah's Ark is not so much appreciated on the soil that it is located on, it is a source of major interest and income abroad.

"The trick is this: there are Christian societies in America. There are all sorts of clergy, various men who commercialize this. They go from church to church and deliver conferences about Noah's Ark. Conferences in America involve money, it costs 10-15 dollars to participate in a conference... The conference speaker says that this is Agri Mountain, Noah's Ark must be there, if we could collect the funds we would go and find Noah's Ark and verify the writings in the Bible... Many Americans were interested in such things and religious people were willing to donate, so when they had collected the money they came here, took photographs, shot films and returned and displayed them at conferences. They said that they did not find the Ark thats year but that they will go again next year, and this cycle continues..."

Ara contacted his journalist friends Lutfu Akdogan and Umit Deniz. They all tagged along after missionary John Libi who had come from America to find Noah's Ark.

"Are you interested? I said. They indicated that they were, so me and the man, Umit Deniz, Lutfu Akdogan went to Agri, our guide was Sahap Atalay who was a first lieutenant at the time... We went to Dogubayazit. There were no hotels or motels then, we managed ourselves at the officers' guesthouse. We climbed the mountain and camped at an elevation of 4600 meters and at the end reached the summit. We sang the National Anthem, hoisted a flag, left plaques, and descended."

At the request of those who sent him to the summit, Ara made a point of remembering to strike poses for photographs of him holding a plaque with *Yeni Istanbul* written on it.

"As a result of the investigation we carried out, we learned that the American was an elevator operator in Boston. He was an old man who had collected money from various churches and came here... Moreover, this John Libi started to come to Turkey every year, took photographs, returned to America, collected money again and would come the next year to ascend and descend Agri Mountain again... What these people do is they go from village to village, give conferences, display slide shows. That was our elevator operator's scam. He has not been here for a while, perhaps he has passed away."

Elevator operator John Libi made statements to the *Philadelphia Inquirer* newspaper about his ascent on Agri Mountain such as *"I saw Noah's Ark but I could not approach it because of blocks of ice"*, but that was not quite the case:

"That was not true at all! However, I became an expert on Noah's Ark thanks to him..."

This intense interest in Agri Mountain was not limited to missionaries. As a result of the pressure applied by conservative politicians in America, the colossal CIA with all its agents and opportunities had been forced to put their regular work aside and investigate whether Noah's Ark was in Turkey or not.

Devout American senators would consistently call the head of the CIA and clamp down on him as to why the U2 surveillance aircraft tasked with monitoring the Soviet Union did not take photographs of Noah's Ark. American intelligence was convinced that such a photograph assignment would not remain a secret but would be displayed in churches.

It was already difficult to convince the surveillance aircraft to deploy from Incirlik airbase. And they did not want to give the impression that this aircraft was collecting intelligence on ally country Turkey. For years, such demands had been countered with divertive responses and backpedalling. The fact that according to the information provided by the CIA on condition that it remained confidential to the American administration and senators, photographs taken by U2 surveillance flights revealed nothing to verify the presence of Noah's Ark did not satisfy the counterparts. They wanted photographs.

"One day a captain came to *Hayat* magazine; Captain Durupinar... from the General Directorate of Cartography. While they were drawing maps over aerial photographs they had noticed an indentation which looked exactly like a vessel around Agri Mountain. Military cartography aircraft was special, the aircraft itself had been manufactured for the camera and it operated automatically. In other words, such mapping aircraft was not designed to aim and shoot. When they were assessing the photograph in the cartography room, they noticed it. That was the photograph that was brought to us, a cartography photograph with the properties of a map. And they decided that *Hayat* magazine could publish it the best. 'It is a gift of the Turkish Army to *Hayat* magazine to be published because we believed that it was Noah's Ark."

Ara was very much impressed with the photograph that was taken during NATO cartography studies in 1959 and kept holding it for minutes. Ara and his friends compared the indentation in the photograph with the description in the Torah: 'Go build yourself a ship from gopher wood. Tar it on the inside and outside and build berths inside. The vessel you build shall be three hundred Turkish yards in length, 50 yards in width and thirty yards high', and the measures seemed to fit.

"We looked at the measurements and they matched but not those on Agri Mountain, on a mountain in the opposite direction... They fit the indentations on Tendurek Mountains. Even Sevket Rado and Hikmet Feridun were excited. However, it is not possible to have a commentary with one photograph of a map so a new expedition for new photographs from a closer distance needed to be arranged; 'I'll do it,' I said."

Well, nobody is perfect. Restless with excitement, Ara went to Erzurum immediately with a copy of the photograph in his hand to present it to the Commander of the 3rd Army General Ragip Gumuspala.

"'My Pasha' I said, 'This is something huge. If you allocate an aircraft for me I can take photographs over the image and we can distribute them to the world. I am going to do this if you help me'."

Ara's proposal pleased the General; however, he did have one demand.

"'I will allocate an aircraft but I want you to take photographs of the barracks I have commissioned here' he says. They did not have proper barracks before, they quartered in inadequate barracks in the cold. The General had commissioned the new buildings and he wanted me to take their photographs."

Ara responded "As you order" after which General Gumuspala summoned his adjutant and issued the necessary orders. Ara took the photographs of the barrack with lightning speed; however, once he was in Dogubayazit and saw the allocated aircraft, he shivered slightly.

"These were canvas artillery aircraft for outposts. Helicopters were non-existent then. The youth who flew me over Noah's Ark was from the Black Sea Region. We made nine dives, the weather was stormy and I felt sick to my stomach. When we descended, I felt really bad. The aircraft had a window which I opened to get a clearer photograph but this time the wind blew in and the aircraft was hard to control."

The indentation that Ara photographed was located on the skirts of Tendurek Mountains opposite Agri Mountain, near Mahser village between Asagi Surbahan and Yukari Surbahan villages.

"We found the place according to the photograph in my hand and the map, looking from the aircraft the indentation really looked like the mould of Noah's Ark. As if Noah's Ark had been grounded on mud after the water receded, then the wooden vessel decomposed and the indentation remained frozen in eternity...That was what it looked like."

Once Ara's photographs are delivered, all hell breaks loose. The long sought after photograph had been found.

"We took the photographs and the whole world stood at attention... I took the photograph, the rest was up to scientists... Moreover, the measurements given for the vessel in the Bible exactly matched the measurements of the indentation in the photograph. I was comfortable in saying: 'If this is the trace of Noah's ark then I am the first human being to see and photograph it."

Years later he was visited by a member of the clergy in his studio in Galatasaray.

"When the Christian pastor entered the door, he drew out his cross and started to pray in front of me in a servile manner. He gazed at me as if I were a saint. Naturally I felt uncomfortable but luckily later he opened up; 'You have proved the existence of Noah's Ark, this was a significant service to religion and for which I thank you on behalf of mankind.' After a while he left, walking backwards. I said to myself: That was just what you needed."

In Sophia Loren's Bedroom

As Ara had started to go to Cannes every year, he had become a regular at the film festival.

During one of the gala nights there were about 50 photojournalists struggling to get a good position on the palace steps to be able to photograph the famous who posed on the stairs. This struggle was in the form of a minor scrap with plenty of the ever-popular French curse 'merde' echoing throughout. Gunes Karabuda was discreetly using his hands, arms and elbows to push aside those who had arrived early, as the latecomers tend to do, when he heard a voice immediately behind him saying: " *Watch out you brute!"*

When he turned in the direction of the voice he saw a colleague, someone about his age, dark, with a mustache, two Leicas hanging from his neck and two on his shoulders. When he said 'Good luck with that' in Turkish. It was Ara himself who answered " *Thanks*".

Dispatching the photographs which were taken in the accompaniment of rivalry and bustle was another problem.

"There is no end to the stress we had. When we went to Cannes how could we send the photographs? Let's say you took the pictures and sent the unprocessed film, how would you know which is what, who is who? That means I had to process the film. I had to process and cut it into single units and put them in separate envelopes so that they did not get mixed up. And then the relevant text needed to be added. How can you write on an unprocessed film? So, when we photojournalists went somewhere, we brought large black papers with us. Then we closed the windows of the hotel, the doors. Then we took out the film processing liquid that we had brought with us or we bought it at the destination. Afterwards we processed the film in the bathroom sink of the hotel, we also brought pins and hung them out to dry. Then we cut and put them into small envelopes with numbers and a corresponding list indicating what each envelope contained. If we didn't do that, who would know what they would have ended up writing underneath the pictures."

Actually, God knows what would be written as captions underneath the photographs sent from Cannes.

"On one of my visits to Cannes – as I went there every year, everybody thought that I was someone significant, I had booked into a bed & breakfast. I had taken my camera and gone off. I was reporting for *Paris-Match*, I was commissioned for the job through some acquaintances there. The famous were staying at the Carlton hotel and the Hotel Marchinez. The front of the Carlton was crowded, full of journalists. I didn't mix with them, I was a fancy reporter, I worked with appointments. 'What's up?' I said. 'Sophia Loren is coming,' they replied. Her flight had landed in Nice and she was coming this way. I was not bothered, I had photographed Sophia Loren a million times'.

An officer was holding the elevator door open waiting for Sophia Loren to arrive.

"I was well dressed, all dapper in bow tie, etc. With my camera under my shoulder, I boarded the elevator and soon enough Sophia Loren and her husband Carlo Ponti arrived. 'Oh, hello how are you' bla bla. Sophia Loren, Carlo Ponti and myself went to the 9th floor. They recognized my face but they did not know who I was, if they knew I was a journalist, they would have had me removed. We got off the elevator and I followed them as if I was a part of their party. We entered the suite and they closed the door. 'Thank God we are saved from the fracas' they said. I looked around because if I did not hang out with someone I would have been discovered, it was not crowded, there were only two other individuals.

Ara steers toward Italian director Alberto Lattuada who was in the room, with great sincerity:

"I went over and said 'How are you?' We chatted, he asked if our Italian films were doing well in Turkey and I answered sincerely. Sophia Loren and Carlo Ponti looked at me and came to a conclusion that I was not a stranger to them as I was talking to our Alberto. Sophia Loren went into the bedroom and took her shoes off and sat on the bed comfortably. I immediately seized the opportunity and said, 'Let me take a few photographs of you, no one has ever seen you like this'. 'Oh, go on then' she said. When I sent the pictures they had written the following text underneath; 'Our reporter in Sophia Loren's bedroom', that was the heading. They printed posters out of it and hung it all over the streets, the sensational news was mine but I didn't have a clue."

The Onassis Yacht of Celebrities

During the hot summer days in 1959 the yacht Christina, of Greek Shipping Magnate Aristotle Onassis, which had hosted numerous celebrities from Marilyn Monroe to John Wayne, from Greta Garbo to John F. Kennedy, and had been nicknamed the 'Yacht of Celebrities' for that very reason had departed from Chios and entered Turkish territorial waters.

Onassis, who had spent millions of dollars transforming a Canadian frigate dating back to the World War II into a luxury yacht, had once again brought prominent personalities with him as his yacht berthed at the port of Izmir where he was born.

Ara was informed that the yacht had left Izmir and had set off for Istanbul. He completed his preparations and rented a fishing boat and started waiting offshore in the Marmara Sea. When the Onassis yacht with its white hull, yellow chimneys and Liberian flag appeared on the horizon, Ara followed the yacht to the Princess Islands area. As the yacht was approaching the Burgaz Island, it changed its course and anchored offshore at Buyukada. Due to the protective circle formed by the police and gendarmerie, it was not possible to approach or see the inside of the yacht.

Ara calculated that the yacht was six meters high and he rented another fishing vessel with a long mast which he climbed to take photographs.

"I was on top of the mast that fishing vessels had. The law enforcement had surrounded the yacht but I could see the deck from where I was sitting. A woman came on deck. She sat down, took out her mirror and was putting on lipstick. I did not recognize the woman. I was making news as 'A woman is coloring her lips on Onassis' yacht'."

He did not know that the woman putting on lipstick was the world famous soprano Maria Callas, nor that the portly man, with his back turned sitting in a wicker chair with a cigar, was the former Prime Minister of the United Kingdom, Winston Churchill. Ara was so engrossed with the beautiful woman whose love life, separations, scandals, dramas he had witnessed, that he did not even pay attention to Churchill. Churchill, who had been observing the ultramarine waters with a sailor's cap on his head, a white suit and cigar in his mouth, and turned around and commented on Ara's photographing technique of perching on the mast as "That is a very good idea".

He tore himself away from the lens as he heard Onassis calling out to him.

'What are you doing?"

'Nothing. I am a reporter for *Paris-Match*, I am taking photographs. "

'Adnan Menderes will be here in the evening at 4:30 pm. You also be my guest. Come and you can have an interview with photographs as well. "

Ara already had what he wanted so he did not respond to the invitation. When it became common knowledge that the love affair of Greek Shipping magnate Onassis and the diva of the opera had started on this yacht tour, the photograph of 'A woman is coloring her lips on Onassis' yacht' was used by the world press in various sizes of format.

In the Shanties of Taslitarla

As the 1950s were reaching an end, the Menderes government which endeavored to establish 'a millionaire in every neighborhood' with American aid and without any clearcut plans or programs, went hunting for votes to sustain the continuity of power.

The DP power started to plunder cities to entice the citizens who had migrated from rural areas to urban areas and added the word "shanty" to its vocabulary.

Areas had to be opened for those who migrated from villages to big cities starting with Istanbul. American made bulldozers plunged brazenly into cities. Istanbul was being demolished.

Hundreds of layabouts, with nothing better to do, watched for hours as bulldozers shoveled the wooden houses along the Aksaray-Bayrampasa line into trucks to open up Vatan Caddesi Avenue.

Hayat magazine, which was pro Adnan Menderes as ever, presented this act vandalizing the historical fabric of Istanbul with the headline 'Toward the Istanbul of Tomorrow' as "*After the most recent reconstruction works, Istanbul which is one of the most beautiful corners of nature in the world has started to be one of the most beautiful cities in the world. The grand metamorphosis of the city is presented to you with these comparative photographs displayed in these columns*".

The job of taking "Comparative photographs" was meted out to Ara. He spruced up his photographs with subtitles such as,

"Some of these areas have not been zoned yet but tomorrow everything will be perfect".

In October 1959 Ara and his reporter friend Orhan Tahsin decided to interview a shanty resident togteher.

Taslitarla neighborhood, where the state had built one-storey homes for migrants from Bulgaria and Yugoslavia, had been transformed into shantytown heaven. The residents of Taslitarla, with a population in excess of 100,000 residents, were renowned for their ability to erect a shanty in two hours.

Their plans did not involve a one-day interview, they were thinking in terms of mingling with the shantytown dwellers and living with them for a while.

"We set off for Rami. First, we had to find a place to stay. We knocked on the door of a house with a 'for rent' sign. We told the lady with the headscarf embroidered in blue who opened the door that 'we are free migrants, we lived in Kastamonu and now we have come to Istanbul. We are looking to rent a room... we saw your advertisement and knocked in response'. The lady donned wooden clogs and walked behind the house to show us a room measuring 2 x 2.5 meters where we would stay for 1.5 months."

The young reporters, who introduced themselves as Orhan and Ahmet for 45 days left the house early in the morning and came back at midnight. They spent the whole day touring the streets of Taslitarla, talking to people, and spent the remaining time playing pishpirik (a card game) in Sen Teahouse.

"One day our landlord stopped us at the doorway and said 'what is it that you do?'. In order to give a reasonable explanation for the camera that I always kept hidden under my jacket, I said I was a street photographer, while Orhan Tahsin said 'I applied to IETT and am still waiting for a reply'. The landlord said 'There is a photography shop in Sarigol. The owner is a friend of mine. He is also an immigrant from Bulgaria. Let me take you to him' and I was over the moon."

Not a day goes by in Taslitarla without a wedding. Ara was going to the weddings and taking pictures of the bride and groom together and 'family portraits' with the in-laws, brother-in-law, mother-in-law, co-sister-in-law, sister-in-law. He did not forget to shoot the guests sitting at the tables. He was putting a card on the table he had shot and received 2.5 lira. Ara was happy because he had acquired the opportunity to take the most colorful photographs ever.

The interview with the information and photographs in it generated a major response.

Taslitarla is a neighborhood with a population of 100,000 comprised of people from nearly 70 provinces. They came with their various traditions, speaking Turkish with various accents and people from three countries in which formerly a Turkish influence prevailed. Hayat magazine portrayed the characteristics of this neighborhood which had remained uncovered to date, their wedding traditions, the gypsy assemblies, interesting personalities through the pen of a reporter and the lens of a photojournalist who lived in Taslitarla for 1.5 months.

The interview did not go unnoticed by those who were responsible for the current uncovered realities.

"The Democrat Party restrained that interview, they did not want it. The Menderes government restrained the second part of that interview. It was revealed that they had distributed the land free of charge to win the elections. They stopped the publication."

One of those who was displeased by the interview was Ara's mother. For years she had been saying 'I raised him in cotton and he becomes a journalist and sleeps under bridges with bums. Lives in shanties in places like *Taslitarla*' ".

"Being a lady of society my mother did not understand what her son did, was he a bum? If you asked my mother she would say "instead of being a man he became a bum.""

Tunes of the Unplayed Kemencha

In February of 1960, as Ara was scanning the newspapers for a news item to engage him, he saw *Hurriyet* newspaper report that a vessel had been grounded offshore the Black Sea. The wild waves of the Black Sea had sunk 120 vessels in 75 years and taken the lives of 1,100 individuals. He decided to set off to Kefken.

It was a Saturday. Unpleasant things always happen on a Saturday. I opened *Hurriyet* newspaper and saw that a vessel had been grounded on rocks, the sea looked vicious with the wave but there is no human in the photograph. I said it was good reporting, I also mentioned it to Ibrahim. I said I would go there and show them how it was done, it would give good photographs, it was good for us. How shall I go? Kefken was the tip of the Black Sea which was a forbidden zone."

Permission had to be obtained from the Coast Guard to go to that area.

"It is different now but at that time it was possible to pass only with a border pass and those were available to the people living in the village. There are small islands further on. I went there and telephoned the Coast Guard. I talked to the Coast Guard and said I was from *Hayat* and they said 'well, hello there'. 'You,' they said 'come to Beykoz, there will be a change in the shift, get on our bus it will take you there'. 'OK' I said. It was 5 o'clock and the shift would be changed at 5. I set off with cameras ready, film ready. I got on the bus and we continued into the night. It grew dark on the way."

Ara did not know what to do so he talked to the Garrison Command.

"I asked where the Garrison Command was, usually the military are helpful to journalists but the individual I encountered that day was obnoxious. I went to the officer on duty who was a first lieutenant and said, 'my name is Ara Guler, I am a journalist for *Hayat* magazine, etc. I need to go to the place where the vessel was grounded, he listened and listened and 'How on earth you come here?!'. 'I took the bus, what do you mean!' I said. 'I am doing my duty as a journalist, are you the only one in the world on duty?!'. He was obnoxious and consequently so was I. Finally, he lost his temper and called the troops and ordered me shut in the infirmary."

Ara who became bored in the infirmary, saw the magneto type telephone and grabbed it.

"I had been recently discharged as a reserve officer. I dialled the military old phone 'Hello this is Fire he said and I learned the password. I said 'Fire, my boy, do you have a civilian phone there with you?' 'Yes commander' he said. 'Dial this number for me' I ordered, I did not mention *Hayat* magazine, I just gave him the number. 'Get Ibrahim for me on that number' I said. 'Yes commander' he said. I could hear him getting *Hayat* magazine. I said 'I shall tell you and you pass it on to Ibrahim'. Ibrahim got on the other end of the line, 'I am Ara' I said. The soldier said 'I am calling commander'. I could not make him realize that my name is Ara (ara means "call") but Ibrahim understood. I said 'Tell him I know the North Sea Field Commander, get in touch with him to get me out of here'. And then the lines got all confused. WhenI said 'Ara' somebody else would get on the line. 'Who are you?' 'It is me' I said 'I am in the infirmary, who are you?' 'I am Erol Dalli, editor of *Cumhuriyet*.' Our officer on duty had arrested all arriving journalists and put them in separate venues. Of course, everyone who picked up the military telephone could hear everything. By this time, we were conversing with Erol about where the other journalists were, etc. This officer was not going to do anything to us but time was passing. We waited until morning when we were all bundled into a jeep and removed outside the garrison."

He was committed to taking that photograph. He got off the vehicle near Polonezkoy.

"There was a villager named Ferdinand, I used to rent a horse from him and ride around. I found Ferdinand and said 'Man where is the horse?' He had a blind horse that I took, I asked him where Kefken was and he drew me a sketch and explained where to go, how to get there. I got on the horse with the cameras and fell off 4 times, I kept getting tangled in bushes, hit by branches and kept on falling. Finally, covered in bruises and scratches, I saw the coast where the vessel was. I descended down a path and took a few photographs. One of the best pictures I have taken is the one where the vessel rests against the rocks like a kemencha, a beautiful composition of 'Tunes of the unplayed Kemencha.'

He set off with the peace of mind having succeeded in his task. He took a horse carriage to Pasabahce.

"From there I went to the newspaper. I submitted the interview, I explained about the photographs. 'Never mind that now there was another job for you, go here' they said. 'What job?' I asked. A vessel has overturned in Izmir... I got on a plane and flew to Izmir. In journalism one event happens and it is usually followed by another which comes on top of it. There are many incidents like this, for example a very poor photograph replaced this beautiful photograph I had taken. The job in Izmir that I went to was a secondary event but it was given full page whereas the other photograph went unnoticed. All that grinding work to get that photograph and they did not use it."

Hospitalization in a Mental Hospital

In the spring of 1960 the King of Jordan, Hussein, and his mother, the Queen Mother Zeyn, came to Turkey. After the official contacts in Ankara they came to Istanbul and stayed for three days. They visited a mysterious address: Ortakoy Sanitarium. The reason the King of Jordan and the Queen Mother Zeyn were visiting this building facing the Bosphorus, within a wooded area, was because the king's father Emir Talal was hospitalized here. Talal had lost his mental health after the assassination of his father and had been relieved of duty and been secluded from prying eyes in this clinic in the woods. The building is currently used as the headquarters of Alarko Holding in Istanbul.

Talal, who sprawled through the many rooms he occupied at the Sanitarium with his body guards, spent all day flogging his adjutants, saluting the trees from the balcony and making a call for prayer at any and all times. The world press vied over who would take a photograph of the deposed King of Jordan, but so far no one had succeeded because of the strict protection.

Hayat magazine, which followed the Istanbul visit of His Majesty Hussein closely, made a plan. Photojournalist Ara Guler would be hospitalized in Ortakoy Sanitarium like a patient and they would beat the whole world to the news.

'The Sanitarium was the Alarko building. I was hospitalized so that I could take a photograph of the King. His wife hospitalized him for insanity. She visits him every year. I bought philosophy books to portray myself as mentally challenged. Only crazy people read weird books. I was hospitalized and the first day I was injected with something; I felt like I had been hit with a ton of bricks. "

The injection was not included in the plan.

"Anyway, I languished there for 4-5 days without giving myself away. The King was kept in the room directly opposite my room. The setting was deplorable, there were police guards all over the place, they were all in plain clothes. One day I set off to the library with my Leica hidden beneath my nightgown. I kept the Leica ready in case I get a shot at the king. My mind created imaginary scenes such as 'The King behind the Screen' but the man did not make an appearance. It just did not happen."

Ara started to feel frustrated among the mental patients.

"One day I finally saw a shadow in the corridor, I said perhaps it was his shadow. Mysterious and all that. The moment I took the shot my arms were grabbed by two men, my feet lost touch with the floor. Talal's guards picked me up and threw me into my room and said, 'If you show your face again you will be shot'. I hung around for a while but my nerves were a wreck. That night I got dressed and escaped from the hospital."

After escaping he went to the editing department.

"I went to the editing manager Ibrahim Camli who had assigned me on the case and said 'Man, you sent me to death, the police did this to me, what if hey had shot me' and he said to me 'you should have let with sheets hang down tied like a rope'. I told him what he could do with his sheets. 'Go down with a sheet he says!' They would shoot me right away, I give you the sheet and let's see if you can go down."

Military Coup Days

When Turkey entered 1960, it witnessed the last throes of the Menderes government which had filled its term. Adnan Menderes, who tried to pin the blame of the fiasco -- generated by the reactionary and populist policies maintained under the guidance of the US -- on the press and the opposition. He commissioned the establishment of an Investigation Commission that was given unbelievable power, such as imprisoning those who criticized him for up to three years without trial, and seizing newspapers and printing presses.

Eventually the methods of Menderes, which were comparable to dictatorial regimes such as the confiscation of the property of CHP (The Republican People's Party), and his attempts to silence and even have the opposition leader Ismet Inonu lynched, made youth revolt. The police attacked students of Istanbul University who hit the streets shouting "Freedom-Freedom," and ended up killing 20-year-old Turan Emeksiz, a student at the Faculty of Forestry, and wounding many others which triggered the downfall of Menderes. The martial law was declared in Istanbul and Ankara did not help, the country was seething.

"I was walking down from Cagaloglu, I had a small camera with me. I needed to collect something from Karakoy and return, when suddenly I witnessed a commotion. Men were coming and crossing to the other side, the bridge opens. I remember taking photographs, it was a sunny day. The bridge opened and I crossed with a rowboat and positioned myself above Ziraat Bank and took photographs. Lots of incidents took place."

Finally, the expected happened and the Army took over.

"My father had turned on the radio at night, something was going on. At 2 am a voice announces 'we are associated with NATO' CENTO'. The first speaker was Alparslan Turkes. Nobody, regardless of profession, was allowed to go outside. Martial law had been declared, etc."

After listening to the radio, he gathered his bag with professional instinct.

"I worked for *Hayat* magazine but I was a reporter for *Paris-Match, Stern, The Time*. The man said that it was strictly forbidden to go out. If we didn't go out, how could we take pictures? We were desperate, we needed to get out, there was nobody outdoors. I had two, three cameras with me. The day was slowly dawning. I was waiting on Galatasaray Square. It was quiet and empty. I looked towards Taksim, I saw a military jeep approaching me from afar. As it grew nearer I saw that it was occupied by only one soldier. I remembered my stint as a reserve officer and before I could stop myself I yelled 'Stooooop' and the soldier came to an abrupt stop. My tone was imperative when I asked 'where are you going?' 'To the governor's office, sir' he said. 'Take me with you' I said. Now that I was in the vehicle there was no stopping me. I passed all the barricades and took pictures one after the other."

The jeep transporting Ara stopped in front of the Governor's office building and the journalists gathered there turned toward the vehicle with curiosity.

"The jeep came to the Governor's office and spinned to a halt, I saw our boys were there. I got out of the jeep like an emperor, the soldier thought that I was some kind of big shot and he opened the door. Imagine, all the editors were there, Abdi Ipekci, Omer Sami, my editor; Ibrahim Camli, he lived in Bebek, imagine when they heard the initial news they walked all the way from Bebek to get here. They all walked and on the way, they were queried a million times. They had been stopped about twelve times until they arrived. And there I was, the rookie Ara Guler getting out of a jeep. They could not believe their eyes, they thought I was law enforcement. I immediate-

79

ly got out of the car and disappeared. During revolutionary times one cannot be sure of anyone. As I got out of the car everyone was looking at me but no one was talking. That was because they thought I was from MIT (Turkish intelligence service) and they did not talk to me for a week."

It is always difficult to work in a military intervention setup but photographs had to be taken for the world.

"The members of the National Union Committee in Istanbul were going to issue a statement so we went to take their photographs secretly from underneath the chairs. We had to take a lot of pictures with what was available. We needed tanks in front of the Hagia Sophia or in front of any monument known to all. I took about 40-50 photographs. I went and processed the photographs, printed the cards, and put them in envelopes until morning. I separated all the pictures into envelopes to *Sunday Times, Life, Stern, Paris-Match*. I had 5-6 envelopes. They had to be put on the first plane. That used to be the way they were sent then. There was no one who could operate a tele-photo in Turkey at that time. I went to Yesilkoy airport in a car. I was accompanied by the Associated Press reporter. I gave *Stern*'s envelope to Lufthansa, the envelope of *Paris-Match* to Air France. The officer in the customs said 'Bro, there has been a revolution and I do not know whether I am even on duty or not. If I allow these to pass I will be punished. In other words, I do not know what they contain, should I allow them to be sent or not? Bring a signature from someone with more authority and then we can send the photographs' he said. The planes departed and the job was postponed to the next day."

His solution was to go to Radyoevi (radiohouse), the favorite venue of the military intervention.

"We went to Radyoevi and a lieutenant commander said to us 'what is it, what do you want?' I told him I was Ara Guler and explained our problem. 'Commander Colonel Kenan is not available, I cannot sign anything' he said. We waited and he arrived. Do you know who he was? He was the man who raided Radyoevi with a machine gun in his hands."

Ara started to explain his problem excitedly and when he said that he represented *Time* and *Paris-Match* he received a very rigid response:

- *Who cares about them?*

The Colonel took the photographs of tanks from Ara's envelopes and examined each one separately as if thinking 'what the devil is this?' and threw them to the ground and started yelling:

"*You* cannot send these photographs abroad. This revolution was made by the Turkish nation, it has nothing to do with soldiers. "

'Sir, if I don't send these pictures nobody will know that a revolution happened here. These newspapers and journals are the biggest press organizations in the world. If these photographs are not sent the revolution you had will only be an article in the foreign press. The revolution will go up in smoke."

"Are you not the man in *Hayat* magazine? You did not attend Ismet Pasa's Topkapi events but you took the photographs of Menderes every time he inaugurated a dam."

"They recognize me..."

The Colonel was decisive about blaming Ara for the pro-Menderes publications in *Hayat* magazine now that he had him there.

- Sir I go where my editor tells me to go. You are a colonel, if they order you to conquer hill number 261 you do not go and conquer hill number 262 because you do what you are ordered to do. That means that my editor did not dispatch me to Topkapi so I did not go. If he tells me to 'Go shoot a turtle' that is what I photograph. I do my job. If you want someone to blame go talk to my editor...

'Who is your editor?"

Ara did not answer. When the Colonel got no response he yelled again:

'Who is your editor?"

Ara replied in a small voice:

'You shout so much I forgot my editor's name."

With this response the Colonel, who thought Ara was mocking him, got furious and issued orders to the soldiers:

'Lock this man up... "

"The soldiers locked me up in one of the managers' rooms in Radyoevi. They put me under guard. It was a rather luxurious room. I was talking to myself swearing. 'I curse this profession. When I get out let everybody spit at whoever is a journalist etc.' Kenan had raided Radyoevi one day earlier. As I sat there I ran out of cigarettes. I smoked a lot. I opened the door to find the soldier with the bayonet and say, 'come here. Do you have cigarettes?' And I finished his cigarettes too. I stayed there until evening. Subsequently Kenan remembered me, he asked somebody about me. 'Take your pictures and go' he said. I was overjoyed of course. But 'these photographs will not be published locally' he said."

He had saved his photographs to be sent abroad but the 'domestic' issue was a major problem.

The Military Intervention of the 27th May caught *Hayat* magazine, which had supported the activities of Menderes without compunction, unaware.

"Two weeks ago, I had photographed Adnan Menderes in Izmit at an inauguration ceremony of a petroleum refinery. We had put Menderes on the cover and dedicated the center section. The biggest problem was we had published the magazine, made the news a centerfold but a revolution happened, how should we remedy the situation, what should we replace it with? Four obtuse photographs were sent from Ankara. We enlarged the pictures I had taken but there was still the issue of the cover. Who would we put on the cover; Cemal Gursel. Nobody knew him. I did my military service at the Davutpasa Barracks, they had pictures of the commanders on the wall. He was one of the generals I said and I jumped in my car and went. I explained the situation to the officer on duty. In the meantime, they were collecting members of the Democrat Party and slapping them around. The officer on duty did not know which one was Cemal Pasa. I looked but I did not find him."

A picture of Mustafa Kemal in his military uniform was put on the magazine cover and a poster of 'Heroic Turkish Military Forces opening a new and brilliant page in our history of democracy' was spread in the centerfold, and the photographs of student protests which had not been used to appear pleasant to the Menderes administration, were published under the headline '*We Narrate the Liberation of Turkish Democracy*'.

The interesting thing was that on the day the military intervention took place, the owner of the magazine, Sevket Rado, was nowhere to be found; he had been taken to the US by the American government to meet colleagues and carry out studies about the American press.

"The principle boss Kazim Taskent came to the newspaper on the first day of the revolution and our administration manager hid him in one of the rooms in the back of the newspaper. All these cohort capitalists were always afraid of military revolutions, they searched for a hole to hide in."

Farewell to Turkish Life

"It was a good thing that the revolution happened otherwise I would have continued to work for *Hayat* magazine."

In the days following the 27th May Coup, Milliyet newspaper was successful in organizing a campaign to fund the Dardanelles Martyrs Monument, which could not be completed due to 'lack of funds' for eight years, and the monument was completed.

Fikret Arit was my editor in *Yeni Istanbul*. He was a very principled journalist. 'Well,' he said, 'if you are not busy let's go and shoot the inauguration on Sunday. They will not manage it before Thursday'. 'If you want I can go. I am not very busy with anything,' I said. He went and told Hikmet Feridun Es who in turn told Sevket Rado that 'Ara and Fikret want to go to the inauguration of the Dardanelles Monument'. He barged in in a state of fury. I was reading a newspaper. 'Damn you reporters, you want to go there. Probably there is a scaffold on the monument. Did you check? You want to go on a jaunt with the magazine's money' he shouted. He was yelling at Fikret, Fikret listened. He yelled and yelled and left. Tears started to fall from Fikret's eyes. He banged his fist against the desk 'damn if I did not have to earn a living, I would not have let him get away with that,' and cried his heart out.

Ara could not bear that Sevket Rado had made his dear friend Fikret cry.

When he cried like that I said 'I shall go and spit in his mouth.' I went to Hikmet Feridun who was opposite me. 'Hikmet Bro, I am beating this man. I shall spit in his mouth, you will see,' I said. I kicked the door open and entered the room. He had taken the centerfold of the magazine and hung it on the walls.

As the door of Rado's room opened with a kick, he jumped out of his skin.
 "Give me my interview with Ismet Pasa."
 "Did you not do it for us?"
 "Who are you, man? I shall..."

Ara was so blinded by anger.

"I belted him one. He realized he was getting a beating so he started running around the room. He ran and I ran after him, I grabbed the paintings from the wall and hit him over the head. I hit him with four paintings. Nobody intervened because they knew that he was no good. He ran out the door of the printing shop and saved his life. He fled without looking back. He was running in front along Cagaloglu and I was chasing him. I gave him two more punches when I caught him. I pursued him until the Governor's office and after that it was uphill so I gave up. I returned to the magazine and I said to the Accounting Manager Ferit Hansoy, 'Ferit, for my resignation you give me my compensation now. If I ever come here again I will come back as the boss' I said. Journalists do not take bosses so much into consideration that is the way it was then and that is the way it is now."

Master of Leica

Ara was relieved now that he had quit the *Hayat* magazine, which sometimes made him feel as if he was shackled.

In 1961, the Italian publishing house Lerici Editori decided to publish the third part of Nazim Hikmet's *Human Landscapes from My Homeland,* which he had finished in Bursa Prison. He delivered it to his publisher in Turkey after being released by amnesty, but no one had the courage to print it. The Italian editors who were going to publish this work by Nazim Hikmet under the title *In Quest'anno 1941* (In this year 1941), requested Ara for photographs. He gave eight photographs to the publisher depicting life in Anatolia on condition that his name was not published.

Human Landscapes from My Homeland was not published in Turkish until the demise of Nazim, but at least he could see the book published by Lerici Editori with the left pages in Turkish and the pages on the right in Italian.

"The books written by Nazim Hikmet were banned in this country for years and then this ban was lifted for all of them. So how many people read these books and consequently became a communist? This means a lot of unnecessary things have been done in this country. As long as Turkey does not get rid of such useless enforcements, it will never achieve modernity."

Now he could devote more of his time to international works.

"There is a time for everything! That is the way it is... I met Marchinez on one of my visits to Paris. Romeo Marchinez. He was a man who has played a major role in my life and the lives of all photographers. He is Spanish. *Camera* magazine was published in three languages in Lucerne, city of Switzerland and it was the biggest journal existing about photography. Marchinez was the editor of this journal. We met, he liked me. He had been a student in the Italian School in Istanbul at one point when his father was deputized there, he was symphathetic about Turkey. He kept asking me for pictures and he used them in *Camera* frequently. One day he said, 'We are going to print an issue about you...' Come on... What do you mean an issue about me! Do you understand? We selected and sent the pictures. An issue of *Camera* was published and it was all about me!"

Camera, which was the official publishing organ of the International Photograph Art Federation, introduced Ara Guler to the work community of photography in its 41st issue published in February 1962.

"10 years later Marchinez printed my photograph and do you know what he said to me? 'I'm waiting to see if you were to become a photographer' You had to be one for at least 10-15 years until he considered you. Tomorrow or the next day the incumbent may become a banker, merchant, a glassman. 'I' he said 'am the editor of *Camera*, I publish the foot soldiers of photography.'"

During the same year when Ara went to Germany to get the new model Leica, he met the editor of *Leica Photography* journal, Heinrich Stockler.

"I had a few photographs with me. The man interviewed me and took some pictures. Time passed. An issue of *Leica Photography* was delivered to me. I looked and saw that I had been declared 'Master of Leica'. Being declared as 'Master of Leica' was very encouraging for me."

The magazine that had declared Ara the "Master of Leica' wrote about him as follows: *"Ara Guler focuses on the human being, on his sadness, joys and fate... that is why no matter where they are he endeavors to capture instant frames depicting the people around him together with their natural environment. This approach in photography, this attitude of esthetics of an exemplary quality are generated with the skills of an artisan as well as the talents of a master".*

Leica Photography, a journal the pages of which Ara could not bear to fold in his initial years as a journalist, like a holy book, a journal which he read between the lines, had declared him "Master".

"A change in the outlook on photography in Turkey coincides roughly with the period when I started to take pictures with my Leica. Currently Yapi Kredi has issued a book. It is a catalogue of our exhibition. It says, 'Photography in Turkey started with Ara Guler's Leica number III B 382418'."

The skills of Ara as the one and only holder of the title "Master of Leica" in Turkey has been registered.

"Leica is the Rolls Royce of cameras. There is no match for Leica. The first 35 mm camera I used was a Leica. A review of the best photographers in the world revealedthat they all used Leicas. The Lenses are very sharp, very good. However, these are technical issues. If you are not a good photographer even using a Leica will not make you one. A person might be wealthy and buy a Leica. I have often heard of people not finishing a roll of film within a year. If that is the case, do not buy a Leica. It is expensive but it is worth it. Can you imagine during the Second World War the American army did not hit the Leica factory in Germany because the bombardment might harm the lenses. It takes 30, 40 years for a lens to dry."

American and British war pilots who subjected German cities to carpet-bombing were told to be more careful over Frankfurt. They were specifically forbidden to bomb the towns of Wetzlar and Solums which were 90 kilometers away from Frankfurt, because the manufacturing facilities of the famous camera Leica were in these towns.

"The American army knew this and invaded this area with bicycle troops instead of air bombardment."

Magnum Gang

The editor of *Camera* journal Romeo Marchinez, who had been a student in Istanbul when his father was working for the Regie Company "Société de la Régie Cointeressée des Tabacs de l'Empire Ottoman", and felt half Turkish, liked Ara's photographs of Istanbul as well as his personality very much.

For this reason, Marchinez helped Ara at every opportunity, opened new doors, new horizons.

He was instrumental in arranging for Ara to meet the legendary head of Magnum Agency, Henri Cartier-Bresson.

"Marchinez called Henri and said, 'I am going to introduce a young Turkish photographer to you'. Marchinez was fond of Turkey, he had gone to the Italian school here. He was planning something from there. Istanbul was important for him. Cartier said, 'I know, I have seen his pictures, I shall come'. We met at the house of Marchinez in Paris. We do not mention Magnum too much. At that time, Magnum consisted of 16 people."

Ara who finally got to meet the founder of Magnum Agency, Bresson, had always appreciated him.

"Cartier-Bresson was very famous even then. We read about him in the journals, he was legendary. Marc Riboud was his assistant. He had brought him to Magnum. He was also new to Magnum, which meant that I was more famous than he was. Bresson wanted someone and hired him. He assisted Cartier, he would admonish him without interruption. I met Marc when he came here and met Bresson in France."

Bresson had impressed Ara very much with his products and stance.

"Henri Cartier-Bresson was a very skillful war correspondent. His realist structure made him the Emile Zola of photography. He was our pioneer, a master. He was aware of many issues. He felt excitement. He was interested in people, in the world. He loved life, people. He objected to things which were not beneficial to people.. For example, Cartier-Bresson was a friend of Gandhi. He was also the photographer in the film Gandhi. Cartier-Bresson was a man who could think very politically."

After their meeting in Paris, Bresson came to Istanbul.

"He was invited by the media. I knew Cartier-Bresson but we were not close. He learned to like me on account of Marchinez. He stayed at the Gezi Hotel on Mete Caddesi in Taksim. I took him all over Istanbul but he also had an official guide provided by the state. We toured with Bresson and got tired and went to see Sabahattin Eyuboglu. Sabahattin grew up in France. Cartier took many photographs of him. There were street photographers opposite the statue of Ataturk in Taksim. He said 'what are they doing?' 'They are street photographers, they take snapshots of people,' I said. After that he started signing his books as 'street photographer'."

Bresson was happy during his visit in Turkey and much impressed with Ara's entrepreneurship and altruism. Ara in turn was pleased to witness the photographs preferred by Bresson at close range...

"The attitude of Cartier-Bresson in terms of what he saw while taking photographs in Istanbul and my attitude were completely different. The photograph depicting the yoghurt salesman on encountering cars in the street became one of my most recognizable photographs. Bresson did not take one photograph there. His attitude differed from mine. His photographs depict instances as did mine. I waited for hours for the emergence of a photograph. So did he. When he captured the moment, he hit the button. That is what a documentary photograph is about. A photojournalist is someone who writes history with his camera; Henri Cartier-Bresson was one of those who did it the best."

Ara's association with Magnum progressed differently than that of other Magnumists.

Everyone misperceived that I worked for Magnum. Magnum was a prestige for me, a symbol to aspire to. It was like a business card whether it is Capa or Cartier-Bresson. It was like having an American Express card. Therefore, my association with Magnum was different, I could not work like other Magnum members, I had fixed duties such as representation, reporting. I gave many of my photographs to Magnum for distribution, my most significant interviews were distributed throughout the world through Magnum... but I was never completely within Magnum, never a full member.

The venues served with photographs by Magnum Agency were venues that Ara represented anyway.

Where did Magnum sell its product? Magnum distributes in four places in the world; Tokyo, London, New York, Paris. All the costs of these offices are countered by photographers. In other words we could not earn money from ourselves. 50% of the fees for our photographs was automatically deducted by Magnum and used for office expenses. Magnum photographers were the boss of Magnum. There is no such place as Magnum, you cannot say that I am going to work for Magnum. Yet not everyone can enter. These choose each other. For example, I said 'Hasan Senyuksel can be our distributor here'. Niko said 'Yes' another said 'Yes' as well. It was a gang effort but it did not earn anything. All income was distributed as salaries to our men there. For example, when Ernst Haas passed away he owed 8,000 dollars. Furthermore, I did not need it because I was already in journalism from another channel. Magnun sells the photographs to *Time*, *Stern*, *Paris-Match*, I was already a journalist why should I have n them a percentage. That was Magnum.

Magnum Agency set off with the notion of its founder Robert Capa: "*If a reporter does not own his own negatives then he is nothing*", and acted like a cooperative with no boss, protecting the property rights of photojournalists and providing the opportunity for every photojournalist to choose their own subjects and go where ever they wanted to go in the world.

"He started photojournalism with the publishing of *Life* magazine. Henry Luce was the founder of *Life*. On the other hand, there was the man calling himself a war correspondent, Robert Capa. Capa was a first-class man who knew his business, a playboy, a womanizer and a gambler to boot. Royalty, millionaires, artists were all his friends. In addition, he had photographers as friends because he was a photographer himself. Capa and his photographer friends wanted to take photographs at will, work without being affiliated with anyone. This was where Luce got involved. He told Capa to deal with the works of *Life* in Europe. That was how the idea of establishing an agency emerged. Yet there was the issue of money. Luce sent 10,000 dollars to Capa. But like I said, the man gambled. He lost the money in his pocket on the horses. If Capa had not lost the money on the ponies, Magnum would never have been established.
But when he won the 10,000, it became 25,000 and hence Magnum was established. The year was 1947. Magnum had five founders. They were Robert Capa, Henri Cartier-Bresson, David Seymour, George Rodger and WilliamVandivert. In other words, Magnum was an agency estab-

lished out of thin air by renowned photographers who had joined forces. The bosses of Magnum are the photographers themselves. They appointed the managers, the employees. In those days, Magnum was magnificent but now there is nothing left. Out of 45 persons perhaps five are old timers like myself, the others are all rookies."

The number of old timers at Magnum can be counted on the fingers of one hand.

"Two troublemakers emerged from the past era, they were very important: Joseph Koudelka and Sebastiao Salgado. The best current visual material was generated by these significant photographers. They were different. They were better equipped. They knew how to look at people. Their taste was more refined. I felt an affinity for this young generation."

He became close friends with Koudelka, who he met at the Magnum office.

"Every time I went to Paris I used to drop by Magnum that was how I met Koudelka. He immediately brought some wine, the cheapest kind... It was like poison. The man drank, he did not have a home, when the nighttime came he spread a sleeping bag on the floor and slept, in the morning he gathered it. He stayed here when he came to Istanbul. 'Come, I have a bed at home.' He refused, he wanted to sleep here, his body was accustomed to the sleeping bag. He got up at 7, left at 8 o'clock until the sun had set... 'The body had to stay upright for eight hours, then it will take photographs for seven hours, nothing else,' he said."

A Film Proposition to the Spy of the Century

When 1962 rolled around the whole world found out that the most important character in the history of espionage, Cicero, was a Turk by the name of Ilyas Bazna. During the Second World War when he worked as a clerk in the British Embassy in Ankara. he stole confidential documents and sold them to the Germans. Cicero was the name that changed the course of the world, however, no one knew what that name was at the time. Even in 1950 when German intelligence officer Ludwig Carl Moyzisch, the officer that Bazna submitted the documents he stole from the British Embassy to, wrote his memoirs titled 'Cicero Operation' the identity of Cicero had not been revealed.

After the book a Turkish film was made in Turkey titled *Ankara Spy*. Then Cicero was the subject of an American film titled *Five Fingers* starring James Mason. However, there were no clues as to who the legendary Cicero was in the book or in the films. Cicero, who everyone was curious about was actually a Turkish citizen of Albanian origin, Ilyas Bazna, born and raised in Prishtina, whose family had migrated to Istanbul when the Serbs occupied their country, He did his military service in Cankaya Palace with Ataturk and started a business and failed after his discharge from military service.

"I met the man for the first time, he was a man who lived in Beyoglu. Everyone knew him. Who knew his name? We found out later that at birth his name was Eliyasa Bazna. He was just one of the types in Beyoglu, one of those men on the street. I think he was a real estate agent, actually it was not quite clear what he did. He was not just one man, he was many. Nobody knew about Cicero so they could not make the association. He came to *Hayat* magazine from time to time, we had coffee and then he left. But at that time, we did not know what his business was."

One day while he was soaping the back of the British Ambassador, Sir Hudge Knatchbull-Hugessen, as he did every morning singing with arias, he took the mould of the key of the safe with cande wax that the Ambassador wore around his neck. This was how he managed to get the secret documents from the safe and photographed with a Leica and delivered to the German Embassy which were directly dispatched to Hitler.

The British Ambassador never suspected Bazna who had even taken a photograph of the letter from the British Ministry for Foreign Affairs warning that 'information was being leaked from the Embassy', on the grounds that 'he was stupid and did not know a word of English'. When Bazna realized that he was going to be apprehended, he took the thousands of pounds paid to him for services and set off for Nazi paradise, Argentina.

However, when it turned out that the £150,000 paid by the Germans was counterfeit money, Bazna had a hard time in Argentina and he decided to get back at the German government for the huge disappointment and write his memoirs.

"When the film came out, eventually the Turkish nation learned his identity. Whereas he was working for the National Security at the time. They deputized him to go to the British Embassy and managed to do so as a waiter. He photographed the documents with a Leica and gave them to the German attaché. The Turkish government had always held the Germans in high esteem. They generated the Cicero incident on purpose, the Turkish government used Cicero to deliver intelligence to Germans."

Ara was the first person that the spy of the Century Bazna negotiated with about the memoirs that would set the world on fire.

"After he left the Intelligence Service he was allowed to write his memoirs. At that time, he said 'OK, now I shall talk, I am free, I can say what I want'. He wanted to sell his memoirs to *Hayat* magazine. He came to *Hayat* magazine and said, 'I will sell my memoirs to the Germans'. I mentioned it in passing to Bob Neville at *Time*, he said 'If he writes his memoirs, we can buy them.' 'How much shall we pay?' I asked. He asked *Time* and they said around 25,000 dollars. I told him. 'No,' he said, 'it is not enough'. Then he went and wrote those books. Bunte did not accept, he went to *Stern*. I said 'forget the American market, the only magazine that will pay for this work was *Life* magazine but if you wanted you could sell your story to the Germans'. He did not hit the jackpot with his memoirs, he only got small sums."

Ara thought that taking the Grand Spy to the film about himself would generate good interview material. At first Bazna rejected the offer but was finally persuaded without difficulty after Ara persisted.

"This man's film was playing on the screen, a film of his life. The Director was Joseph Mankiewicz, one of the biggest names in the world. I took the man to the movie, he laughed a lot but did not talk and did not explain why he laughed. The film was shown at Cinema Melek."

When Ara failed to do the interview, he wanted to try his luck once more.

"Goksin dropped by and said 'Let's do an interview', I told him about Cicero. I said 'I went to see him but he was not interested, he is not talking, we offered him 25,000 dollars for his memoirs but he would not budge'. "Where does he live?" they asked. I inquired around. I got an address in Sehremini. We went there. We went up to the first floor and knocked on the door, the door was opened by Cicero himself. 'What is it?' he said, 'what!'. I said, 'I have brought Goksin to you etc.', 'F..... off you b....' he said. He pushed us and slammed the door in our face. That was the last time I saw him. Then he went to Germany and died."

The German government gave the spy of the Century a pension and Ilyas Bazna was obliged to work as a night watchman to support himself. He died in poverty in Munich.

A Fragrant Film

In 1963 Director Elia Kazan came to Turkey to shoot the scenario for *America, America,* which he had written. The hero of the film which narrated the adventures of 20-year-old young Stavros, a Greek of Turkish origin who was born in Kayseri and sets off to the America the land of dreams, was actually Kazan's uncle.

Elia Kazan who was excluded from the Hollywood society because he blew the whistle on eight of his friends as being communists when he was giving a statement to the House Committee on Un-American Activities established by American senator McCarthy in 1952, was obliged to hang out as 'marginal'.

> "Elia Kazan came here in 1963 to shoot a film. I knew him, he had been here previously. Elia Kazan was born in Uskudar. He wanted to see a Turkish house, the house of actor Behzat Butak was very nice so I took him there. This time he came to shoot a film, 'help me, find me a venue' he said. At that time, there was a vessel stationed at Unkapani, it was always there unloading coal. He imagined a scene like that and I showed him the place. The film takes place in 1910 or thereabouts; his father emigrated from Kayseri as a porter or something. He was shooting the film America America. All journalists came for an interview. The headline written by Dogan Uluc was 'Elia Kazan is filming porters in Turkey'."

The media was very interested in the film set and the journalists found it strange that Elia Kazan paid the porters on the dock to tear their outfits, and paid for the windows of the century- old-wooden houses and the balcony woodwork to be damaged, because he wanted to portray the poverty setup of the era narrated in the scenario.

The news starting with the sentence of Journalist Dogan Uluc, "*In the film America America which will be released next season, American movie lovers will be introduced to Turkey as a land of miserable laborers in the 1900s living in ramshackle houses*", was enough to cause a commotion.

As a result of consecutive and similar news items, law enforcement raided the film set and two representatives from the Ministry of Tourism in Ankara were deputized to monitor the film closely. When the team was shooting in the Golden Horn, one of the officers who accompanied the team at all times stepped in front of Kazan in an attitude of excitement:

> *"Wait do not shoot!"*
> *"What is it, why not?"*
> *"Do you not see the sea smells, everything is filthy!"*
> *"I am not shooting a film with smells!"*

Elia Kazan could not resist the pressure and had to cancel the shooting of the film.

> "The law enforcement stopped the film. We told Ecevit that the man had gone off to America. They cracked the whip and stopped the film. How did they expect the man's father, a coal porter, to be dressed when he was migrating, should he have been wearing a tie or a bow tie? Those scenes were shot in Greece. I shot the buildings that needed shooting in Kayseri and they were eventually reconstructed there. Do you have any idea what that cracking of the whip cost, was this journalism? And who you were ripping off; Elia Kazan. He is always going to be Elia Kazan but you will be nothing."

The Cyprus Crisis

In the middle of 1964 all Turkey was focused on the massacres in Cyprus. The Greek EOKA gang members who had killed the spouse and three children of Major Nihat Ilhan in the bathroom where they were hiding on Christmas day in 1963, had accelerated the scale of their attacks. The Greeks intended to eliminate the Turks living on the island and annex Cyprus to Greece. They were burning the houses of Turks, killing hundreds and burying them in pits.

This massacre, which was witnessed by the whole world without generating a reaction, made Turkey respond. Turkish Air Force Aircrafts carried out warning flights over the island while rallies were held in the four corners of the country to protest the massacres in Cyprus. As the Greek gangsters carried out their agenda brazenly, the Inonu government announced to the world that it had decided to intervene in the situation as "Guarantor State", as stipulated by the 1960 London Convention, and all hell broke loose.

US President Johnson sent his famous letter where he let Ankara know in no uncertain terms that American weapons could not be used in any possible military intervention, but by that time it was too late: Turkish Air Force aircrafts bombarded Greek positions and had submerged two Greek assault boats bearing Cyprus flags.

Turksih pilot Major Cengiz Topel, whose aircraft was downed during the operation, escaped with minor injuries, but he was tortured to death by the Greeks.

In August 1964, Ara received a telex message from the headquarters of *Life* in New York, asking him to prepare a Cyprus operation interview.

"The incident they wanted had happened and was done with yesterday. But since they wanted such an interview, it had to be repeated and that was impossible. I put the telex in my pocket, took my cameras, film and Perihan, and set off to Ankara."

Shortly, Ara and his friend Perihan Kuturman, who worked for the American News Center, were in the Office of Air Force Commander General Irfan Tansel. Tansel was involved in the transport procedures of the body of martyr Cengiz Topel, which had been retrieved from the Greeks with a heavy heart.

"I asked around, after the bombardment no journalists were able to contact the Air Force. 'Do not bother trying, nobody can see anyone, they do not even answer their telephones,' they said. I knew the General from before. I went to the command's door in the morning. His adjutant went to tell him I was there; 15 minutes later he came back saying 'he is waiting for you'. He did not receive any journalists, only me. How are you... etc. 'Look I even shaved for you,' he said.
We sat down as if I had come to take his photograph which I did. Then he said 'what is going on?' The Air Force bombarded Cyprus. 'Look, according to the instructions from America I need to go there and take pictures. This is the first-time Turkey goes to war,' I said. 'All right, I shall give you my jet and you can go to Incirlik' he said."

Ara was so excited he could not stand still as he watched Tansel Pasha reach over to press the buttons of the intercommunication device on his desk and said to the answering commander, *"I am sending you Ara Guler, he wants to take some pictures, he will tell you what he wants, do what ever he asks for,"* and then intervened by saying *"My Pasha I have my friend Perihan with me."*

They were taken to Etimesgut Military Airfield with the jeep that was allocated to them.

"I sat in the front while Perihan sat in the back to the aircraft. An officer was waiting at attention. He says that the aircraft is ready for our orders with so much fuel. We boarded the plane. We were going to Incirlik. 'What did you do during the bombarding?' I asked. 'Initially we had a briefing' they said, 'so do it again' I said. Again, an alarm was sounded, again, the men came running. They thought they were really going again. Nobody told them that it was only an exercise, only the commander knew. We had the briefing and I photographed it. 'What did you do next?' 'We attached the bombs'. Who attaches the bombs? The sergeants. There they came with full gear. I found a high place, a crane and got on top of it to photograph. I could see the whole fleet. I said, 'I want five of these aircrafts to be airborne'. I went to the head of the strip and took pictures, it was not necessary but whatever, I ran out things to photograph, I finished with the Air Forces."

After finishing with the Air Force element of the operation, Ara went to visit Admiral Necdet Uran of the Navy Command which shared the same building with the Air Forces.

"He greeted me with a slight reproach and his first sentence was; 'Times have changed, the Navy used to be the favorite, now the journalists think the Air Forces is more popular.'"

In a very short time Ara had won over the heart of the commander and he was already negotiating about Submarines.

"I said I would be taking fancy photographs of the war, order of the navy and added 'It would not go amiss to have a few Submarines'. In the meantime, I asked where the Navy was deployed. Mersin, he said. Whereas I want it to be in Iskenderun, there was a mosque opposite the bay and I could take a photograh with the mosque in the forefront and the fleet in the background that would have been good. The admiral said 'OK'. 'They will be there by the time you get there' he said. I was going by plane so it was not a problem. As the aircraft turned around Cyprus I took photographs. I commissioned the deployment of the Navy from Mersin to Iskenderun, imagine the cost I was incurring?"

At that time, Ara found out that there was a Cargo plane going from Incirlik Airbase to Iskenderun.

"I said 'how can I get to Iskenderun?' They said 'we have a cargo plane you can board if you like but the bottom of the plane is open.' At first I was standing, the center of the plane was open and I was afraid of falling, then I went to the head where the machine gun was nested. It was so windy. We were around Cyprus. I was going to take photographs of the vessels, the vessels went into action, they were all over the place, they were never side-by-side, how could I get a picture? This would not do. There was also glass which was reflective so the photographs were very poor indeed. I was waiting to land in Iskenderun. Finally we arrived, I was at the tip of the aircraft, the runway was short, there was a row of birch trees at the end, the aircraft came to a halt with three meters to go to the trees. I was scared that we would hit them and get crushed. I disembarked but I could barely stand from fright. I felt better after I had some coffee."

Ara felt restless because he could not shoot the composition he had imagined in his mind. He was told that the Southern Sea Area Commander was expecting him.

"I went to Southern Sea Area Commander Neriman Pasha, he was also a Leica man, loved it. He had 12 Leica cameras. I was worried about how I would be able to get the photographs there on time and he went on about his Leica. I said, 'Bro, let's talk later about this, I need to take these pictures'. 'OK' he said. I went to the Coast and saw that the tide was up."

They approached the flagship in the attack boat that was carrying him and the troops accompanying him, but the sea was rough so it did not appear to be an easy task to get on deck.

"We approached to the flagship, I handed over my camera bag to one of the sailors. I had to adjust my position with the waves to be able to reach the rope ladder that they had dropped down, otherwise I could get squashed between the two vessels. The sailor went first and I remained behind. Everybody was waiting for the famous *Paris-Match, Time* reporter, I was down waiting to get over my fear. I felt a surge of courage and jumped but my foot remained in the air, a wave came and I got wet to the bone, I did manage to go up but my position was in reverse like a fish in a net; the first thing that I saw as I got on deck were my shoes."

Ara was completely wet so he was taken to a cabin to get dried up and he was given a new recruit uniform to wear.

"I started taking photographs, the vessel, the submarine, you go this way, you move a little that way. The sun almost set but I did manage to take a lot of photographs. I had my coffee but then it was time to go back and I was thinking how I was going to get down this time? Descending was much worse, the ladder kept moving. So, what if worse came to worst, I would jump down. When I thought I was quite near, I jumped and fell; I was covered in scratches and bruises."

Solitary Wheel Rolling on Its Own

He did not care about hurting his eye, or the waves of the attack boat making it sway like a cradle and turning his stomach. All he worried about was getting the photographs delivered on time.

"They said the matrix vehicle of *Hurriyet* was going, I said goodbye to the Admiral and got in the car. I was sitting in the front while there was a lady in the back. The road was smooth, we were approaching Adana when suddenly I saw a wheel rolling ahead of us. 'What is that?' I asked the driver. 'A wheel,' he said. How many times in life could you see something like that; a wheel rolling on its own...'The axle broke' he said. So, what happens now? 'Hold tight dude,' he said. We continued for a bit but the driver was unable to control the vehicle any longer and off we flew. We were flying in the air I think, but this thing was not going to stay in the air, it was going to hit something. I put my cameras at my feet, I had 30 rolls of film shot, aircraft, vessels, submarines..."

The vehicle, managed by Mehmet Ayyildiz, rolled on the shoulder of the road with a lot of noise near the Misis Bridge over Ceyhan River.

"The car hit the ground with a bang. The front window was shattered. Thank God, the vehicle was an Impala or Chevrolet or something, a vehicle with a chassis, otherwise we would have been goners. We rolled and hit a tree and stopped. I breathed, I did not have any holes punched into me, the head is fine, the feet are good but I tasted salt in my mouth. Yet I felt no pain. I looked at the vehicle, it had been crushed like a tin can, the driver was on top of me, he had cut his ear which was bleeding. I heard voices from outside 'how it flew'. I yelled help, they came but they did not see us, it was dark. "Oh, look they are alive." They used a stone to break the window and pull me out. I said there is a lady in the back and they pulled her out too. We had flown off the Misis Bridge. The driver was unconscious. Another Impala collected us and took us to Adana. They asked which hospital we wanted to be taken to and I said to *Hurriyet* first."

The driver was seriously injured, his friend Perihan had broken feet, Ara was in a bad shape but he worried about his photographs. The vehicle that took them to the hospital stopped by the *Hurriyet* building first and after Ara called to the *Hurriyet* staff about the accident, they proceeded to Adana State Hospital. He never let go of his camera bag.

"They took us to Adana State Hospital, there was no doctor, no beds, whatever. Finally, four beds were found in the children's ward, the beds were for children so they were small, if you lie down, your feet stick out. I was all right but we had to hospitalize the lady and the driver. I had beaten all the journalists to this scoop, they were just realizing what was going on, my problem was something else; would they steal my film rolls or not? That was why I was carrying the bag all the time with me and I did not explain anything so they did not find out."

He was so concerned about his film rolls that he did not notice a strangeness in himself:

"I did not feel any pain, now that was not normal. I saw a mirror and went to look at myself, I let my arms down freely, one of my hands appeared to be lower than the other one, I could not believe it. Actually, my shoulder had been dislodged, my ribs were broken, I had a sprain and one side was paralyzed. I felt like I was looking at those distorting mirrors in the amusement park. That was when I started to feel dread."

Governor of Adana, Mukadder Oztekin, heard about the accident and came to the hospital to get information.

"I requested the Governor to provide an ambulance to take me to the airport to catch the 6am flight to Istanbul. The ambulance came and I flew to Istanbul. I put the film rolls in envelopes and I wrote the texts for the photographs on the plane on the way from Adana. I had a friend who was the Cargo Chief with PANAM. I said to him 'I am not fit to do anything, sign for me and send these to the United States'. I turned myself in to the American Hospital in Istanbul and was hospitalized for one month."

Chasing the Pope

In July of 1967, Pope Paul VI came to Turkey. The objective of the Pope's visit on this hot summer day dominated by searing heat, was to melt the ice between the Catholic and Orthodox churches. Journalists had invaded Yesilkoy Airport waiting for the Pope's plane to land. The moment came which hundreds of local and foreign correspondents werewaiting for, sitting on the the baggage cars in front of the terminal building, and the plane landed on the tarmac. Cameras and photography equipment started operating at full cycle but the plane which had landed was not the Pope's plane.

The plane on which all the lenses had been focused was carrying American journalists on duty that were working for the largest agencies in the world, United Press International (UPI) to follow the Pope. Ara became deranged when he saw the American photographers disembarking from the plane rapidly and moving to the special area allocated for them. He was very upset and swore because the Americans had been given an advantage while his line of vision and working conditions were difficult and doomed to a baggage car. Just as a scrape was about to be initiated the PANAM aircraft with 'Saint Paul' written on it emerged.

The Pope, in his red cape and skullcap, descended the aircraft stairs and to the astonishment of President Cevdet Sunay, Prime Minister Suleyman Demirel, Minister for Foreign Affairs Ihsan Sabri Caglayangil, ministers, The Governor, The Mayor, Mufti, The Patriarch, everybody who had come to greet, he sunk to his knees and kissed the ground. At that moment when nothing else could be heard except the clicking of the camera buttons and the voice of Ara's competition, Goksin Sipahioglu, could be heard trying to get Ara Guler's attention:

"I *adjusted the camera to F8 will I get a good picture?*"

Ara answered without taking his eye away from the lens:

"*It is the Pope, 8 will do, so will 11, anything will do.*"

After the Pope's visit to Dolmabahce, he departed from the group of journalists without telling anyone and went to the Hagia Sophia, the next stop on the program. He had heard the Istanbul Department of Security would allow a limited number of photojournalists to enter.

> "There were so many journalists. The police did not know who was a journalist and who was not so they had been ordered not to allow anyone entry from there, they were doing their duty.
> Caglayangil was the Minister for Foreign Affairs, he was also a friend of the Pope. We were touring the Hagia Sophia and I was taking pictures. Suddenly right in front of the altar he stopped. He sank to his knees and started praying. All the Italian journalists cried 'Hiiiii Mamma Mia', the Pope was praying in Hagia Sophia that was something that could not be missed. For 500 years, the sign of the cross had not been displayed in the Hagia Sophia, nobody had prayed. It was the greatest monument in the Christian world. The fact that the Pope has come after 514 years to a place which had been closed was a humongous event, everybody was all over each other, etc. I was in a very convenient position and started shooting away. Caglayangil was standing behind him, what could he do, he could do nothing. The Pope kneeled, bro. From the Turkish perspective it was a faux pas but in terms of Christianity it was a significant moment. Everybody inside took that photograph. But they did not take everyone inside, many could not get inside. I took that picture and distributed it to the world."

514 years after Istanbul was conquered by Sultan Mehmet, the Pope attained his desire to pray at the Hagia Sophia, after which the next step in the Pope's program was the pilgrimage to the House of Mary in Ephesus.

> "We were following the Pope; he would visit the House of Mary. There was live television coverage by official television channels, RAI was broadcasting. I saw the RAI team, there was an archeological ruin ahead and they were standing in front of it, they almost fell. I was up a ladder, there was no place further to go. I was watching the Pope. He was short. Suddenly the Pope was blocked out of sight by people around him. The RAI team become volatile. I pushed, shoved, kicked, whatever. I stepped on somebody's neck as well as somebody's foot because on the other side there was an excavated area 15 meters deep. There was no room, I had to step on his foot, neck, head to take photographs with one hand. The man said 'take your foot away Ara Guler.' I said, 'I can't, I'll fall.' I looked and saw that the man was Caglayangil."

Ara knew no obstacles as he followed every step taken by the Pope on his visit to Turkey, which was televised live to 1 billion people throughout the world.

> "These are all places where I have taken photographs, I know them by heart. I know there is a window behind the House of Mary. Only one photographer will be allowed to go inside and that will be someone from their group, the place is very small. I said there is a window out back, let's

dismantle it. Further along I saw a ladder. Goksin and I took the ladder and went to dismantle the window. We hid the glass and put the ladder back in its place. I saw the altar from the window. We saw the place where the Pope would pray. The best possible location. We took turns shooting or one of us would use the cameras; the objective was not to miss the moment. We had it made bro."

In the Family Homeland

At the end of the summer of 1967 Ara's father Dacat reproaches his son, whose days are very busy, by saying:

"You come and go, your interviews are in the papers, we read them, look at your photographs but you are of no use to us."

"What do you mean?"

"Have you ever taken me anywhere?"

"Where should I take you? You are the boss, you can go where ever you want."

"Have you ever thought of taking me to my hometown, to the house I was born in? I want to see the house I was born in. You should see it, too. If you take me, it will be significant, otherwise all villages are the same."

These words uttered by his father penetrated his heart. He arranged his business and they set off to Giresun by ferry and took a taxi to Sebinkarahisar.

"As we kept going along the road, the mountains kept getting higher. The flora changed, as the elevation increased the trees turned into pine trees. As we continued a gray mountain appeared suddenly before us, I could not remember its name but apparently, it was a well-known place. We had diced lamb fried on an iron plate there. It was enjoyable. I looked at my father, it was clear that he wanted to be a man of this terrain. But I knew the situation. He had been sent from Sebinkarahisar at the age of six to study in Istanbul. He had become an urban kid when he was a village kid. Subsequently I remembered that he had told how from time to time they would cross these mountains in one week to get to the coast that is Giresun. I think of that time, perhaps the 1910s. A child from the village going to the big city, to the center of the Empire to go to school. That was a significant opportunity. Going to the school in Ortakoy Istanbul with a clean school uniform, singing in church in the choir of Gomidas, playing with urban children who were your peers, being able to laugh. And as years had gone by now we were going to the village."

They still had eight kilometers to go to reach the village of Yayci of Sebinkarahisar, where his father was born. They found out that it was only possible to go on a tractor because there was no road.

"Finally, we managed to find a car with a high body and reached the village. Everybody greeted us. We talked, had ayran, all the village men came to say hello one by one, we had some more ayran. Then we all started off to the village. My father searched for the house, we turned right, we turned left and finally he said 'this is it'. There was no house standing in the place which he indicated. It was in ruins. There was a wall formed with large stones. It was evident that the house had been demolished over time. Suddenly he turned to the villagers and said, 'there was a fountain in the square in the village, with many water outlets. Where is it?' 'Ah here it is' they said.

We went to the fountain and my father drank water from each outlet to his heart's contentment. 'Oh wow!' he said, 'that is what water should taste like.'"

They were sitting in the village square when his father suddenly asked about the threshing field. The villagers immediately pointed it out.

"We went there also. 'I used to ride this all the time and kept turning,' he said as he pointed out to the idle threshing sled. 'Perhaps my mother made me ride it to add weight but I still enjoyed it very much.'
The villagers Ahmet, Mehmet, Yusuf, Isa... all looked at my father and finally blurted out what they were thinking. 'If you want to ride it again we can prepare it immediately,' they said. One of them brought the horses, someone else attached the threshing sled to the horses; my father re-moved his jacket, got on the threshing sled and with a stick in his hand suddenly he was six years old again. The horses walked, he was sitting in the sled, for all we saw he was turning around but who knows what he was thinking. Just like in the old days who knew when his mother would say 'That is enough', 'Come here'... but his mother was no longer there to interrupt his revelry. He kept turning, my six-year-old father while the Ahmets, the Mehmets observed as did I... for per-haps half an hour, maybe more. The horses wearied and finally my father got off the threshing sled and the horses stopped.
When he joined us, his eyes were moist. Who knows what all he was missing. Like the former days of childhood which were gone forever. 'Well that is how I would circle on the threshing sled when I was six years old' he said."

They said goodbye to everyone and left Yayci village as it was getting dark. When the vehi-cle was 2-3 kilometers away from the village his father stopped the car.

"Wait, let's take a look at the village from a distance" he said.

"I got out of the car, I followed him. He looked long and hard at the village underneath the hill, was he looking for his mother, his father, I do not know. Then suddenly he turned to me and said, 'Let's go'. We proceeded from Sebinkarahisar along the Susehri Sivas road. From Sivas we con-tinued to Istanbul. He was happy, he talked about the village to all his friends who came to the pharmacy. He had been encompassed by a different kind of will to live."

"Look, we went to the village, we drank water from its fountain, we talked to the men, we rode the threshing sled, had ayran which is all well and good but we forgot something. We for-got the most important thing. I forgot!"

"And what is that?"

"We forgot the dried nuts and fruits, dried mulberry, fruit pulp, apricot... I would fill my pockets with them and eat them, I liked them very much. We forget to buy and bring them. Now I remember, when I left the village to come to Istanbul to go to school my mother pre-pared a bag of them for me and I ate them along the way."

"Never mind, we shall go next year, you can get as much as you want then."

"He gave me a reproachful look, something was missing. After going to Sebinkarahisar he had started to be a happy man. 'My son took me to my hometown, let me see my village, walked me along the streets I had walked as a child, I drank water from the fountain, I watched the sun set, we just forgot to get the dried mulberries'."

Four months after Ara took his father to the village of his birth to drink the waters of his childhood, he lost him.

The Greasy Notebook

"My father had a heart attack and died. We brought a doctor, it was around 11 o'clock at night and he died towards 4 am. He had heart attack three times, on the first two we took him to the American Hospital, the third happened here at home and he died here."

Ara's heart sank every time he remembered and regretted that he had told his father to forget about the dried mulberries, fruit pulp, nuts.

"I was waiting at home to go to the funeral. My friend, poet Nevzat Ustun, who is now deceased was also with me. The funeral ceremony was going to start at two. There was still more than half an hour to go. The doorbell rang and I went to open it. Two people were standing at the door holding a rather large wooden crate. I felt I recognized their faces from somewhere. 'Come in,' I said. 'We are looking for Dacat Guler. We brought this for him from Yayci village in Sebinkarahisar,' they said. I remembered. They were the villagers from my father's village who offered us ayran and brought the horses to hitch to the threshing sled, the Ahmets, the Mehmets, the Yusufs. I cannot remember all their names, perhaps they were neither Mehmet nor Yusuf, but it was them. My father's villagers."

With a sense of confusion Ara bid the guests to enter.

'My father passed away,' I said. 'We are going to the funeral, come if you like, it is near by.' They were also surprised. There was a silence. I opened the box, it was full of dried mulberries, fruit pulp, nuts and lots of it. I was dumbfounded. They spoke: 'Dacat is our villager, he came, toured but he left before he had a chance to taste the dried fruit. We were coming to Istanbul so we thought we would bring some. Perhaps it was not meant to be.' Nevzat and I were speechless. My father's words came to my mind:
'We went, we toured, drank the water but came back without tasting the dried mulberries, fruit pulp, nuts.' By now it was time to go to the funeral. I found three small plastic bags; I filled the bags with two, three fistfuls of dried mulberries, a few pieces of fruit pulp, some dried plums. The villagers supplied the nuts that he had longed for and I filled the plastic bags with them,
'Let's go' I said. I put the bags into the coffin that my father was buried in...

After the ceremony at the Beyoglu Uc Horan Church, his father's body was laid to rest in the Sisli Armenian Cemetery.

"It saddened me, but I did not cry. Only once in my life did I cry after a demise and that person was journalist Abdi Ipekci. (He was murdered by Mehmet Ali Agca who later shot Pope John Paul II)"

Shortly after burying his father he learned that he had debts.

"After my father passed away, the house had a mortgage which I kept paying but there was no end to it, I ran out of money. With these debts hanging over me, I was moping about when Kemal from *Tercuman* came. The big boss of *Tercuman*, Kemal Ilicak, was my friend. He used to be a reporter. 'How are you, why the long face? Come with me' he said and we went into his office. 'Tell me what is wrong,' he said."

Ara explained how his father had gotten involved in something he knew nothing about, and the debts that had been generated with the unsuccessful management of his business with his partners.

"My father went into business with some partners. I do not know what the business was but whatever it was it was unsuccessful. He mortgaged the house. Now that my father passed away I was left with the mortgage debt. The last payment was this many thousands of dollars. 'Never mind it is only money' he said and pressed a button. A female accountant came in. Pay Ara this much money,' he said. No guarantees, no papers. The man paid my whole debt. Nobody ever did something like that for me."

Ara was at peace with himself for having paid the debt of this father who had given him every opportunity when he raised him.

"Kemal never asked for that money. He never said anything, neither did I. I made interviews for him. Nazli (Kemal's wife) has no knowledge of this, neither does his son."

The pharmacy business, which had thrived with the personal efforts of Dacat and his acquaintances, petered out after his demise and the assistant could manage the pharmacy for only one year. They had no choice but to close down the pharmacy.

"We transferred the pharmacy and I moved the contents. I brought the mortar and pestle and such equipment home and put them in the attic. My father had a greasy notebook. I gave the notebook that name because my father held it with his oily hands and he was always writing in formulas and what to mix with what and how many grams, what temperature was needed. He would always look in that notebook and prepare his mixtures. My father was a great chemist, I wish I had kept that notebook, I was foolish to lose it."

With Philosopher Bertrand Russell

In 1968, Ara visited his publisher friend Felix Gluck who lived in London. His editor friend procured photographs from Ara for the publications issued by bookmakers in the United Kingdom and, as they were sitting in the publishing house his editor friend asked Ara:
"If there is anything you want to do in London, let us help you."

Ara replied without hesitation:
'I want to interview Bertrand Russell, I would like to take his photographs. "

"Of course," said his friend Felix and reached for a book on a shelf and extended it to Ara:
'This is his last book. If you look carefully there are many pictures inside. Even books about philosophy are made like this now."

While Ara was examining the book of Bertrand Russell, one of the greatest philosophers in the world, with interest, Felix called his secretary and asked her to get an appointment with Russell.

As they were chatting, the secretary returned to say that an appointment had been arranged with Bertrand Russell for the next day. She explained how he could get there, including a road map where she had marked where he should change trains, and the departure and arrival times of the trains and handed Ara the relevant notes. The publishing house had even procured the tickets.

When Ara saw the name of the place he was going to, PENRHYNDEUDRAETH, he felt slightly alarmed.

"The word was so long and so full of consonants that I could not manage to read it. It could have been the name of a dinosaur species."

Ara put the notes in his pocket and left the publishing house with Bertrand Russell's new book.

"The train was moving forward. The land was green and flat. I looked at the plan that I had been given although I could not tell where I was. We were going in a direction that I was unfamiliar with, I had trouble reading the names written on the paper, never mind pronouncing them. There was only one thing I was sure of and that was I was going into the central regions of the United Kingdom. The train slowed down progressively and finally stopped in front of perhaps the smallest train station in the world, a miniature station built of wood in the shape of a square."

Ara disembarked on this small station in Wales and started waiting with his camera bag.
After a short while a car approached him, "Mr. Russell is expecting you, let's go. "
The vehicle passed through the narrow streets of the village and subsequently through endless greenery until it stopped in front of a wooden house on a hill covered with leaves. As soon as he was inside the house he realized that although the house had plenty of windows it was dim indoors and his heart sank. The light was not suitable for photographs. Furthermore, all the chairs in the room had been collected in the center which was not at all convenient for photographing.

"Just because this and that were not suitable did not mean that I was not going to take pictures. 'Ara Guler, perhaps everything is technically adverse, not everything in the world is going to be adjusted according to you,' I said to myself. 'Do not forget you are in Bertrand Russell's house!'"

A tall, slightly hunchbacked man with his head leaning toward his left shoulder filtered into the room. His slim silhouette approached Ara. He said in a hoarse voice, "Hello". Russell shook Ara's hand and sat gingerly on one of the chairs which was most unsuitable for photographing.

"I thought of myself, Bertrand Russell, and the photograph... In terms of light the situation could not have been worse. How was I going to take photographs without lifting this old man from his chair all the time and moving him to other corners of the room? Although the man opposite had been jailed a few years ago when he was eighty-nine years of age for engaging in sit-ins. But how was I going to convey my dilemma?"

He sat in the opposite chair. He explained that he was a photojournalist from Turkey, that he had worked as a photojournalist for many journals and newspapers in the United Kingdom, that many of his interviews had appeared in *Observer* and subsequently in *Times*, and that he had been nominated as one of seven star photographers in 1960 by *British Photography Year-book.*

"I presented a lengthy discourse about photography. I don't know how much of it he understood with my English languge skills. However, he had a benign look on his face, he even smiled from time to time."

Ara, who had started to sip his tea served in blue English porcelain with sugar and lemon, could still not dispel the stress he was experiencing. He had read all Russell's books translated into Turkish and he wanted to have the atmosphere felt in this room that he inspired in his readers

"I thought that at that moment, taking photographs was more important than talking. He had said whatever he was going to say and would say. In view of his presence I could not have been more than a momentous witness. If I could have been a good witness perhaps I could have contributed something to what he intended to say. I sat Russell in front of the writing desk. I took a lot of black and white and color photographs of him in front of this desk where perhaps he had written many of his works. As I was taking his photographs, I did my best not to stress him. Afterwards I took him out into the garden and took pictures of him with his house and with his wife who had joined us. A background with all shades of green with Bertrand Russell upfront ..."

He spent approximately three hours at Russell's house. Just as he was thinking that it was time to leave he remembered the book given by Felix.

"At that moment we were both standing in front of the desk. I opened the book and showed him the blank page behind the cover, 'would you sign this for me?' I asked. 'Of course,' he replied and signed the book with a black pen: Bertrand Russell. He forgot to date it and I did not dwell on it."

As I was leaving Russell asked me for a favor. He said, 'Can you send copies of the pictures you have taken, we would like to use them in the Foundation Brochures.' 'Yes of course,' I said and noted his address and he said, 'There is no branch of the Russell Foundation in Turkey', 'Where-as there are Bertrand Russell Peace Foundation offices in many places in the world. We would like to have such an office in Turkey also.' I was flabbergasted. I had to give an answer immedi-ately. At that moment, I was only concerned in disentangling myself from this business. 'I am a journalist,' I said, 'I am only involved in the visual side of things. I do interviews. Perhaps if I were a writer, I could think differently. Furthermore, politics is not really my cup of tea. But if that is what you want then I shall give you an appropriate name that is just what you require. Get in touch with them. They will probably be over the moon. Thus, you can have a contact in Tur-key.' I gave him the name of Turkey Labor Party. Then I added: 'It is a major left-wing party. You can find out the address and contact its administrators that would be good.' As a result of this, they found a dear appreciated friend of mine, Mehmet Ali Aybar."

Years later as he was strolling along Shaftesbury Street in London which had many bookstores, Ara, who was looking at photography books saw a book in the showcase with Ber-trand Russell's name on it. Russell had passed away. His curiosity was piqued and he entered and asked for the book.

"I started turning the pages. I had four photographs in this book. They were the pictures I had tak-en at his house in the village that day and my name was also mentioned. An era had come to an end with a black cover. However, I am confident that Russell's idea, his philosophy, and views will live forever."

Historian Arnold Toynbee

In the first half of 1968, British historian Arnold Toynbee came to Turkey to meet with the Head of CHP (The Republican People's Party), Ismet Inonu. Toynbee was the editor of 'Blue Book' which is a British psychological operation brochure alleging that Turks carried out genocide to the Armenians in 1915. During the World War I, Toynbee worked as a staff expert in the British War Propaganda Bureau. He confessed that he had commissioned the preparation of a provocative document with controversial contents as war propaganda material, to ensure that the British Government and the US enter the war as early as possible. In fact, he had developed a sympathy for the Turks. Ara was invited to Ankara to photograph the meeting of British historian Toynbee and Inonu during those days when the waters of the Mediterranean were starting to simmer due to Cyprus.

The event had been organized by CHP Secretary General Bulent Ecevit.

"The Secretary General of the Republican Peoples' Party of the time, Bulent Ecevit, took me to the Pink Mansion to take special photographs of the Pasha (Inonu) as well as to document the visit of the renowned British historian Arnold Toynbee. We arrived in Ankara and first visited Ecevit's home in Bahcelievler, Ali Ihsan Gogus was also present. I took many photographs there."

Journalist Mete Akyol was making an audio recording of the meeting. Osman Okyar, Cambridge graduate and son of Fethi Okyar, a close colleague of Ataturk, was interpreting and Ara was taking photographs.

"Toynbee and Ismet Pasha were both older than the other, Ismet Pasha was thrilled. Finally, when it was over 'I will take him to his hotel' I said. I took him to his hotel and took some more pictures at the hotel. He said, 'If you ever come to London look me up'. I go there frequently anyway so when I went to London the next time I had the pictures processed, telephoned him to inform about my visit and gave him the pictures. We became friends, he took me to his private club. He hosted me a couple of times, I also took photographs in his home, etc. You know there was an article in *Time* about the establishment of the republic in 1923 with Ataturk on the cover. Do you know who wrote that article? It was Arnold Toynbee."

Arnold Toynbee, who was deputized by the Turkey Desk of the British Ministry for Foreign Affairs Intelligence Department to monitor the Dardanelles and Independence Wars, operated against the Turks at one time but subsequently became a fan. In fact, he lost his appointment to the London University because of this sympathy.

A Life and Death Situation

In October of 1968, Ara set off with Fikret Otyam to prepare an interview with the agricultural laborers in Cukurova. Painter Orhan Peker was going to draw the patterns. The first thing they did on their arrival in Adana was to go to the flea market to get themselves second hand clothes. They were going to mingle with the laborers and work with them picking cotton. The Adana Bureau Chief of *Cumhuriyet* newspaper, Coban Yurtcu, who was familiar with the region, and his son Isik were included in the team to oversee them. They went to the plot of land where they are picked as daily agricultural laborers with trucks.

Fikret Otyam, who was well-prepared for his role, was not shaved for 15 days; did not have a haircut or cut hisbeard or nails. As he was blended so well with the other laborers waiting at the intercity bus terminal in his old and filthy outfit, he was stressed when Ara could not distinguish him among the others .Otyam could not even call out, '*Damn, Ara here I am*'. After a while Otyam was relieved to see Ara leaning on the fender of a car photographing the agricultural laborers but this time the laborers were uneasy.

When the laborers started to think ill of Ara, believing him to be a tourist, Fikret Otyam immediately intervened to pull his colleague away from there.

'Off you go about your business yallah!"

Their attention was disrupted when the trucks collecting the agricultural laborers appeared.

"We were together with Fikret, I would take his photographs. Somebody came and took us, he was taken elsewhere as was I. You go to the labor market to look for work and somebody comes and picks you. We thought that the man would choose both of us but eventually we were chosen for different places. Somebody else chose me. We never thought of this way. Where am I, in what part of Cukurova, I do not know."

The team split up on the first day.

"Anyway, I went and worked in the field picking cotton; I took photographs. The man asked, 'Why do you have camera?' 'I am an amateur, I like taking pictures,' I said. With a Leica in my hand, ha! I was taking photographs but Fikret was not there, how were we going to do this interview? My writer had gone missing. I was picking cotton, I was a laborer. I slept in the field, those with families had brought beds but as I was a bachelor, I had to curl on some dry weeds. There were snakes, centipedes, lizards."

Ara was exhausted from working like a laborer picking cotton on one hand and taking photographs on the other.

"I worked in the cotton fields for one week. The day I got paid I escaped. I walked for five kilometers to get to a paved road; I did not know which paved road it was."

Ara tried hitch-hiking but no cars would stop for him when he raised his hand.

"Nobody stopped for me when they saw my circumstances. I had the unkempt laborer's outfit that I bought from the market. Finally, a person stopped for me and brought me to the city. I went to *Cumhuriyet*; our place of coordination Shepherd Yurtcu, do you see? 'Damn, I am dying, get me a room at Erciyes Palas,' I said."

Erciyes Palas is the first hotel in Adana with air conditioning. Ara who was unrecognizable by this time threw himself into the hotel.

"I was so filthy. The first thing I did in the hotel was to run the hot water and place a stool in the bathtub, I sat under running water for an hour to get cleaned, bro. I even began to feel cold."

Ara was affected by the temperature difference from 30 degrees Celsius in the shade to an air-conditioned environment, in addition to lingering under the water for so long, and he got a lung infection.

"I was lying in bed with a temperature of 40 degrees. I did not get sick there but later when I returned. Fikret found Orhan Peker. As I was lying in bed with a temperature of 40 degrees, I felt as if the walls were collapsing on me, the windows were turning upside down, etc.."

The team hovering at Ara's bedside was anxious. Fikret Otyam leaned to whisper in Ara's ear:

'Please Ara hold tight, don't die or anything, I am sending you to Istanbul tomorrow morning at seven o'clock, if you are going to do something do it there."

Regardless of his illness as soon as Ara arrived in Istanbul he processed and printed almost 500 pictures and sent them to Otyam. The interview 'A Matter of Life and Death' was printed in *Cumhuriyet* newspaper as a series and caused a major commotion.

15 Vodkas, 4 Cameras

In May 1969 Ara was attending the Cannes Film Festival for the 11th time. The favorite of the festival that year was Soviet director Sergey Bondarchuk. Everybody was talking about the most expensive film to date being 700 million dollars which was *War and Peace,* and the making of which had lasted seven years. 120,000 Soviet soldiers took part in the film and the director had commented that "*I lead the 7th largest army in the world*".

Ara who had watched Bondarchuk's film had been mesmerized.

"They played this magnificent film *War and Peace*, it was wonderful. There are great scenes in the film and I wanted to interview the man. I was accompanied by Gunes Karabuda. We got an appointment from the man and went to his hotel room at the Carlton Hotel. It was 10 am. We were just going to take a few portrait pictures of the man and leave. The man did not know English, French or any other language and we did not speak Russian so what else could we do? We smiled at each other."

Bondarchuk raised his finger and made a sign for "*one minute*" and took a large bottle of Stolichnaya vodka out of his suitcase. Bondarchuk went to fetch the toothbrush glasses from the bathroom, which he filled fully to the brim, and offered the glasses to his guests.

"The man said 'vodka' I said 'vodka.' He filled the glasses, drank it as a shot and I was getting sips .He waited for me to finish, and then he filled the glasses again. We had a few drinks like that and one hour later before noon I was so drunk I could barely go down the stairs."

When they were out on the street Ara felt something was missing and he asked Karabuda:

'Where are your cameras?"

'Where are yours?"

The vodka consumed in the morning hours had hit the duo so hard that they laughed until tears streamed from their eyes.

They had forgotten and left a total of six cameras, out of which four were Ara's and two were Karabuda's, in Director Bondarchuk's room and left.

Ara, went back to the director's room staggering slightly and returned with the cameras:

"It is a good thing we left, the man has opened a second bottle!"

Here It Is, Istanbul Bashing

In the summer of 1969, Cetin Altan who was a writer for *Aksam* newspaper, had arranged to meet with Ara to ask him how to operate a recently-bought camera.

"Cetin was holding the camera in his hand and asking stuff like, 'How does this work, etc.'. I saw he was deadly serious so I said, 'Let's walk'. These words generated 'Here it is, Istanbul". At that time, he was a member of parliament from Istanbul. "

Cetin Altan and Ara made a plan. They were going to tour the neighborhoods of Istanbul one by one.

They toured coffeehouses, junkyards, manufacturers, shantytowns and listened to the problems of the Istanbul residents in these areas. As Cetin Altan talked to people Ara would photograph them. Altan did not want to broadcast the fact that he wrote for *Aksam* which was known as a left-wing paper, and that he was MP from Turkish Labor Party (TIP), which was associated with communism. So he told those who asked that his middle name was Huseyin. There were times when Ara was obliged to confess that he worked for foreign agencies.

For most of the three weeks that they toured, they were greeted with the curious gazes of people. However, they were not always welcomed with the same understanding. When they set off on the dirt road from Ihlamur to Mecidiyekoy, they observed women living in the shanties in the central point of the valley who had spread rags onto ground covers and were stuffing them into mattresses. Ara did not want to miss this scene and jumped from the vehicle and started taking photographs.

"We were driving uphill. Altan had a Volkswagen car. I said stop, those ladies have spread something on the ground. They had spread wool and were airing it in front of adjacent apartment buildings painted in all colors. I thought it would be a good photograph. I got out of the vehicle and started shooting. After I had taken quite a lot of photographs the women started grumbling."

Suddenly the women went crazy and a young woman picked up a rock and just as she was going to throw it at the car Cetin Altan intervened:

"But sister what are you doing, does it suit you to throw rocks? Let the stone on the ground. "

"Why are you taking our pictures?"

"I am sure you have problems and complaints. We want to show these pictures to those who ignore your problems, your complaints and make them understand. "

"And that can be done by taking pictures, you say?"

The women were not impressed with the literary speech of Cetin Altan; "Dishonest pimps," "Sons of so and so," they shouted and went into an offensive.

> "The women attacked me. I started chasing them to frighten. They went to bring their husbands. They came with sticks. We got a good thrashing. We hardly got into the car. At that time Cetin did not want to be noticed because he was an MP. If he got thrashed it would be an MP getting thrashed. So, we were obliged to flee out of fear."

An Old Friend in Paris

Every time Ara visited France, he would visit his loyal friend Marchinez at his wooden house from the 16ᵗʰ Century.

The discourse about photography would continue until the late hours between Marchinez, his wife Jacqueline and Ara, in the accompaniment of cognac.

Ara enjoyed this discourse very much and he listened carefully to anything Marchinez, who he believed to cover a significant area in his life, had to say.

> "This man has always inspired me with excitement and strength. Perhaps he has not said anything that is not known but for the photographers of my generation he was like a battery, an accumulator."

Marchinez would introduce Ara to his friends, inform him about any new developments and protect and watch out for him when necessary.

> "The father of Italian photography, Paolo Monti, and Marchinez came here with their wives. I toured them for one and a half months. We were having a slide show, I was showing Turkey to Monti as well as some others. Fulvio Roiter took notes without interruption. He kept asking: 'What is this, how do you get there? Can you show it on the map?' He watched my slide show and then went to shoot the same pictures and made a big book of these pictures with Freya Stark. He was admonished quite severely by Marchinez one day: 'He told us about these places, are you not ashamed to go and take the same shots?' he said."

Once Marchinez, who loved Ara like a brother, was sick and he was afraid that he was going to die. He did not hesitate to bequeath the rarest pieces of his photography collection, which was his only wealth, even the priceless Daguerreotypes, the first photographs to be produced on glass, to him.

> "At one time when Marchinez got sick he was engulfed in the fear of death. I was there at that time. 'You can have these,' he said and gave me the Daguerreotypes. He gave me the Atgets, the Steichen used on the cover of Camera, Demachys, the Puyos."

Marchinez, who could not do enough for Ara, discovered that Ara was trying to reach the American avant-garde artist Man Ray who lived in Paris, and rushed to Ara's aid.

> "I said to Marchinez that I was going to take pictures of Man Ray. He got me an appointment. I went to his studio and said that 'I bring greetings from Marchinez'. 'I know, Marchinez has pre-

pared an issue for you and you are the photographer,' he said. He went and brought issues of Camera journals. 'This is you, right?' he said. He had taken them before. Now there was a young girl with him, he kept pinching the girl's cheek, sort of hitting on her. I started to take photographs. I shot as he pinched the girl's cheek, as he embraced the girl, pictures like that. Do you know who the girl was? There was this famous model he used, the one with the violin slit drawn on her face... We had beer, the studio was glass on top; the old Paris, I really liked it. It was a wide big space. Of course, it did not get warm, it never did, we were freezing. It was over and I left. Then a few years later I remembered and processed the photographs and intended to give them to him."

As Ara called Man Ray to give the photographs he was thinking about getting a few works from him, and with that thought he set off to the studio.

"I went there. 'This is my young photographer friend,' he said as he introduced me to his wife. 'He has brought the photographs,' he said. Whereas I had taken his picture with the girl which was why I could not give them, I tried to avoid giving them, I kept putting him off. He had a new book which had just come out; I talked about the book, I asked him to sign it. Stuff like that. Finally, the woman said: 'Let's have those pictures.' No, there was no place to escape any more. I gave the envelope. She took it, took out a few pictures and looked at them. It was evident that she was not pleased. She looked at the other pictures and got even more mad. The photographs showed Man Ray pinching the cheek of a young girl, hugging her etc.... The woman was furious. They started to fight because of my photogaphs. The woman yelled, threw the pictures and slammed the door and went."

They were left alone with Man Ray in the hangar-like studio.

I looked at him and he looked back at me. He was ashamed, 'shall we have tea?' he said. 'Let's have it,' I said. 'You have been coming here for some time now, I have not given you anything, let me give you something,' he said. 'There is no need,' I said. What did he give me? He gave the picture that was known throughout the world: La Baguette!
Do you know how many thousands of dollars that is worth? That was what he gave me. The one painted in blue. I held it in my hand, it was perhaps 200,000 or 500,000 dollars!
'Now I can't possibly take this,' I said. 'Why not?' 'You had a fight with your wife, there is a strange situation here; that is why you want to give me this whereas I would prefer you give me something that you wanted to give,' I said. 'I don't want it,' I said. 'Go on take it' etc.... Finally, I left there without anything."

Marchinez who was never tired of opening the doors of opportunity to Ara had even determined Ara's ten-year target.

"One day when we are eating at the house of my old friend in Paris, photograph man Romeo Marchinez, he suddenly stood up and said, 'You continue to take pictures of men you call artists and show them to be, you believe they are artists. Whereas if you brought these three men together and took their picture that would be the photograph of the century and that would be it', he said."

Ara asked with curiosity *"Who are these three men?"*.
Marchinez opened his eyes wide and approached Ara and counted off the three men in one go:

"One, Charlie Chaplin; two, Albert Einstein; three, Pablo Picasso."

"Perhaps what he said was right. This dream remained riveted in my mind."

Standing Guard at Charlie Chaplin's Door

Einstein had passed away so that opportunity was lost but Charlie Chaplin and Pablo Picasso were still with us.

Ara had admired Chaplin as an actor, director, scriptwriter and composer of film music ever since his childhood. The character he created, Charlot, with his walking stick, flabby pants, funny walk, satirized the ruthlessness of the capitalist world on one hand and made a stand against fascism on the other. Because of this oppositional stance Chaplin, who had given the name of Elia Kazan to the McCarthy Committee, had been forced to leave the US. Ara knocked on every door to reach the great man he adored, he used all his acquaintances to get a foot in the door but when he failed to get results he went to the man's door.

I went to Vevey in Switzerland where he used to live, it was about half an hour or 45 minutes from Geneva. I sat in a taxi I rented for days in front of his house regardless of the weather which was winter and snowy. He lived in a house like a chateux with a guard at the gate. The house was surrounded by a high wall and a guard dog at the gate. I told the doorman I was a journalist but I did not get anywhere so I decided I had no choice but to write a romantic, sincere letter and said:

Dear Chaplin,

I have been collecting photograph material for the past 15 years for a book that will come out in the near future titled 'The Creatives of our Times'. It is not possible for this book to be completed if you, whom I have great admiration for, are not included. I am a Turkish photographer living in Istanbul and I am touring Europe at the moment. I came to Switzerland with the hope that you could allocate 20 minutes of your time to me (without bothering you with a flash, etc.) To this date, I have photographed many celebrities who are essential elements of this work. However, for me you are the most important man in the world. No politician measures to your significance. Although I have no other wish than to meet you I would appreciate the opportunity to introduce myself and for you to pose for me.

With my most profound respect.

However, there was no reply... Three days later I was back at the door. Again, it was raining, the same dog was there, the same result... For three days, I came and went away. On the last day, it was not raining. His wife invited me in and offered tea. I was in his house.

Chaplin's wife was Oona, the daughter of the famous playwright Eugene O'Neill, and she had taken Ara in because she was afraid he was going to freeze outside.

"His wife invited me in, we had tea. I knew that Charlie Chaplin was upstairs, I was having tea downstairs with his wife but no pictures were being taken. Now I realize that what the man did was right. Why? Who is Charlie Chaplin? The most active, mobile, agile man in the world. He does this, he does that, he does whatever, that is the image he had established. You have come to take this man's photograph now that he is paralyzed and in a wheelchair and that is adverse to his image. He cannot move from one place to another on his own and he does not want to portray himself in this condition that is why I cannot take photographs. His wife said 'He does not like to have photographs taken any more, I hope you understand'. He said we can talk but no photographs. He did not want a photograph taken in his present condition because that was not the image he wanted to leave. He knew as well as I did that the camera in my hand was merciless."

The words of Marchinez were still in his mind.

"Charlot was the greatest man on earth. There are three men in the world like Charlot. One of them is Picasso, the other one is Einstein. As to the rest it does not make much difference whether they lived or not..."

Picasso was next.

A Photojournalist Carries Scissors in His Pocket

Jacqueline, the widow of American president John F. Kennedy who was assassinated, and who had remarried Greek shipping magnate Onassis five years later, had come to Istanbul. Goksin Sipahioglu, who heard that after touring the Topkapi Palace with an army of journalists Jacqueline Onassis was going to tour the Hagia Sophia but no journalists would be admitted.

Without alerting anyone the duo sneaked off to Hagia Sophia and hid inside.

Although Jacqueline had remarried, she was still the widow of a former US president and therefore under the protection of the American Secret Service. It was not long before they discovered Goksin and Ara.

"The American police were chasing him because he was tall. He refused to give his camera to the bodyguards. Actually, they did not want the camera, they were trying to get us out of there. A Turkish journalist would be offended by such action in his own country from an American. I entered with a lot of noise saying 'How dare you treat a Turkish journalist this way?' Anyway, they settled down."

They managed to stay inside. As Ara started to take photographs immediately, Goksin had no experience in photographing in environments with limited light and did not know what to do.

"There was only me and Goksin. Our guide was Inci Pirinccioglu, she was explaining in English. I was taking pictures of the woman inside the mosque. Goksin knew nothing about cameras, he did not have a clue about instantaneity. He kept asking, 'what diaphragm shall I use, what diaphragm?' I said 'put 5.6' but I was shooting with a 2. I did not know what I was using in that commotion and he asked me. I said 5.6 etc. and he went for 5.6."

When the duo was processing the films in the studio in Galatasaray, they saw that Ara's pictures were perfect, however; Goksin's films were pitch black. Goksin had adjusted the diaphragm erroneously but Ara was the one who advised him.

Goksin said to Ara *"At least give me a few pictures so I can send them to the foreign press. After all I took you there,"* and Ara did not give him a single frame.

Everyone was trying to fob each other off, looking to get one over. In fact, in that time camera flashes had cords so all photographers carried scissors in their pockets. When everybody went to events and saw somebody they knew there they would mosey over and say 'oh hi so you are here too!' They would act all friendly and ask about your health and in the meantime, look for an opportunity to cut the other party's flash cord on the sly. In other words, in those days a photojournalist was a person who carried scissors in the breast pockets of their jackets.

As I was enjoying the Jacqueline victory the studio telephone rang. I answered the phone and it was the editor of *Paris-Match*; 'Ara look at the photographs you took, if you have a picture of Jacqueline and Onassis next to each other I will give you 10,000 dollars, let me know immediately'. I was excited, I started to put all the negatives I had taken on the light table to look for such a picture. I was actually sure I had not taken such a picture but that was hope for you. Indeed, I did not find one so a good opportunity was lost.

Mister Shah

Ara wanted to meet with the Shah of Iran, Riza Pehlevi, but forget about convincing him about getting an interview, it was impossible to get even an appointment. Ara thought of the Minister for Foreign Affairs Ihsan Sabri Caglayangil.

"I told Caglayangil about my problem and he mediated. They were kind of relatives with the Shah."

Caglayangil's son-in-law was Iranian and his association with Iran Shah Pehlevi was so close that the Shah had insisted on inviting Caglayangil to Teheran, and when he was there he had told him that "*There will be a military coup in Turkey in a few months,*" and thus informed him about the coup to take place on the 12th of March, months before it happened.

In January 1969 Ara, his girl friend Perihan Kuturman and colleague Aysegul Dora were in the Shah's Niyavaran Palace in Teheran.

"Don't forget that the man is the head of the Persian Empire, one of the most important empires. I was going to do a special interview with the Shah of Iran. I thought it would be original to have the interview when he was skiing in Iran. A special zone surrounded by bodyguards was allocated for the Shah to ski on the Elburz Mountains. Now we should take the lift and go up, then we should ski down, I would be on skis and take photographs. The Shah was walking in front of me towards the lift when he suddenly fell. 'My God the Shah fell,' I said, that is a great picture for me. I held the camera, just as I was going to shoot he looked at me, as we were there looking at each other I had to give in of course. I lost a great opportunity. The Shah was very happy that I did not take the photograph."

The Shah was very much impressed with Ara's gesture. Ara who was so at ease and reckless to call after the Shah "*Mister Shah! Mister Shah!*" and pull at his lips to make the Shah smile, succeeded in making the Shah who displayed a cool profile, to laugh out loud at his jokes. In the evening, at dinner the Iranian Prime Minister approached to Aysegul and said, "*Tell Ara, the Shah has not laughed like that since he was six years old".*

'This time we went down, we would get on the lift, that is we should be jumping on it as it is moving. I jumped... Actually, I could not jump, I almost rolled to the bottom of the gorge. The Shah pulled me inside, in other words, he saved my life. *"*

Ara, who had captured the Shah after a long struggle, enjoyed this opportunity.

"I stayed there about two months. I ate black caviar from morning to night. Of course, there were important personalities in the vicinity, I knew some of them. One morning the Shah was coming and I would take photographs. I was trying to adjust my camera to the morning sun. There was ultraviolet etc. on the Elburz Mountains. Obviously, I had to askwhere the Shah generally sat they showed me and I asked one of the fancy men there 'can you grab a corner of this table so we can move it'. The man turned out to be the Chief of Staff!"

The headline of the newspaper for the great interview prepared by Ara Guler, a photographer from Turkey who made a name for himself in Europe, was presented to readers as 'Fifteen days in the palaces of Iran with *Sahbanu Farah...*'

Ara and his correspondent friend Aysegul were back in Teheran 15 months after the interview.

Aysegul was a family friend of Farah's daughter Leyla. She did not want to leave her alone as she was having a baby. Three hours after the baby was born, Aysegul had the baby in her arms and was pinning a Cumhuriyet gold coin and mashallah on the baby's frock. Ara was taking photographs of this new member of Iran's Royal Family and distributing them to the world press.

After they finished their interviews in Teheran, they set off to Beirut, the capital of Lebanon.

In the Palestine Guerilla Camps

After the Six Day War between Israel and Arab countries in 1967, Beirut had become a haven for the Palestinians who had been expelled from their territory. Millions of Palestinians who had been displaced from their settlements after the Israeli invasion were trying to sustain their lives in the refugee camps of Lebanon and Jordan.

Aysegul Dora wanted to go to the bases of the Palestine Liberation Organization (PLO), which gathered numerous organizations which were fighting for the Palestine cause under its umbrella in Jordan, and interview the women who were trained there.

"Aysegul went and found the guerillas in Beirut. I don't know how she did it. She said 'Bro, let's go to Jordan and find the women guerillas or something.' We wanted to do something. It was really dangerous, the men were armed with machine guns, if they touched the trigger we would be in smithereens. The guerillas, there were clandestine, FLN, you know? I still have those Palestinian badges. I dispatched the first photograph of Arafat to appear on the cover of *Time*, you know. Aysegul went and talked to the National Liberation Front."

Ara was anxious. He called the Beirut Representative of Associated Press Agency, Henry Kondakciyan.

"I said 'My colleague wants to go, is it possible?' He said 'Do not go, they will stop you on the way and shoot you, they won't bother to ask who you are, they don't have the time. They will shoot and go on.'"

Heavily armed Palestinians who had invaded important areas in Jordan under the title of 'democratization' and were about to seize control in the country, were living waywardly and making their own rules in the areas they occupied. Ara, who was concerned about this situation, tried to convince Aysegul without success.

"I said 'woman, don't go, I won't let you' etc. We argued 'I insist on going' she said. Whatever, I arranged the car. She put on her anarchist outfit and went over land. I said 'if you get there without being killed, come to the Turkish embassy in Jordan, I will wait for you there'. I did not know who the Turkish ambassador was. However, our Orhan Kologlu was there. I went by air. I went there and settled in the Embassy in order to wait for AysegulFinally, she came."

In July 1970 they were in a Palestinian camp 90 kilometers South of Amman.

"At that time, we carried out interviews there, there were lots of women, girls, men, guerillas. It was rather horrible, there you were eating dinner, men armed with machine guns came to get money, don't you dare not to give! I took a photograph of a woman, who became very well known afterwards; Leila Khalid. She raided London airport. She was a young girl then."

The interviews about 'Commando Girls in the Palestinian Army' with photographs of young girls with scarves around their necks, carrying Kalashnikov rifles, crawling on the ground, and walking tightropes, were announced with the headlines 'Young girls learn to fight instead of how to make love, how to use firearms instead of how to dance in Palestine' by *Gunaydin* newspaper.

Ataturk Culture Center Fire

It was not only the Palestinians who learned to use firearms in these camps; people from all over the world including Turkey were here learning to 'fight'. Just like numerous Turkish youths such as Deniz Gezmis and his comrades, who were founders of the Turkish Peoples' Liberation Army (THKO), had received weapons training in these guerilla camps.

In 1970, Turkey was witnessing the comprehensive spread of terror and violence and the days that started the right wing – left wing conflict at universities.

On the last days of the year, a fire broke out in Ataturk Culture Center while Arthur Miller's play *The Crucible,* which allegorizes the hunt for communists during the McCarthy era in the USA, was being shown.

"I was returning from an interview in Ankara, I was on an airplane. I saw the fire from the plane, I had my camera with me. As soon as I landed I came here and took pictures while it was still burning. The next morning, I came again to take some more pictures; by that time, I was just taking pictures of what remained. Many rumors were fabricated, like the fire was started by left-wing elements, the fire started on its own. I don't know from where they fabricate these rumors. I was given a job when the Ataturk Culture Center was being built. The electricity works of the center were being carried out by the German company Siemens. A new theater was being established in Turkey and it was a significant theater. I was asked to have an interview about the works of Siemens, the building of the theater, etc…. I had an architect friend Hayati Tabanlioglu, he was published in *Stern* at that time. So, I was involved in the building phase of the structure and then I got to photograph it when it burned to the ground so I was also involved in its finale."

The Suleyman Demirel government of the era alleged that the AKM fire was 'arson', and started the simmering of the witch's cauldron and a subsequent hunt for communists in the country. This incident was used as a reason to establish pressure on left wing intellectuals although no evidence of arson or sabotage were found in subsequent investigations; it was determined that the fire had been caused by an electrical short circuit.

The Fisherman of Halicarnassus

Author Cevat Sakir Kabaagacli, who was exiled to spend three years in Bodrum by the Independence Tribunal for writing an article criticizing the death penalty given to deserters without trial, liked Bodrum so much that after the mandatory three years he did not want to stay in Istanbul and returned to Bodrum.

Oxford graduate Kabaagacli, known as the Fisherman of Halicarnassus, tried to make a living in the early 1970s with his weary and tired body by guiding tourists through hills and dales and translating.

The Undersecretary of the Ministry of Tourism and Promotion of the time, Mukadder Sezgin, who heard about his circumstances and who was an old friend of Kabaagacli, engaged the Fisherman in the consultants' cadre of the ministry and proved to be a true friend. In fact, he even commissioned the preparation of a book 'Anatolian Civilizations' on behalf of the Ministry for Foreign Affairs. The Fisherman accepted the proposal for the preparation of the book with joy. When he received the copyright fee in the post, he happily wrote a letter to Sezgin who had arranged these opportunities for him:

'It is not clear whether we are drawing pistols or brandishing machetes. I felt myself swell with pride. At that moment, I felt like a fat-ass swaggering bureaucrat. Hehey!.."

The Fisherman prepared the English text of the book "Anatolian Civilizations" which was more than 250 pages, in a very short time in his handwriting. It was planned to distribute this book abroad for promoting Turkey. Then the idea of Ara Guler photographing the venues mentioned in the book was suggested. When the General Staff agreed to the allocation of a helicopter, the proposal was made to Ara.

"We were offered the preparation of a book by the Foreign Affairs Culture Department. The name of the book was planned to be 'Anatolian Civilizations'. The Fisherman was going to write the text directly in English while I was going to tour all the areas and take color photographs to be put in the book. The Fisherman was very satisfied with his life. He had great faith in me. This book with multiple photographs was going to be a mirror of Turkey on its 50th anniversary. I toured for months taking photographs. The Fisherman completed the text. We prepared a mock up of the book and submitted it to the Ministry. The 50th anniversary came and went, even today the book is searched in the Ministry and either the mock up with the photographs is found, the text is found or not, the photographs have been misplaced. In the end the Fisherman passed away without seeing the book..."

The incident 'Censorship is applied on the Fisherman of Halicarnassus' caused sedition among the intellectuals, and the Head of the Culture Department of the Ministry for Foreign Affairs at the time, Semih Gunver, wrote the following sentences in his notebook of memoirs:

"I met Ara Guler for the first time when I took up my position at the Culture Department. He resembled one of the statues depicting former Anatolian civilizations revealed by the excavations, this artist with his tall stature, gray-white beard and tousled hair of the same color. I had difficulty hearing his words through his lips which were lost among all that beard and mustaches. He seemed to be grumbling rather than talking.

The Ministry had commissioned the Halicarnassus Fisherman for a book on Anatolian Civilizations. Cevat Sakir, who was over eighty, had accepted the offer. There had been repetitions in the book. Apparently the old 'Fisherman' had forgotten what he had written previously and repeated the same parts. It was necessary to review and shorten the book. On the other hand, Ara Guler had prepared a series of photographs comprised of 80 slides. These slides had started with ancient artifacts in the Van area. My predecessor as Head of Culture Department of the Ministry for Foreign Affairs, Melih Ergin, could not have the book published. One of the *main reasons was that although Professor Ekrem Akurgal, archeologists and scientists appreciated the fact that the Ministry for Foreign Affairs was funding such a work for the first time, they had protested that the work had been commissioned to a daydreamer such as the Fisherman of Halicarnassus.*

The text written by Cevat Sakir could not be published as it was, it needed reviewing.

Ara Guler wanted his photographs to be put in the same book. There was no necessary allocation for printing the book. Printing prices had increased very much.

Ara Guler visited the Ministry a few times. He quit making an appearance. The shortening of the book was commissioned to an English writer. The Fisherman of Halicarnassus bought himself a radio with his copyright fee. Ara Guler collected his fee. Yet the book failed to be printed."

Ara had also witnessed the complexity of the Fisherman's narrative style:

"When he started talking about something everyone listened to him. He would encompass his listeners into the image he created and pull them into his world. As he narrated suddenly he opened a parentheses to explain something and this parentheses became the main issue. He established a world on this and once more captured us into it. The details got bigger and bigger and became a second subject. Just like the pages attached one after the other for long imperial mandates. There were so many assimilations in his narrative that mythological parentheses had to be opened in order to be understandable. In order to know something thoroughly,it is necessary to know its background and history."

Ara knew Cevat Sakir from way back. He was also witness to his interesting lifestyle:

"Years ago Fikret Adil, Husamettin Bozok and I went to Samim Kocagoz's house in Izmir Karsiyaka. We spent about 10 days with all the artists in Izmir: Necati Cumali, Attila Ilhan, Sabahattin Batur and most importantly the Fisherman. The Fisherman lived an old neighborhood in Izmir in the 1950s, on a hill in a two-storey white painted house with Greek style shutters. Fikret, Husam, Samim and I went to visit him. I can't remember which one it was but I was on the verge of finishing one of his novels. At that time, it had attracted my attention: The Fisherman did not write pages as we knew them, he wrote on long sheets of paper which he attached to one another."

Every time Ara went to Izmir he would call the Fisherman, go and say hi and take new photographs. He took this old man who had trouble walking because of his age down to the seaside, his favorite place.

"I wanted to a take a picture of the Fisherman in a place with the sea. I took him to a bay in Izmir. There were boat repairmen in the area. It was a great day on my part. There were clouds in the sky and the sun would be setting soon. As I was photographing him on the shore, I felt like I was taking the picture of a man arguing with nature. The clouds in the sky were turning reddish with the setting sun. The Fisherman was watching the sun set, looking at the clouds changing from color to color. I am approaching the Fisherman and trying to compromise his silhouette and the colors in the sky with the Fisherman in my mind. He engrossed in the clouds and me in my shooting. He was issuing orders to the skies with his silent looks. He was just like I had imagined, a man of the land in the middle of the sea. After that I never saw the Fisherman again. Perhaps he never went to the seaside after that. He was very old. He knew what I was going to photograph that day which is why he came to the shore with great difficulty. Perhaps we were watching the last sunset of the Fisherman together."

That evening Ara took the Fisherman out to dinner.

"He always wanted to tell me something. For some reason, he found me close to him. However, whatever it was that he wanted to tell me he had failed to do so all these years. That day when I took him from his home to the shore in Izmir and as we were having our raki in the evening at dinner I felt this for the last time. There was someone else with us that night who poked his nose into everything and meddled. From time to time the Fisherman got angry at him but the man ignored him, he was sassy. Subsequently the Fisherman was exhausted. The raki was finished anyway and it was late. He wanted to go home. As if he was saying to himself: I could not say what I was going to say to Ara Guler."

Ara could not help but wonder what it was that the Fisherman of Halicarnassus Cevat Sakir Kabaagacli had failed to tell him until he found a note written in the Fisherman's handwriting among the books...

"Hello!
I am sorry I am late. But with age comes illness, etc. You repair the roof and this time the walls give in. You fix the wall the roof caves in. Every time I say 'hello' to someone it feels like I am saying 'goodbye' at the same time. However, I am happy. I guess when God was creating me he said 'I have left this subject bereft of wordly goods such as money and wealth so I must at endow him with happiness and joy that are accepted by none!' That is why for no particular reason I am as happy as if I had won the lottery. Goodbye Ara. Thanks a million. Hello.
Cevat Sakir"

The work of the Halicarnassus Fisherman which was not published by the Ministry for Foreign Affairs because it was found objectionable, was published years later after his demise as a book titled *Turkey in Europe* with nothing less than the signature of Turgut Ozal, the prime minister of the era...

"It was printed in a rather amateurish way with no captions beneath the photographs, etc. Nobody noticed anyway. What better way to snuff a work."

Picasso

After the day that Ara photographed Picasso at the Cannes Film Festival from a distance, Ara had been churning with the idea put into his head by Marchinez about an interview with Picasso, but he had to wait until April 1971 for this.

Initially he tried his luck with painter Edouard Pignon who was one of Picasso's closest friends. Ara took Pignon, who was both a close friend as well as a comrade of Picasso, to Abidin Dino's house. Ara took a lot of photographs of him to convince him to introduce him to Picasso. Regardless of all the efforts of Abidin Dino, Pignon did not have the courage for this. Even though Pignon's wife Helene Parmelin was a special biographer of Picasso, he preferred not to heed this request.

Subsequently his friend the Count Mario Ruspoli invited Ara to his house for dinner to introduce him to Picasso's son Claude and his new German girlfriend. They thought Claude would take Ara to Picasso. However, Claude said, "*My father does not like me, he does not even want to see me. Furthermore, he is angry at me*".

One day Ara was walking around feeling regretful about Picasso in Geneva. He dropped by Skira Publishing House that published the albums of world famous painters as well as reference books about the art of painting. That day Albert Skira, the proprietor of the publishing house, was very cheerful and explained the reason as he took Ara to the Cafe du Commerce:

"Picasso has given permission for us to do the book *Metamorphoses et Unite*. In fact, we have to go to his house to work. I am thinking about collecting our Maurice Babey and proceeding to shoot there. It will be great."

Ara was about to burst with excitement and looked at Skira with begging eyes:

'I have wanted to take pictures of Picasso for years. I never had the chance. Everybody is too scared of him to do anything. Whereas you are going to work with him for days. You can't even take photographs.'

"Babey can't do anything more than taking pictures of his paintings and you will just stare at them. If I come with you, I can photograph Picasso in his daily life. That would be a significant document. I have been waiting for such an opportunity. Everything has been arranged anyway. If you don't take me with you, I won't take any pictures for your publishing house or give you any photographs ever."

Skira finished his cognac, asked for another one from the waiter and replied with the flair of a boss:

"The idea is good. You can take photographs of Picasso's daily life, the atmosphere in the house. Of course, you can come."

Ara was over the moon.

The team was making work plans at the boutique hotel near Picasso's chateau, nine kilometers from Cannes squeezed between the hills in the Notre-Dame-de-Vie region.

"While we were talking, I noticed that the barman was listening and smiling slightly. I was interested in the man because I knew he was listening to us. Then he asked 'do you think Picasso is going to accept you?' he said. Babey said 'Of course', 'We have an appointment tomorrow morning at 10 o'clock.' The man smiled again. 'What is it?' I asked, 'You do not seem to have much faith in this?' Cynically the barman said, 'It is never certain,' he said. After a while he narrated the following: 'Picasso is a very strange man. He says something and then forgets. Furthermore, nothing is important for him.
As far as I understand he lives only for the moment. Let me give you an example. Right in this room where you are sitting now, the Ambassador of Russia in Paris waited for exactly twelve days to give Picasso the highest medal in Russia which is the Lenin Medal. Picasso had forgotten that the man was waiting here. He was reminded that 'the Ambassador is waiting, he has come here to give you the Lenin Medal'. Picasso said, 'Dear sir, good and well but what difference does it make whether I take the medal or not? Lenin is my friend, they should give the medal to somebody young, it will be wasted on me and this way the path will be paved for somebody young' and the Ambassador had to leave with his medal. That is why I am not confident about your seeing him."

The barman's narrative had caused Ara's blood to freeze. He was reminded of the 10-15 photojournalists who waited at the door of Picasso's chateau every morning to take a photograph. But he consoled himself by saying *"Of course Picasso will accept Albert Skira and us. If Picasso painted pictures it was Albert Skira who introduced them to the world with his books. After all we are going there to prepare a new book for Picasso".*

After a stressful journey, they arrived at the chateau. A car came from inside the garden and a man stepped out of the car to open the garden gate saying *"Hello, follow me,"* and then got back in the car. They followed him climbing toward the chateau.

They were at Picasso's house.

Just as they were entering they ran into Picasso at the door who said to Albert Skira, *"Hello Albert, welcome. Go in and wait. I will be back within an hour. Enjoy yourselves. I am going to the man I fear the most,"* he said. When Albert asked *"Where is it you are going?"* Picasso replied, *"To the dentist".*

The team turned one of the rooms in the chateau into a studio and toward evening they started working with hundreds of original Picasso paintings. They were supervised by Picasso's butler of 30 years, Miguel, like a detective. While the master of reproduction, Babey, was photographing the paintings, Ara stuck with Albert Skira who was talking and laughing about adventures in their youth with Picasso. Picasso's large Afghan hound stuck with Ara.

"While I was hanging around the gate Miguel came. This time he was not his gloomy self, he was smiling. 'Is he in?' I asked. 'Yes' he said, 'and he is along'. My Leica and I went in. Picasso was sitting in a rocking chair and humming a tune, probably in Spanish. When he saw me he said: 'Come, come sit down'. I sat opposite him. I was facing a giant. I wanted to take pictures. He just sat there rocking in his chair. I took many photographs of him in this position, I think he enjoyed it too. He seemed to be making fun of me. Every once in a while I would ask something. You cannot ask men of this order flimsy questions like 'What do you think about art?' I learned that years later when I was interviewing Picasso."

Ara asked to see Picasso's paintings.

"The large room was filled with paintings. They had been strewn about as if they were of no consequence. He made a pretense of showing me a few of them and I took their photographs. Some of them were curled on chairs while others were leaning against walls. 'I want to see where you paint,' I said. He smiled and said 'Come, follow me'. He had a large keyring attached to his belt. I took the keyring and proceeded to a door in the room and opened it. We entered. It was a rather dim room. When my eyes adjusted to the light I noticed something: we were walking on the original carpets that Picasso had made fifteen years ago. He walked in front of me, a silhouette with keys in his hand, going forward while I fearfully step on the Picassos. He opened another door, this room was even darker. It was a large room. The walls are bare. In the center of the wall there is an easel, an old chest, newspapers on the chest which are covered with paints. Opposite the easel is a camera reflector and that was it. It was like the operating table of a surgeon. I realized that Picasso filtered what impressed him outside and then painted those impressions in the dark. He did this because he painted the inside instead of the outside. He painted most of his paintings in the light of the projector. That is why I photographed him always in the dark room: everything is black, empty space and a man in the space."

By now Picasso was accustomed to Ara following him like a shadow, he called out to him "Turco Turco". One day when he was carrying out his routine work and Ara was quietly taking photographs he turned to Ara and said *"Look here. You remind me of my old friend Cézanne. Have you seen my Cézannes? Come let me show you some real pictures".*

"Again, he took out the bunch of keys. He opened a door, then another door. We passed through the room with the easel where he worked to open another door. We entered a large room like a warehouse. It was very dim inside. There was a large table in the center with large size rolled canvases and lots of dusty paintings piled up against the walls. All of them were facing the wall. I guess he knew where everything was by rote because he immediately extricated a Cézanne from the lot. He was clearly excited as he showed them to me. He went a bit further and removed a Renoir. Then he revealed an Utrillo. Then he turned to me and said: 'When I was a young painter I would give them five paintings and they would give me one in return'. As I listened to him I took pictures without interruption."

After this we turned by passing through all the rooms again. Picasso looked intently at Ara's face whose beard was just starting to turn grey and said *"but you really look like Cézanne. Wait, let me draw your picture,"* and started to look for paper.

"I was flabbergasted. My hands and legs trembled. It was surreal. The greatest painter of the era, Picasso, was going to draw me! I would not have dreamed of such a thing. But he looked for a paper and there was not a single paper in the room that had not been drawn on. I was afraid that if he failed to find paper to draw on, he might have got distracted, forget and decide to give up. Actually, it was simple, very simple. The only thing to do was to find a blank page of paper. When Picasso gave up looking for paper I started to look. I looked and looked, no paper! In a room full of paper, it was impossible to find a blank sheet of paper. I was squirming. Suddenly a pile of books stacked in the corner caught my eye; these were various books written about Picasso, there were forty or fifty of each of them. The front pages of the books were blank I thought to myself. I grabbed a medium sized book from one of the stacks and turned the first pages. I immediately handed the book to Picasso."

The book that Ara put in front of Picasso in a state of excitement was a special edition of which there were only 50 copies in the world, and therefore very rare and very valuable, prepared by Norman Grantz, a friend of Picasso.

"He took the book and when he saw a blank page he was thrilled. He sat on a chair and took a pen from a nearby table and started drawing. I was so excited. I did not know what to do with my hands and arms. I was curious to see what he was drawing but I did not dare to reach out and look. Every once in a while, he looked at me and then continued to draw. At one point Madame Skira came in to take a picture, I immediately went to her and handed over my camera. 'Picasso is drawing a picture of me. I shall stand next to him and you can take our picture together,' I said. The woman approached Picasso with hesitation while I immediately rushed over and hunkered down next to Picasso. Picasso was not even aware of anything, he continued to draw. Madame Skira hit the button twice, with those two photographs I was eternalized with Picasso in the same frame."

Picasso had finished his drawing and was just about to sign it when Ara intervened: *"Wait."*
"What is it?"
"Can you sign this picture in my name?"
- *"Of course".*
When Picasso asked for his name Ara took the pen out of his hand and tried to write his name on a packet of cigarettes on the table to facilitate him, and when he did not succeed in writing on the packet Picasso took the pen from him and did not forget to admonish him:
"You are breaking my pen."
It was their last days at the chateau; Babey had almost finishing photographing the paintings, Albert Skira and Picasso were exchanging stories about womanizing. Ara learned that one

of the most important large works of Picasso, the *La Guerre et La Paix* was near by in Vallauris, and he jumped into a cab, set off to a dark building built in the French style of the 16th Century with arches, and viewed in admiration the way on one side the paintings *La Guerre* (War) and *La Paix* (Peace) joined at the ceiling, depicting how close war and peace were to one another.

"Again, I was reminded of my photojournalism and I thought to myself:
'If I took Picasso and put him in a picture with War on one side and Peace on the other that would be the best photograph in the painting world of this 20th Century.' I returned immediately. It was early evening. I found everybody having tea. Our team had finished their work. Of course, I could not tell Picasso let's go to Vallauris and take photographs. Picasso said, 'Come Cézanne, where have you been, you are late for tea!' 'I went to Vallauris, I watched War and Peace' I replied. 'Really, having tea is better' he said."

While everybody was sipping tea, Picasso's butler Miguel entered the room. He was holding a list. He approached Picasso and whispered something in his ear. Picasso nodded his head as if to say yes. Miguel opened the drawer of a desk in the room and took out something that looked like a check book and handed it over to Picasso. Picasso looked at the list, first one, then two, subsequently three, then four… He wrote four checks in total and signed them. Miguel took the signed checks and left the room.

"Albert Skira and Picasso continued their conversation. Babey and I went out into the garden. The Afghan joined me immediately. We sat on the stone steps. Miguel joined us. Babey said, 'I presume Picasso signed a check?' he asked. Miguel smiled, 'Yes' he replied, 'He always makes small payments with checks. That is what he does up to a few hundred dollars. That is mainly because nobody cashes checks with Picasso's signature on them, they prefer to keep them as mementoes. That way people get to own something with Picasso's signature on them.' That was quite a fine thought. This way Picasso ended up not paying for a lot of stuff, his money remained in the account."

As Ara was thinking in the twilight what a significant opportunity it had been to spend four days with Picasso, Miguel told an interesting story:
"A friend who lives near Cannes sent an invitation to Picasso to come to his wedding during the week. Of course, Picasso never minds going, he forgot about the whole thing. Time went by and they met somewhere. The friend was reproachful and said, 'I sent my wedding invitation. You did not even bother to come'.

A few days later Picasso went to his friend's house 'give me your house keys. Take this air ticket and go on a trip with your wife and come back in two weeks. I shall give you your wedding present,' he said. Subsequently they enjoyed themselves, had a few drinks and the man gave his house keys and went on a trip with his wife. When they returned home in two-three weeks they saw that all the walls were covered with Picasso's paintings. They were overjoyed, 'This is the greatest gift in the world! What could be greater?' They said and thanked Picasso.

Unfortunately, it was as expected. The man rented the house and when the landlord heard that the house was covered in Picasso's paintings he raised the rent three-fold. He accepted with difficulty and continued to live there with Picasso's pictures. Since they could not extract the Picassos on the walls they were obliged to comply with the landlord. However, that was not all, the municipality applied to the landlord and wanted to buy the building and said they wanted to turn it into a museum. The municipality offered a tidy sum so the landlord sold the building.

Then the municipality opened a court case to evict Picasso's friend; although the case did drag on for quite a while in the end they were obliged to vacate the building. Thus Picasso had wanted to give a gift to his friend and instead had got him into a lot of trouble. Poor man, imagine he loses his Picassos as well as his house. Isn't that strange? I heard this story when I first started working here. It was evening and the team felt sadness as they were preparing to leave.

"Perhaps we would never find a chance in our lives to spend another four days like this. Those four days opened new horizons for me. It was like a magic wand, like a magic flute. Those four days that I spent with him are the most privileged days in my life. He enlightened me, Picasso changed my outlook on the world."

Chagall from Buyukada

Two months after the Picasso interview, Ara was visiting his editor friend from Skira Publishing House, Lauro Venturi, in his house in Geneva. The two old friends were talking about pictures and sipping their drinks when Ara asked:

'Do you know Chagall?'

'Of course I do.'

'If you are close enough, do me a favor and get me an appointment, I want to interview him and photograph his portraits. The great Skira does not have a photograph of Chagall! That is why I should go and take his pictures.''

Lauro was convinced; when he said, he would call Chagall in the morning, Ara could not sleep.

"Chagall and his paintings have danced before my eyes since last night.
Those were the ones I knew about, who knows what works he had, I remembered the ceiling of the Paris Opera building, but I could only see details. If only there was a Chagall retrospective that I could visit...
So, I could be pervaded by the atmosphere of Chagall... and I take photographs of the painter with that vision... such things were on my mind."

Time stood still and finally at noon he went to Skira Publishing House. As soon as he entered Lauro's room to ask whether there were any developments with the Chagall business he got the good news.

"When Lauro saw me he said, 'OK', 'I talked to him. He is in his house in Paris. This is his telephone number, get an appointment. I work with him a lot as Skira. Don't worry, he is a good man if he does not have a tantrum."

Ara immediately went to Paris and booked into the *Hotel d'Angleterre,* where he regularly stayed. Since it was evening he did not want to bother Chagall and waited until noon the next day.

"He answered the telephone himself. His voice was calm and he spoke slowly. He understood from my accent that I was the photographer that Lauro had mentioned. He said, 'come tomorrow toward noon'. I was surprised that something I had been so excited about could be handled so easily."

He was too excited to stay in one place so he left the office of *Life* magazine and went to the Turkish Tourism Office, from there to Magnum Agency and toured all the cafes in every corner in Paris.

When it was time for the appointment he was standing in front of a two-winged large wooden door which was reached with a wooden staircase with a carved ornamental balustrade. He rang the doorbell.

"It was a modern, silly doorbell. I pressed and it sounded a silly tune in line with the era. I did not like it one bit. Never mind, it is only a doorbell... The door opened, in front of me stood a pink faced white haired Chagall who was over seventy. He invited me in. It was a large room. The light was pretty good too. The bad part was that the room was empty of any composition, there was no appropriate furniture, a chair, pictures, nothing. It is as we are standing in space in this room.
Chagall was right there but I needed to integrate Chagall and his world. I wanted to seat Chagall in line with my dream and record his world with visual material and take a photograph which said 'There, this is Chagall!' and I wanted to add a fancy signature under it."

Chagall was not a talkative man. Ara was endeavoring to create an atmosphere of communication by talking about the publishing house and the photography books published about him. On the other hand, he was busy looking for material with which he could establish a composition in the room;

"There was a plant with large leaves in a corner; it was tied to a rope to make it grow straight. I took a chair and placed it next to the plant. I asked Chagall to sit there and look directly into the lens. He did as I asked but the pose was diffident... I took one more photograph, then another and another; I took a lot of pictures but none of them were satisfactory. In short Chagall and I struggled in that room. None of the frames I shot had any character. "

Tea came, they sipped it, chitchatted, but Ara was not satisfied with the photographs taken in this venue. He thought of the bends in the staircase.

"I thought perhaps I could photograph something there. I proposed this to him and he accepted. We went to the stairs. I took a lot of photographs close up, from a distance, sitting on the stairs, leaning on the balustrade, many other positions. There was no doubt that these photographs were much better because I had been freed from the painful pressure of the gloomy atmosphere of that room. But still my pictures of Chagall were not exactly the way I wanted them to be.

"When we went back inside, Chagall's wife said "I assume you will give us copies of these photographs?" I replied "I will bring copies myself within the week".

Ara who was not very happy with the frames he had taken hesitantly said: "*but I am not satisfied with what I have taken. I would like to shoot some more.*" He relaxed a bit after the Chagall couple agreed. He thought they would open up once they saw the photographs.

The film was processed and printed in the laboratory of *Life* magazine in Paris. The next morning, he went to Chagall with the photographs in his hand.

"The prints were good but in my opinion the photographs were not so good. I had two copies printed of those that I liked. He looked at the pictures for a while, he liked them very much. I thought to myself if he liked these so much I guess he did not understand photography at all, yet I put one of the large photographs on the table and asked if he would sign it which he did. In the meantime, his wife came into the room. She took the photographs and looked at them, looked more carefully and finally said she liked them. It is a good thing she did because I found out later that Chagall made no decisions without her knowledge, her approval; even when selling paintings. I guess Madame Chagall liked me a little and liked these silly pictures. She knew I wanted to take more photographs. She gave me the address and telephone number of their summer house in the south."

In the meantime, when *Paris-Match* dispatched Ara to Saintes Maries de la Mer in the Camargue region to interview gypsies, he thought that it would be a good idea to call the Chagall couple as he was in the south of France. He was relieved when Madame Chagall answered the telephone and said that they were expecting him. Ara came to the couple's house in a taxi and was astonished when he saw the land that the house covered. Chagall had bought the whole hill where the summer house was, which he built years ago, on the forest area at the top of the hill. The fact that Chagall's doctor had told him that he needed to walk in the evenings had a major impact on him buying the place. Chagall preferred to buy the whole land to walk in peace.

When he came to the front of the sliding doors in the courtyard entrance of the house Ara heard a sound. It was the butler:

"You are just in time. He went for a walk a few minutes ago that way, he will not be back before one hour, and he walks fast. If you run perhaps you can catch him."

Ara put his heavy camera bag to one side and took two Leicas with him and filled his pockets with roll film.

"I spent over ten minutes looking all around for Chagall in the forest. There was neither hide nor hair of him. I was not about to call out 'Hey, monsieur Chagall!' Well what could I do? I could not do anything else than walk in the woods. I started walking faster. I got going yet there was no end to it. Then suddenly through the lower branches of the trees from I saw the silhouette of somebody in a hat far away. 'There he is,' I said and started running toward him. When I gained on the silhouette in the hat he heard me coming, stopped and turned around and saw me. I was out of breath, I slowed down and stopped. 'I guess you ran, did you tire?' he asked. 'You walk very fast,' I replied. 'That is the way I must walk otherwise it is no use' he said."

As the rays of the sun which would be setting in an hour were filtered through the green the image took on a mesmerizing pastel color. Chagall, who had started to walk slowly to facilitate Ara who was taking photographs nonstop, turned around suddenly.

"Why do you insist on taking my picture? There are a lot of photographs of me in books. Everybody takes my picture but this photograph business has no end."

"And it never will, it will always be like that. Because you are Chagall."

"Is that so? Well who else have you photographed?"

"Many people. And not just painters, I take photographs of important people in all forms of art. Poets, writers, scientists, actors, directors, composers, painters..."

"Well did you photograph Picasso?"

"Yes I did. For four days."

When Chagall heard this, he stalled and the expression on his face changed. He took strength from his walking stick, stood straight and they started walking again.

After walking for a bit he stopped and said, 'I know Constantinople ...' he immediately corrected himself and continued by saying, 'that is I know Istanbul very well. We lived there for two years, on Buyukada. We lived in a wooden house on Principo. We could see the other islands from the windows. Do you know it? Have you taken photographs there? If you have then I would appreciate if you sent me a few. We have some good memories there, we remember those days. After we fled from Russia we came to Istanbul first and after staying there for a few years we went to Paris over Rome. At that time, I was trying to paint, or to put it more correctly, I was trying to discover this work...'

This was the first time that Ara heard that the Chagall family had lived in Istanbul for a while.

"Since I heard from him personally it must be true. Then I learned that Chagall was a Russian Jew and he had been forced to migrate in those days and had come to Istanbul first and then settled in Paris after a while. I guess if he had stayed in Istanbul he would not have become Chagall, he would have been the friend of Nurullah Berk and Bedri Rahmi at the most; they would not have made him a teacher at the academy because they were jealous of him. He would have boarded the ferry every evening from the bridge to go to the island and lighted one of those flat non-filter Yenice cigarettes and blown the smoke towards the Marmara Sea."

Ara said that next time he would bring photographs from Turkey and Chagall made him an incredible promise:
'In that case. I will give you a small painting or sketch.'

'This was a very important sentence for me. 'Imagine Ara Guler' I said to myself, 'has an original Chagall'. That would make me the only owner of an original Chagall in Turkey. It would be enough to show off. Private collectors would burst with envy..."
But it did not happen.
When he returned to Istanbul he sent some of the photographs he had taken and all the photographs of Buyukada that he had, to the address in Paris, and received a thank you card signed by Chagall. A few months later he heard the news that "*Marc Chagall, one of the great painters of our era has passed away*".

Salvador Dali

As violence escalated in Turkey in 1971, the 12th March military intervention known as 'Sledgehammer Operation' targeted the left wing. It took place while Ara was in France chasing after Salvador Dali. He had received a tip from one of the expert correspondents of *Life* magazine, famous for its resounding interviews:
'Dali has a man, a former British soldier named Captain Moore. He handles Dali's business. They are staying at the same hotel. If you contact him perhaps you can get a result."
For years Dali had lived with his wife Gala in Paris in a suite at the Meurice Hotel near the Louvre Palace.
Ara went to Meurice Hotel and found John Peter Moore. He explained that he was a journalist and wanted to make a comprehensive interview about Dali. He told Moore that he was a photojournalist for magazines such as Paris-*Match*, *Time-Life*, *Stern* as well as many other newspapers. If he succeeded in interviewing Dali he could distribute the interview to all press organizations. Moore listened with an expressionless face and said *"Do not come before 12*

o'clock. His room is on the first floor, room number 101," and left Ara in the lobby. It was 11.45. Ara tried to spend time at the bar having a cognac and planned on how he would get into room 101.

"In front of me was a two winged rather heavy door probably from the 18th century; I turned the handle and stepped inside. There was plenty of light, in fact it was so bright I couldn't see anything. When my eye grew accustomed to the light I realized I was in a large room. In my opinion this was an old-fashioned pile of French fashion. When I could see better I observed weirdly dressed youth sitting on some of the chairs and chatting, I saw a young girl drinking something from a slim glass, two people sitting in the opposite chair were engrossed in an argument. I left my bag by the door and took some steps forward when I saw a tall silhouette with a cane rush towards me. Suddenly we were face to face, his nose was only two centimeters away from mine. I understood the situation. Dali had waited for me to enter the room and when I entered he rushed toward my nose. For a while we stood there like that without retreating… It was clear that his man Captain Moore had told him I was coming a little while ago."

'So you want to photograph me? Why?"
"Because you are Salvador Dali."
"I am a very famous man. I want twenty-five thousand dollars for ten minutes of shooting. Which journal is it for?"
"*Life Magazine.*"
"Twenty-five thousand dollars!"
"I do not have that much cash with me. Anyway, ten minutes shooting is not my style. Perhaps I will need one hour, perhaps two. I cannot carry so much cash on me. Let me go to the bank and withdraw some money and come again…"

"Suddenly he became angry and held the back of my neck and my belt and dragged me towards the door. Regardless of his age his bony hands were very strong. As we approached the door, I opened the door so I would not hit my face. Dali pushed me outside, I remained between the two-winged door. I turned toward him and said, 'I am getting the money and coming back'. He looked at me with his big eyes. I did not forget to take my camera bag which I had left on the threshold, that was how our first contact with Dali took place."

This strange event had a strong impact on Ara and when he met his girl friend Ginesta Kohen for dinner he told about what had happened:

Do you know what happened today? I went to see Salvador Dali for an interview, he threw me out."
"Really? Never mind. He is my godfather. He named me Ginesta. Let me call him, I have not spoken to him for some time now. This Dali will be instrumental in my calling him."

Ginesta got up to make the phone call and returned shortly:
'It is OK, he is expecting us tomorrow after 11 o'clock."

"When Dali caught me with strong hands and took me to the door I had felt that this was a beginning, that we were sparring in the warming up round and that the rest would be played out eventually. In the morning, we met in the lobby of the hotel and opened one wing and then the other wing of room number 101 and entered. The place was again full of model wannabees, pop artists, jockey designers, etc. I think Dali enjoyed such strange people around him. Some of them were having heated conversations, some of them were sampling the food. Dali sat in the right corner in a chair facing the windows. When he saw us he got up, opened his arms wide and shouted 'Ginesta!' With a magnificence which befit kings, and embraced Ginesta. I understood that he knew Ginesta well. We sat in the chairs that he showed us. "

Dali started to talk with Ara's girl friend Ginesta. While Ara was busy observing the strange people in the room at one point Dali said, *"I recognize you from somewhere, your face seems familiar"*. Ara who did not even want to remember the incident the previous day said "*Of course you know me from the press conference in New York. I did an interview with you for Life magazine, then we bumped into each other nose to nose...*"

Ara had never been to America let alone New York. Dali continued by saying;

"I am a great film maker. I made the greatest film in the world. There will be no greater film in world history. Have you seen my film?"

'I was surprised. Well I'll be damned, I was straining my brain, I could not remember a film made by Dali. I seemed to have a foggy idea but I could not fix it anywhere. "

"So, you don't know my film? Its title is Un Chien Andalou *(Andalucian Dog). You must see it,"* said Dali and rang a bell for his special servant and instructed that the cinema hall in the hotel be readied after dinner to show his film. Furthermore, he instructed a small drinking party to be organized for the guests after the film.

"While Dali and Ginesta were talking, I was taking photographs just to do something. It was as if I was warming Dali up for photography. At one point, I said 'would you sit over here?' and I sat him in a rather large chair in front of the fireplace; I took nearly a roll of black and white film's worth of photographs; from a distance, close up, portraits, various other poses… What I took was not too bad but the work had no substance. Furthermore, there were too many unaccustomed people around to my understanding. I could not reach Dali the way that I wanted to. At that moment, an elderly thin sunburnt woman with loose folds of skin hanging about her body in a black bikini went to lie down on the sofa in the corner. That was Dali's wife, Gala".

In the evening, there were around ten to fifteen people in the cinema hall of the hotel. Dali was standing up in the front as if checking who was there. After a short speech the lights went out and the film started.

"When Dali asked, I did not make the connection but I knew this film very well. It was one of the most talked about films in the world. Dali did not make this film alone, he worked jointly with Luis Buñuel. Apparently, I had memorized the film as Buñuel's work. After the film was over everybody drifted towards the refreshments, including myself."

Now that they had become acquainted, Ara started to drop by room number 101 at the Meurice Hotel which was very close to *Life* magazine.

"I needed to keep the embers glowing so that Dali would not forget me because I wanted to take a lot more photographs. Most of the time I would walk to Dali's hotel and mingle with the crowd of parasites and have lunch in room number 101 with white wine. After a while I became one of the extras, in other words one of the invisible men in room number 101, I could do whatever I wanted."

Ara printed copies of the black and white photographs that he thought Dali would like. He enlarged some of them. He took the photographs with him when he was off to one of the lunches and pulled Dali into a corner after and showed him the pictures. He looked long and hard at all of them.

'These eyes knew how to look at a photograph or more correctly he knew how a square surface could gain meaning. In short, Dali knew about composition and perspective.'

"Are you giving these to me?"
"Yes, all of them. But I would kindly ask you to sign this one"

"Without saying a word, he took the photograph from my hand, went to the desk in the corner and took out a thick felt tipped gold color or ink pen and scribbled a round shape on the black-white photograph that was half drawing and half signature. There is no doubt that this was a great moment for me. How many journalists in the world have been so fortunate, I thought to myself. The signatures of Dali, Chagall, Picasso... Those are already half of contemporary artists. Others can have the rest!"

Dali's signature would not dry.

I could not put it in an envelope because it was wet plus there was no envelope. I had to keep the picture elevated in the air without touching anything until it dried. I could not put it down because one of these crazies would come and sit on it. I waited there with the picture in my hand. I went downstairs to the reception floor and sat at a table. The time just would not pass and the picture would not dry. I had three espressos followed by a tomato juice and ended up by having two sodas. When I left the hotel, I noticed the signature still had not dried. I got into a taxi, me and my picture signed by Dali arrived home safe and sound. I put the photograph on a table in the corner with no wind to keep it safe. Next morning the first thing I did was to look at the photograph. I was thrilled to see that it had dried...

Ara was not very happy with the photographs because of the crowd which was inseparably around Dali. Ara wanted to shoot Dali alone:

'I would like to take a close-up portrait of you like the photographs in encyclopedias. That is why we should be alone in the room. I want a photograph of you looking at the lens. I can also take other compositions of course."
"In that case come early tomorrow before all this racket starts. Then you can do what you want."
"If that is the case then I shall come early tomorrow and you must instruct Captain Moore not to give an appointment to anyone during that time."

Actually, Ara knew that regardless of what he said this was not the way that it was going to happen. He went to room 101 where Dali was staying early the next morning.

"My materials and cameras were ready. When I entered the room, Dali was talking on the telephone. I was not listening to what he was saying but I could not help hearing that he kept asking the question 'what is the formula of tar?'. I did not know what the person at the other end was saying but Dali kept asking 'what is the formula of tar?' This continued for a while. Finally, Dali hung up the telephone in a fit of rage. I was sure if I was to say something he would have asked me what the composition of tar was. In fact, I was careful not to look his way or ask anything."

At that moment, his aide Moore entered the room with three youths. He walked up to Dali and said that the three persons were journalists and sat them opposite Dali. Dali leaned toward Ara who was watching the goings on with puzzled eyes and whispered *"I will finish with them shortly and send them on their way,"* after which he sat opposite the journalists, put both hands on the silver knob of the walking stick and started staring at the young journalists.

He was gazing into the eyes of all three of them. They appeared to be very much impressed. Dali turned to first journalist and said, *"You! Tell me the formula of tar!"*

The young journalist squirmed, looked every which way and could say nothing.

This time Dali turned to the second journalist and insisted, *"You!"* he said and asked the formula of tar again.

He was speechless as well. When he asked the third journalist the same question and received no response he opened his hands, which had been on the knob of the walking stick, wide and said with a majestic manner, *"The formula of tar is H2C4K812B418"*.

The journalists were looking at him in a state of confusion. He wanted to repeat the formula but because he had made it up he could repeat the first part of it, he could not remember the rest. Then he lifted his silver knobbed walking stick into the air and roared:

'If I take this walking stick and stick it into tar that is worth 1,000 dollars. If somebody else does it they will be considered crazy and their walking sticks will be dirtied. Now gentlemen, you write your articles as you see fit based on my statement. That is the difference between me and other mortals."

Then he spoke in a forbidding tone *"That is it. The press conference is over".*

He grabbed the three with his arms and threw them out just like he had thrown Ara out. When he reached the center of the room he called to Ara:

- *That was the shortest and most clear press conference in the world. Now if you are ready we can work.*

"While I was holding one of the cameras and checking the view finder, Dali went into another room and came with a dueling sword from the middle ages. He waved the sword at me and started to duel. Of course, this was a subject for me but the light in the room was so poor and that I could only shoot with low instantaneity. In fact, every photograph I took was either cloudy or shaky. After a while I noticed that Dali was completely engrossed in this business and he was brandishing the sword in the manner of a royal knight. As I lifted the camera he waved his sword at me and every time I had to retreat. After a lot of cloudy photographs like this I suddenly stopped and asked him to sit in a chair."

Ara barely escaped with his life by making Dali sit. Suddenly a thought occurred to him and he turned to Dali and said, *"You should pose as a matador"*. But red fabric was needed for that. Both of their eyes strayed to the curtains covering the windows.

The curtains were not red but they had red dots; it was better than nothing. 'If you wrap yourself in these you will look like a matador with a sword,' I said. Suddenly he was happy, he liked the idea too, perhaps he thought of something, who knows... He got up and rushed to get the curtains down. After a few pulls the cornice became detached from the wall, started hanging and finally broke off and fell to the floor. The broken plaster created some dust but after it settled the atmosphere cleared up. We helped each other by taking off the knob of the cornice and separated the curtain from the cornice. We were the proud owners of a piece of fabric which was five meters long and one hundred twenty centimeters wide manufactured from the most expensive silk fabric with red dots on it."

Dali grabbed the curtain in the manner of a Roman emperor and threw it over his shoulder.

"I asked him to pose for me, I told him to follow my instructions slowly. He did whatever I asked. Perhaps he liked my compositions. I took photographs without interruption, until I was satisfied. I understood from his eyes that he was also pleased. The historical truth was that we had started to demolish room number 101 in the Meurice Hotel. When the cornice was pulled out pieces of plaster fell into the room and scratched the furniture. I cannot remember how many of the objects d'art in the room were broken. Dali and I had engaged in battle so we could not think about details and the damage we incurred. We both fell into chairs. I was both laughing and enjoying myself on the inside. I was happy because after so much coming and going I had finally captured Dali's atmosphere."

Dali pressed on the button to summon his special aide to request him to have the room cleared before the regulars started drifting in. As Ara was collecting his cameras and packing them in a bag, Dali came to him with an incredible proposal:

-I have a place on the seaside in Castellaras in Spain. Come there. There is a swimming pool in the center immediately on the coast. Maybe we can create some compositions there. For example, I can put flowers on the tips of my mustache and stand in water up to my chin. In the background there are women with faces painted in all colors, naked men...and an angry bull at the bottom etc. ... or something else. We can think of compositions like that.

"What he said was very significant. Considering that he invited me for such a reason he must have liked my working humor. After that day, Dali never saw me again. He did not see the last photographs that I took. Because I did not attend the lunches nor did I send him the photographs. That composition in the pool in Castellaras that he talked about was always on my mind. But how was it going to happen? For some reason this idea created a massive hesitation inside me. I knew – because he had told me – he was trying to discover three dimensional pictures."

Pitch Black

In the last days of 1971 Ara was in Moscow. He was going to interview Aram Ilyich Khachaturian, one of the leading composers of the century. Khachaturian was born into the world in Tblisi to a poor Armenian family, to become selected into the Conservatory of Moscow and even became a professor due to his talent, although he had not had any education in music. Ara went to the house of the musical genius in the slums of Moscow to meet with him.

"This place was like a site for musicians and composers, it was rather luxurious but neglected. It included concert halls, opera stages and sections for chamber music which are ready for functioning, do not forget that Moscow is the center of music and ballet."

Ara and his guide Vera met Khachaturian who lived on the 18th floor of high-rise blocks.

"Vera took me to Khachaturian. Not Vera the wife of Nazim Hikmet but the Vera who was a tur-colog. Vera Borisovna Feonova, a true friend of Turkish literati who had translated many works which endeared Turkish literature to the Russians. Vera had to be somewhere, she introduced me in Russian, explained the situation etc. and then said 'I have to go, I am late, you manage the situation, I told him what we want but be aware that he does not speak Armenian'. This last sentence meant disaster."

After Vera left, Ara and Khachaturian were sitting and looking at each other across the table and started smiling.

"I did not speak Russian and he did not speak English or French. I spoke Armenian thinking he might understand, after all it is a language that he should know, perhaps he might recognize something familiar from other languages but that did not happen. I started to take photographs to save the day but his poses were very amateurish. It was like a photo shoot from the 1920s. Subsequently, I decided to use light."

Ara refrained from using a flash indoors and preferred to use 1,000-watt bulbs to generate the dramatic light he wanted for pictures.

"I prepared two quartz bulbs and connected the cables. I sat Aram in front of the piano and signaled for him to play. Just as he started playing I plugged the lamps and when I turned on the switch to light the lamps, the power was cut off."

It was completely dark.

"Just as I was thinking what language I should use to ask where the fuse box was, it turned out not to be necessary."

When Ara turned on the switch it was not Khachaturian's apartment that was short-circuited, the whole block and even the neighborhood was without electricity.

"The whole housing estate was without electricity. All power was cut off and we were left in the dark of night. We looked for candles in the house and found some. Can you imagine, there we were sitting opposite each other in the candle light with one of the greatest composers in the world? The man was Armenian but he did not a speak a word of the language. We did not talk at all."

They sat across each other for hours without talking.

"Even if I wanted to go I could not because the elevator was not working. As we waited and waited we became hungry, we opened the refrigerator, we looked for food in the refrigerator with a candle and find some cheese. We found knives and forks and sat across each other and ate. The electricity was out for hours, all concerts were probably suspended. They had built a huge housing complex and all it took to cause trouble was to connect a 1,000-watt bulb."

Ara had managed to bring life to a standstill in that part of Moscow.

Control Officer Perihan

Perihan Sarioz, who was 23 years old, was a clerk in the PTT (General Directorate of Post and Telegraph Organization). She was a fanatic admirer of Ara Guler. She cut pictures of Ara

Guler from journals and kept them, and followed everything he did. She had memorized Ara's telephone number and address from his records at the PTT. Every time she went to Beyoglu she would look at the building off the corner of Galatasaray High school without understanding whether it was a residence or a work place. If anyone was with her she would point to the building and say, *"This is where Ara Guler is"*.

Everyone who knew Perihan knew about her fixation with Ara Guler. The young woman had arranged the pictures she had cut from newspapers and magazines on her desk under glass. Perihan's desk attracted the attention of everyone as well as her supervisor, Hale. She looked at the pictures covering the desk and said, *"My girl if you like this Ara Guler so much let's ask him for an original of one of these pictures"*. Perihan gave the memorized telephone number to Hale so she dialled:

"Hello sir, I would like to speak to Ara Guler?"

- "Speaking!"

"Sir I am calling from the Telephone General Directorate Collection Section."

"I do not have unpaid telephone bill, I have paid all my bills!"

"I am not calling about a telephone bill sir, we have a request, I have a young daughter, she admires you very much and wants to have your photograph..."

"What does she want my photograph for? I am not an artist... She should ask Cuneyt Arkin for a photograph!"

"No, Mr. Ara, she does not want your photograph, she wants one of the photographs that you have taken."

"Oh, that is different, good, of course I can give a photograph, which one does she want?"

"If you like I will put her on the line and she can tell you herself."

Perihan was tongue-tied with excitement as she tried to explain the photograph she wanted...

"It looks like it was taken in Eminonu, a horse cart etc...."

"Oh, yes the one where it is snowing, is that right? A tramway passes..."

"No not that one, there is no tramway, it is not snowing, there is a yoghurt seller in the foreground..."

"My dear I have taken a thousand photographs like that, I have plenty of them here, tomorrow you can come here and you can look which one it is that you want..."

On a Saturday towards the end of May in 1974, Perihan was in the office of Ara Guler that she had watched from afar.

"Come in, welcome!"

There was an open suitcase in the room that Perihan entered hesitantly.

Ara pointed to a pile of 40 x 60 photographs against the wall that had been returned from an exhibition.

"Why don't you look if the photograph you want is among those?"

The photograph Perihan wanted was not among them but for fear that he would give up, she took a photograph titled "Bahcekapi Tramway". Ara Guler gave her the photograph of "Woman and Allah".

"Take this one also, this photograph is like my signature."

Ara who was in a haste to pack, offered Perihan tea and gave her some foreign magazines.

'I need to go somewhere. I will be back in 10-15 minutes, you drink your tea and wait... Here, let me play you some music so you don't get bored... "

When he returned, he explained the reason for his excitement.

'Tomorrow I am going to America. I shall take photographs of Americans who have created the 20th century."

It was going to be a long trip. On one side, he was filling the suitcase in the center of the room with his materials and on the other side he was checking his photography materials and putting them into bags. He held one of the cameras.

'There is some film left in this one, let me finish the roll by taking your photographs. "

After he had taken photographs of Perihan he quit filling his suitcase and sat down. He took a piece of paper and wrote a poem which started with the words "*I am so glad you came Perihan*". He had been thinking about things to do before going and what he needed to pay people, and this had tired him until Perihan came. The poem was about how he could put this chore on hold and relax for a while, and finished the way that he had started with "*I am so glad you came Perihan*".

Before he left the office, he asked for Perihan's address so that he could send the photographs to her. Ara flew to America.

Three days later Perihan was holding a large yellow envelope in her hand marked "*Do not fold*". Perihan opened the envelope in a state of excitement and found the photographs that had been taken that day as well as a small note.

"*I thought that if I postponed the processing of the photographs until after my trip I could forget so I processed them as I was leaving. My contact address is below, inform me when you get the photographs.*
ARA"

Perihan wrote a short thank you note to the contact address in New York.

Creative Americans

Ara replied to this letter with a short note saying "Not at all!".

Thus, a period, which Perihan and Ara wrote letters or sent postcards to each other without waiting for the counterpart to reply, had started.

Ara wrote short funny letters all from different states marked with "Air Mail" and "Par Avion" labels and with the words 'WITH AIR MAIL' in capital letters. Ara would write things like, "*Shortly we shall board an airplace and go to Oklahoma, damn I am so scared,*" and Perihan tried to interpret meaning into these short letters while she envied his active life and luxurious fobias.

While PTT Control Officer Perihan was daydreaming about the man he adored another Perihan was accompanying Ara on this trip. Ara's partner on the trip was his girlfriend Perihan Kuturman who was also the organizer of this trip. Perihan worked for the Istanbul office of American News Center (USIA) which had invited journalists from all over the world for the promotion of America on which it was going to celebrate its 200th anniversary in two years' time.

Ara was among the 10 photojournalists invited to the New World but he was not that eager to go. He believed that the USIA where his girlfriend had worked for long years, and which had been established during the Second World War, had been transformed into an "Office of War Information" which was an extension of the CIA.

"They invited me to America. I said I did not like America but if I am going there to do something then why not."

On this condition, his friend Perihan had prepared a program with the American officials to which Ara would not object. He was going to America to meet close to 40 prominent names who had made America what it was and have a photo-interview with each of them.

This was not an opportunity that was given to just anyone. He was offered a golden opportunity to visit the American News Center, which was responsible for US propaganda, as well as meet prominent names from various sectors from famous cinema director Alfred Hitchcock to Minoru Yamasaki, the architect of the Twin Towers in New York, from Dr. Jonas Salk, the scientist who found the polio vaccine to Master of Jazz, Herbie Mann. There were appointments in Ara's diary with Photographer Ansel Adams, Dancer Alvin Ailey, Playwright Edward Albee, Demographer Lester Brown, Jazz pianist and composer David Brubeck, Composer Aaron Copland, Photographer Imogen Cunningham, Economy Professor John Kenneth Galbraith, Reformer John Gardner, Director George Roy Hill, Philosopher Eric Hoffer, Actor Dustin Hoffman, Comedian Bob Hope, Photographer Andre Kertesz, Director Sidney Lumet, the first female director in Hollywood, Ida Lupino, Writer Arthur Miller, Art Director Vincente Minnelli, Sculptor Louise Nevelson, Composer Richard Rodgers, Economist Paul Samuelson, Historian Arthur Schlesinger, Pedagogue Dr. Benjamin Spock, Feminist Writer Gloria Steinem, Producer George Stevens, Architect Edward Durell Stone, Novelist John Updike, Rocket Engineer Wernher Von Braun, Human Rights Advocate Roy Wilkins, Film Producer Robert Wise, Painter Andrew Wyeth. All Ara had to do was call them one by one to fix a date and time. An officer at the State Department helped him with this. It was not possible to reach the famous director Alfred Hitchcock. The master of horror films Hitchcock, who was known as the 'Contrary Old Man', was finally reached with the help of cinema director George Roy Hill.

"Hitchcock was a contrary man. He did not accept anything. The secretary was trying to organize something but he objected. I took photographs of Roy Hill but I really needed him to reach Hitchcock. He took me to Universal studios and Hitchcock was contrary again. He sat on a chair and gave me such a dark look that I thought I would suffocate. I was acting also trying to put him in the mood. I asked him to put his legs on a table which he did. Then I asked him to make similar moves. I guess he liked my style because he was really getting in the mood and posing for me. He went from one pose to another. He liked me very much .... He opened a hidden bottle of whisky because his wife did not allow him to drink. 'Nobody can interfere with us now because we are working. Come on let's have a couple of drinks' he said. We really cut loose after that. Nothing was forbidden any more. Imagine I took 200 photographs. He gave me the best poses so far. He really knew how to add something special to a pose. He managed to add the element of fear into photographs."

He caught famous actor, Dustin Hoffman, in his office in New York enjoying cheese, olives and bread on a newspaper spread over a table.

"We met in Dustin Hoffman's office in New York. He was keen about flowers that was immediately evident. His office was worse than mine. We talked for a bit. Then I started taking photographs. After taking a few pictures I stopped and he asked 'why did you stop?'. I looked at the setting and it was not going to help to ask him to move from one place to another so I said 'the venue is not appropriate, let's go out'. He was going to the ballet school to pick up his wife. We set off to the ballet school directed by a Russian madame. No fans attacked Dustin on the street. I took pictures of Dustin with his ballerina wife. Then we went into a bar. We became friends. He was a very funny man. We toured New York for a week."

During the photograph shooting Dustin Hoffman had become aware of Ara Guler's obsession with his nose so two years later, through journalist Leyla Umar, he sent a message to Ara, *"You have a famous photographer by the name of Ara Guler. Last year when he was taking my photographs he tried really hard to display the prominence of my nose but his nose is more prominent than mine. I liked the man, pass on my greetings."*

Another appointment he had in New York was with Historian Arthur Schlesinger. Ara thought he had some time to spend before the appointment hour so he went to a bar to have some beer. When he needed to go to the toilet he found out that the beerhouse did not have one. He went out and walked for two blocks to another beerhouse. He was obliged to have some more but then he found out that they did not have a toilet either and he was obliged to go into a cinema.

After he bought a ticket from the booth he learned from an officer that the cinema had no toilet and he threw himself into the street. With pain in his kidneys and feeling like his bladder was about to burst he took refuge in the first skyscraper that he saw, with glazed eyes. Ara hastily boarded an elevator and got off on the floor of destination. He found himself in the doctor's office waiting with the rest of the patients.

He ran to the secretary and said *"I do not have an appointment but I am sick. I shall wait to see the doctor,"* and had his name added onto the list. After a reasonable time, he asked the secretary where the toilet was and relieved himself. Then he sat with the patients again for about 10-15 minutes and then told the secretary that *"I can't wait any more. Give me an appointment for tomorrow,"* and ran off to his appointment with Schlesinger.

Ara was much impressed with the renowned philosopher Eric Hoffer who lived in San Fransisco.

"This man worked as a porter for years in the docks. Imagine, the only philosopher in the United States was a former porter. He published a lot of books. He donated his money elsewhere, he did not touch it. Money was never a tool for pleasure for him. There was a chair, a bed, a desk and a typewriter in his house. Just like the room of Cartier-Bresson, there was no other furniture in his room. Every now and then he went to the docks to stay with the dock workers. When he saw me, his first words were in Turkish 'Padisahim cok yasa' (Long live my Padishah). It turned out that his closest friend when he was working the docks was a Turk. First, he called me Ara Efendi and then he started to call me Ara Pasha. The man knew everything, he was aware of everything. He was not a stranger to Turkey. He was the only man in the United States who talked about Catalhoyuk to me."

Bob Hope, who had been born in the United Kingdom but was the greatest comedian in the United States, was adored by all America. The fact that he was the first artist to go to the front to give morale to the troops in particular made him a legend. As soon as Hope entered the house he put Ara into a room.

"He showed me a photograph of a man peeing. It was a picture of General Patton. In the Second World War, he had said that when they reached the Rhein he was going to pee into it. They took his picture when he was fulfilling his promise. Bob Hope said 'I paid a lot of money for this photograph'. I wanted to photograph him with his grandchildren but he refused saying it would make him look old. This man who always made us laugh was actually so very serious. When I said to him that the 'years had not left their mark on him' he said that 'you can come and say that to me any time'."

He was on his way to the Preservation Hall in New Orleans where all the masters of jazz played.

"Here all the former jazz masters, famous jazz pianists played classical New Orleans jazz. Famous stars such as Sweet Emma who passed their prime met with the people, everybody sat together and listened to jazz. It was reminiscent of colonial cities with a French influence such as Bourbon Street etc. At night it was a fairground. This small place has a tradition which continues. Duke Ellington, Louis Armstrong were raised this way."

As Ara was enjoying the jazz he thought he saw a familiar face in the crowd.

"I think the man's eye caught me too. I approached him as the the jazz continued. He had taken his shoes off and was sitting on the ground. I tried talking but I could not make my voice heard. Finally the jazz was over. The team was changing. I said, 'I recognize you from somewhere'. Your face appears familiar too' he said. 'I am a journalist from Istanbul,' I said. 'I hope you are not the journalist who took my photograph in the hamam,' he said. That is when I recognized him. It was Tennessee Williams. He had changed, gained weight."

Ara's visit to the U.S. was mentioned also in the local press.

"When I told the officers from American Ministry of Foreign Affairs that 'for years you have been presenting in movies Indians on horses but I have not laid eyes on a single Indian since I have been here!'. They immediately got me a flight ticket to Iowa and dispatched me to Sioux City. The place was a town surrounded by men who were doing animal trade business with radiophones but no Indians. The local guides said that the Indians lived in the hills and that if I liked they could take me there."

The next morning Ara was in Indian Territory.

"I interviewed the Indians and I met an Indian Chief in a pool hall. He took me home and showed me different kinds of teeth, stones and pieces of bones. He tried to tell me that these were magical tools of fortune telling, that they manifested news from the great beyond."

Ara's problem was that the Indians wore regular clothes during their daily life instead of the costumes that he had observed them wearing in films which he wanted to photograph.

"After trying for a while I convinced the Chief to put on his national apparel and a hat with a feather on his head, after which I sat him down on his motorcycle. I took a lot of photographs."

The Indians liked Ara.

"One night they lit fire. In order to become blood brothers, he Chief's son and I cut our wrists and held them together. I had become a Sioux and I guess I still am; Turkish Sioux Ara Guler. They did a television show about me on the local television network."

News about Ara Guler in Sioux City was not limited to this. The *Sioux City Journal,* published in Iowa, wrote lots of details about Ara Guler and photographs of his friend Perihan Kuturman with a caption saying "*how the Guler couple had been married for 16 years in harmony and how she accompanied him on all his trips*".

Ara Guler had not been married a day in his life so either this information was whispered by Perihan Kuturman or the correspondent who admired the couple had come to the 'conclusion' that such harmony can only be achieved by a married couple.

Ara was very emotional when he saw Imogen Cunningham in San Francisco who he believed to be the greatest photographer in the world. He was so affected by this elderly lady who was a master of portrait photography that he remained immobile for quite a while. One thing lead to the other and soon they were reciprocally pressing buttons...

"The greatest surprise of all. The oldest eyes which looked from within my world. Should I hug and kiss her, should I sit down and cry? We ended up by taking photographs of one another."

Human rights advocator Roy Wilkins was also one of the faces that Ara admired:

"This man equaled the rights of blacks with the rights of the whites. We visited a school where black and white students studied together and all the children ran to greet him as if he was their father, surrounded and hugged him. This meant that Roy Wilkins had started to have an impact on the rights of blacks and whites."

Not everything went according to plan during his six-month US trip.

When Ara asked Tennessee Williams, "*Who is the greatest playwright in the world?*", he replied without the slightest hesitation "*William Saroyan*".

"For me, this person was the best diologue writer in the world and he was telling me that Saroyan was the best. It was only years later that I understood. We were displaying a play by Saroyan. The name of the play was "My Heart's in the Highlands". It was a very well written play. Even the pauses had meaning. There was a whole world of accumulation concealed in those small sentences, those short pauses. Saroyan taught me about the magnitudes in small worlds."

Now he was in Saroyan's country and his name was next on the list.

"My assistants made telephone calls, sent telegraphs, they knew Saroyan was in America but they could not find him. Finally, I was given a list of addresses as well as telephone numbers. There were names of people who could help,... 'They know, they can find Saroyan for you. The addresses are in New York, San Francisco...'
I went to Los Angeles, telephone calls, questions. Result: none. There was only one thing left and that was to write a letter to all these addresses. I wrote a letter in English and sent it by special delivery to the addresses.
If the mishaps had been limited to that, fine and good."

When Ara was taking photographs of director Vincente Minnelli in Hollywood, the heart of American cinema industry in Beverly Hills, which was of the most expensive neighborhood in Los Angeles, he thought of the director's daughter, Liza Minnelli.

"I said why don't you call your daughter and I can take your photographs together. He called his daughter immediately. We found out that Liza Minnelli had a concert in Las Vegas one week later. I went to Las Vegas to take their pictures one week later. She was getting ready for the stage. She said, 'I do not have time. Take my photographs when I am on stage'. Taking pictures while the object is on stage was not my style so I responded by saying 'Who do you think you are!?'. She started shouting at me 'God damn you'. I left, slamming the door. I can't shoot someone on the stage. What am I, some kind of street photographer?"

He was unable to take photographs of anti-war poet Irwin Allen Ginsberg and Jane Fonda, known for her critical stance regarding American policies. Fonda, who was a serious activist, scathed Ara by accusing him of "*serving American imperialism*":

"That was Fonda's most active time. She had just returned from Vietnam. 'I cannot pose for anyone who glorifies the US government!' she said. No matter how hard I insisted that I was left wing myself she did not budge. So that was one session that did not happen!"

When Ara encountered such setbacks on the trip that he was not too eager to make in the first place, he was prone to make some critical statements about the New World himself:

"When I went to America for photography I found myself in a world that had been deformed compared to Europe. Everything was new, everything was different and everyone was trying to remodel the beauties, habits and culture that had prevailed in Europe for centuries according to their mindset and then endeavored to sell this to the world under the title of 'Novelties from America".

After the trip which was executed on the invitation of the US administration, Ara opened his exhibition 'Creative Americans'. He named the 100-page catalogue featuring the exhibition, comprised of 43 Americans he had photographed in or outside the US, the *Ara Guler's Creative Americans*. Romeo Marchinez who wrote the preface for the catalogue drew a very clear Ara Guler photograph:

"I had always sensed that with his understanding of photography, his sensitivity for perception, talent and technical knowledge Ara Guler would be a brilliant taker of portraits. However, I did not expect him to be able to overcome the spiritual obstacles, repulsion in the core of this type of work so rapidly and with such awareness. It is true that the secret of a portrait must be searched in the emotional bond formed by the reciprocation and generosity to be established between the photographer and the subject being photographed. You have found your path, may your path be open Ara Guler..."

The exhibition, which attracted a lot of attention, was then taken to Pakistan and was open for one month in Karachi for visitors. Ara, who was staying at the home of the cultural attaché of the American Embassy in Pakistan, received an offer to photograph politician Zulfikar Ali Butto during his election campaign, which he accepted and roamed the villages and mountains of Pakistan for three months.

A Serious Business

PTT Control Officer Perihan, who corresponded with Ara with letters when he was in the US, had not been idle during this time. She deduced that a customer around age 60 who came to the collection service could be a friend of Ara, just because he had a beard, and she walked up to him, took his invoice and processed his business. In the meantime, she spoke of her interest in photography and aked the bearded man whether he knew Ara Guler and she received the antici-pated reply of:

- *"Of course, I do, he is my friend, I can introduce you if you like."*

The bearded man was the editor of Ara's *Hayat* magazine Ibrahim Camli. Perihan told Camli that she knew Ara Guler that he was in the US, that she wanted to become more closely acquainted with him and gather information about him.

Camli asked *"I understand your passion for photography but why do you want to know Ara Guler better?"* to which Perihan responded without hesitation by saying:

"I am going to marry him!"

Ibrahim Camli was dumbfounded. *"That is not possible, you can't marry him,"* he said and tried to explain to the young girl who had made her mind up a long time ago why this marriage would not be possible.

"You will see," said Perihan with conviction.

Perihan had come to this conclusion after seeing him for 1.5 hours and a few short notes, and while Ara was in America she often visited Ibrahim Camli's office to gather information about her future spouse and put the fruits of her investigation on the table with the return of Ara in Istanbul, which she had waited eagerly for.

As they were talking, she referred to issues which she had learned from Ibrahim Camli and which were not known to everyone. When she asked Ara to confirm some special information, Ara went crazy and started shouting:

"Where have you learned all this, most of my friends do not know these things, tell me are you an agent from MIT, are you the police, are you a spy, what are you?"

Ara, who thought Perihan was an MIT agent, started to swear at her, at her chief and su-pervisors. Perihan noticed that she had gone too far and when she explained that she had met Ibrahim Camli and got the information from him Ara calmed down.

"But still I did not like you investigating me behind my back, I did not like this" he said.

"Well why did you do it, what do you want from me?"

"I want to marry you..."

"What! How can this be, marriage is a serious business!"

'So, we'll get married seriously. "

'How old are you? "

'23. "

'Eee, I am 46, that is double your age, when you are 35 I will be 70. That is not good. Well maybe that is passable but when you are 40 I will be 80 what happens then?"

Perihan saw that there was a mathematical flaw in Ara's calculations so she told him to think about it for one month. Months passed.

They did not see each other very often; every week Perihan would visit Ara's studio twice in Tosbaga Street in the evening and stay there for a few hours. There were always people in the studio and while Ara and his cronies chatted, drinking cognac, she sat on a stool opposite the fireplace and sipped tea and listened to the conversation. She liked this world which differed so much from her world, as well as the people. As winter was drawing to an end, Ara said to Perihan "*Let's get married*". But it was impossible for Perihan's family to approve this marriage. She gave her identity card to Ara to start the marriage proceedings without her family's knowledge. But Ara had to go to France, so the marriage had to be postponed. They corresponded again and Ara proclaimed his love for her in his own style in a letter sent from Paris.

William Saroyan from Bitlis

When Ara arrived in France he pursued William Saroyan who he was unable to find in the US or in Paris. He dialed the telephone number in his address book countless times without receiving a reply.

"One day when he was in a café near the Avenue de l'Opéra I dialed a few times again just in case. After three or four rings the telephone was picked up. A voice said 'Yes?'. For a minute, I was flabbergasted. The voice spoke 'who is calling?' and I said 'I am photojournalist Ara Guler from Istanbul'. Then I continued: 'I was in America for four months. I looked all over for you. I telephoned every number. I became desperate and wrote a letter to all your addresses. Suddenly the voice seemed to recall, 'Ha, Ara Guler' he said and added: 'I remember, I received all the letters. I did not respond because I knew you would find me. Where are you now?' 'I am in a café near the Opera' I said. 'Come immediately,' he said, 'I am on the top floor, my name is written on the door.' I hung up and left the café."

Ara hopped into a cab immediately and was in front of Saroyan's building. He rushed to the sixth floor and when he got there the door was opened by a tall, unshaven William Saroyan in a t-shirt and strong white mustache.

"There was practically no furniture in the house. Two wooden chairs, a folding wooden table, a few dried-up flower pots on the window sills on the balcony side and late 17th Century French style fireplaces in both rooms. The floor was made of wood, the bed was by the wall, books strewn all over the place. It was as if he had known me for a thousand years. I harbored the same feeling. 'When I was in Turkey you were not there,' he said. 'I was abroad doing an interview,' I said. 'What is Yasar Kemal doing?' he asked. I explained about Yasar for a while. 'Well what about Fikret Otyam?' Then I talked some more about Fikret. 'Well who did you photograph in America?' he asked. I listed nearly forty names."

Saroyan went inside to brew tea after which they were immersed in a profound chat.

"His best friends were Ernest Hemingway, John Steinbeck, John Dos Passos, William Faulkner... We grew up reading them. *Tortilla Flat, Grapes of Wrath, Of Mice and Men, The Old Man and The Sea, the Snow of Klimanjaro, For Whom The Bell Tolls...* I took a lot of photographs and then he said, 'Come let me introduce you to my friends'. This was a very desirable offer for me. Then I understood that he wanted to leave the details of his life for my documentation. He wanted me to know him."

They started to walk the streets of Paris. They entered a small shoe repair shop on Rue La Fayette.

He introduced me to a man. He was elderly, short in stature with eyes like a genie. When he found out that I was from Istanbul he said that he had come to Turkey years ago. Then the man took a shoe and started to repair it on his leather apron and talked at the same time. I was taking photographs as well as thinking to myself. Now I understood Saroyan's world better. Saroyan wrote about the lives of these people. Wherever Saroyan took me I met the same sort of people. I met a tailor on the second floor of a business building, a street vendor, a lottery ticket seller, etc. He liked these people. In the end, I concluded that Saroyan was interested in people not events.

They were swilling their beers in the café on the corner of Rue Lafitte.

"His tailor friend, the shoe repairman was also there. Saroyan was the kind of person who would always question people. They talked and eventually it was my turn. 'What does your father do?' he asked. 'He was a pharmacist but he passed away a few years ago,' I replied. He paused and then asked again: 'Where were you born?'. 'I was born in Istanbul but my father was from Sebin-karahisar,' I responded. He looked at his beer, extended his hand but did not pick it up and drink. He stared into space. 'My father was born in Bitlis,' he said. 'Fikret Otyam and a couple of friends took me there once. Is Sebinkarahisar near Bitlis?' 'Not really but they are in the same region, sort of,' I responded. 'Tell me a story from there,' he said. I thought about what he said. He had gone there, toured the area, he had a longing for the place. He wanted to hear something from there. That is why one of his plays is titled *My Heart's in the Highlands*. What could I tell him? 'Let me tell you my father's last story,' I said. 'Do tell,' he said. So, I did."

When he told them about Dacat's visit to his village and drinking water from the village fountain, yet passing away without having his dried mulberries, fruit paste, dried nuts and fruits, Saroyan's and the shoe repairman's eyes were filled. They finished their beer and left.

"When I prepared the catalogue for the exhibition in 1975 I wrote the following caption under his photograph: 'Do you know the little people in your neighborhood? For example, if you are in Spain do you know your neighbor the small-scale shoeshiner, or the leather master on Rue Lafitte if you are in Paris, or the ice cream seller in Copenhagen? Even if you do not know them William Saroyan knows them all and their worlds as well. He was born in Fresno but he has become a man of the world. Observing the world through his perspective is superior to discovering the world for the second time. Saroyan teaches us how important the smallest things are.'

A Modicum of Marriage

After Ara declared his love for Perihan in his letter he accelerated the marriage proceedings when he returned to Turkey in the summer of 1975. He telephoned Perihan to inform her of the wedding date as soon as he got it:

- *The wedding is tomorrow at 2 o'clock at Beyoglu City Hall.*

Perihan walked to the city hall on Istiklal Street and Ara, who was waiting for her at the street corner greeted her, with "*Where have you been, we are going to miss the ceremony.*"

Perihan's marriage witness was the editor of *Cumhuriyet* newspaper Cetin Ozbayrak. Ozbayrak's spouse Nazan was reproachfully saying, "I never saw such a wedding in my life, how carefree they are!"

Ara's witness was Yasar Kemal.

There were three people sitting in the section reserved for guests: one was Nazan Ozbayrak, the others were Ara's mother Verjin and the third one was a photographer from *Cumhuriyet* newspaper. Ara failed to collect the photographs that were taken that day so there is no photograph to commemorate the ceremony. After the wedding ceremony was completed and the witnesses left, followed by Verjin, Ara asked Perihan:

"What shall we do now?"

"I don't know but I think I should not go home any more, I should stay with you."

"Here take these keys, I shall go to Cagaloglu, see you tonight."

The newlyweds were going to stay in the studio flat in Galatasaray where Ara's mother Verjin lived, until they could find a house with a sea view. The dream of a house with a sea view never materialized. They lived in Ara's office where the kitchen and bathroom had been transformed into a dark room throughout their marriage; they used Verjin's apartment two floors below for requirements such as breakfast, food, and baths.

"Perihan played the guitar for three days, made candles for five days and married me for a bit," said Ara, and clues as to why their marriage lasted 3.5 years are in the dialogues about photography.

"Please let me have your camera, I want to take pictures on my own."

"No way, just like a horse, a woman and a weapon are not loaned nor is a camera, a camera is the photographer's weapon." "What now, do you take photographs too?"

"You know what they say, if you tie a donkey next to a donkey they will adopt each other's habits..."

"Cat."

"What cat, there is no cat in the picture..."

"That's it, that is why there is something missing in this photograph, a cat should be passing there in the street..."

...

"Electric wires."

"What can I do, there are electricity poles, no matter where I take the picture I will get the wires..."

"Do not take it then, is it one of the Ten Commandments that the picture has to be taken from there, Do they beat you if you don't?"

...

"Rowboat..."

"There was no rowboat in the sea."

"There would have been if you had waited."

"Well would this picture have been good if there was a rowboat?"

"What, if my aunt had a hat she would be my uncle, what can I say to that..."

"Ara don't pull my leg, please take me seriously just a little..."

"I am not kidding boy, but you are giving a man shoes with no laces, then you say try it on is it comfortable, put the laces on first and ask the man to try it on for comfort when its good and ready. You don't try shoes on without laces!"

...

"Please give me the camera, I want to take photographs and enter this competition."
-"No, you can't enter this competition."
"Why not?"
"Because I am on the jury of that competition is why."

Perihan and Ara got married quietly and got divorced the same way. Their divorce was witnessed by Sahin Kaygun.

The Censored Yavuz Documentary

In the summer of 1973 Ara was following a sad farewell ceremony organized in Golcuk.

All military personnel as well as civilians who attended the ceremony were in tears; it was the ceremony of scrapping the armor plated Yavuz battlecruiser, which had served the Turkish navy for years.

> "I was the correspondent for *Stern* magazine... When news came out that Yavuz battlecruiser was to be dismantled, German *Stern* magazine showed interest because it was the former Goeben Battlecruiser, and asked me for a feature on the dismantling. That was why I was photographing it."

During the First World War when the German war ship SMS Goeben took refuge in Turkish territorial waters to flee from the British Navy, the vessel was donned with a Turkish flag and named "Yavuz Sultan Selim" and the crew were given red fez to wear.

Although the vessel was entered into the inventory of the Ottoman Navy it remained under the command of a German admiral, and when it entered the Black Sea and bombed Russia's Sivastopol and Odessa cities it was instrumental in the Ottoman Empire joining in the First World War.

Ever since it was manufactured in the shipyards of Hamburg, Yavuz battlecruiser had been repaired many times for the battle wounds it had sustained from the mines it had hit in the wars and the bullets it had taken. It also took its place in the history of corruption in Turkey because of Ihsan, the Minister of the Navy. He was deputized with the repair of Yavuz. He took advantage of the situation and granted the French company, which would repair the vessel, various privileges. .

When this became common knowledge, his immunity was removed and he was referred to the Supreme Court and found guilty, after which Ataturk gave Ihsan the surname of Eryavuz when the Surname Law was enacted, so that he would feel ashamed of himself. The task of transporting the casket of Ataturk from Dolmabahce Palace to Izmit was also given to Yavuz which was a flagship of the Turkish Navy.

> "Until its last days Yavuz sat offshore of Heybeliada billowing smoke. That smoke never stopped. Once it stopped it could not be re-operated. That vessel probably used half of the coal in Zonguldak."

TCG Yavuz Battlecruiser operated successfully until 1950, when it was discarded from the inventory and moved to Kavakli port near Golcuk. For nearly 20 years it was left to rust in peace and the historical battleship was a home to seagulls.

In 1969 on the declaration of the General Staff that *"there is no point in maintaining Yavuz Battlecruiser any longer, it has no further function"*, the government of Suleyman Demirel sold the flagship to Makine Kimya Endustrisi (Mechanical and Chemical Industry Corporation).

In 1973 Yavuz Battlecruiser bid farewell to the Navy with a ceremony. It then was towed to Seymen dock by MKE and dismantled into weapons and technical parts. The sale of the vessel was advertised in *The Wall Street Journal* and it was purchased by an Italian company to manufacture razor blades. The inglorious end of this historical vessel which had left its mark in the past of Turkey had a great impact on Ara.

"Imagine paintings were made, poems, songs were written about Yavuz plowing through the waters. Those who had done their military service on Yavuz felt pride and then their hero was dismantled into parts. It was cut with welding machines into pieces. It was a sorry situation, a full drama, it was impossible not to feel pain. I am a nationalist. They were going to sell Yavuz, sell it in kilograms. Make razorblades. "

Ara rebelled at this tragedy and destruction of Battleship Yavuz which had left its mark on an era, and decided to make a film about it.

"*Stern* asked me for a feature regarding Battleship Yavuz. They wanted historical photographs etc. I went to commanders, admirals and found some old photographs. I took reproductions of all of them. Anyway, I made the feature. I saw that I had a lot of material. I said this material was enough for a film. After that feature, I thought about making a documentary about Yavuz for a long time. Should it be a film or something else? I was not sure, it was still there. It took about five years from the idea brewing in my mind to get to the shooting phase."

Ara visited the dismantling site at every opportunity, like visiting a loyal friend, and took photographs of every phase.

"They were dismantling Yavuz, but it was not easy to dismantle. It took exactly 10 years to dismantle. I thought I would shoot the film first and think about the scenario later. Now they were killing the hero... the name of the film was the *Hero's End*. Slowly, I started to shoot. I was shooting 16 mm. From time to time I would go and shoot in Seymen, the workers had become accustomed to me. 'That bum is here again...' they said. I kept shooting and shooting and then it was done. Yavuz was the size of a hand. The film was done."

Ara's film called *Hero's End* features Ismet Ay, Necdet Akin and Semsi Guner. The shooting of the film had been completed and Ara took it to France for montage.

"I went to France. I went to Henry Langlois. He was the man originally from Istanbul who established the French Cinematek . I said to him, 'Bro organize a montage room for me'. Montage was going to cost a lot of money. He said to me 'pick any room and work'. I found a montage room free of charge. Then I found a woman to do the montage. She said 'pay me one thousand francs per week and I'll work'. The woman did the montage work for the films of Orson Welles. I took her out to dinner etc. She became friends with my wife. Now I needed sound. How would we do the sound? Ilhan Mimaroglu had this electronic music I liked very much. We made the sound with that music. The welding machines, rusty irons, just as the iron was being dismantled, there was a shout of *Aaahhh.....* The music was great, it was surrealistic, bro. Just like how my mind is. My film about Yavuz was worse than Buñuel's Andalucian Dog."

In terms of both shooting technique, as well as form of narrative and the music used by Ara, the film was eccentric and a far cry from Ara's realistic style. Ara showed the film to Fazil Husnu Daglarca and Salah Birsel who did not react in the way that Ara expected them to.

"I showed this film earlier to Daglarca and Salah Birsel and I had been disappointed that they did not react the way I expected them to. I can't really define this work as a film or a photograph or even a documentary. It was not clear what it was. If you think of it as a documentary then yes perhaps it was a documentary of something. However it was more like a poetic version of various accumulations in my life from the perspective of a photographer. What I portrayed was a poetic story of the sad life of Yavuz. Something underground. Yet at the end of the day, I was very much satisfied with my work."

Ara took his film to America and showed it to Ahmet Ertegun, the owner of Atlantic Records, one of the major music companies in the world, and on his approval started off for Turkey.

"Bro, I brought the film to Turkey. We were passing through customs. 'I have a film with me which I want to declare. I shall submit it for censorship and I would like for it to be processed immediately,' I said. 'All right,' they said, made a protocol and took the film. The film was viewed by the censorship delegation. They said 'This is a local film, we watch foreign films. This film has to go to Ankara'. Well, what to do now... the film entered customs again. Another protocol was prepared. I took the film and went to Ankara. It was the 1970s, the worst era in terms of censorship. At that time I was taking photographs of Fahri Koruturk (former Turkish President). Koruturk knew that I was making a film about Yavuz. He kept asking me 'when are we going to see it'. The Navy Commander was also interested. 'I will take the film off you, don't worry,' he said. 'Bro there is no film. What are you going to take off me?' I said. 'It will come out don't worry,' they say."

Ara started to await the outcome of the film, which he presented to the Film Control Commission in the capital.

"Bro, the film had been shown in Ankara. Everybody said it was good. One person said 'no'. It was a man from the Ministry of National Education... he was obsessed ... there was no speech in the film. There was only electronic music. They said, 'This is a French copy'. So, it was a French copy but there were no words in the film. There was not so much as a cough. If it was a French copy what could I do...? The commission sat down and took an unanimous decision as this film was banned from Turkey. They seized the film. The message of the film was this; if Yavuz was a hero, it was renowned, why was it dismantled? Was it dismantled because someone condescended/deigned to five-cent iron? It should have been transformed into a museum. They killed the hero. 'Well yes, you are right etc. etc.' I saw they were squirming. I said 'God damn you'. Probably they sold it in kilograms but I still have the negative..."

The dismantling of Yavuz took 12 years so it was inevitable that the completion of Ara's film also took 12 years, after which one of the vessel's propellers was brought to the Navy Museum in Besiktas and the foremast was erected on the dock of Navy War School. The negative of the film is in Ara's home on the fourth shelf of a bookcase.

When Europe Meets Asia

The first Bosphorus Bridge was launched for service on the 50th anniversary of the Republic of Turkey in October 1973. Ara followed every phase of the construction which took approximately three years. Ara went into action when *Stern* magazine ordered a feature for 'The Meeting Point of Two Continents".

> "I convinced the Garrison Commander. He allocated a helicopter for me whenever I needed one. 'When will Europe connect with Asia?' I was wondering. Who knows how much fuel I made the army spend on my flights. But Europe was going to meet Asia, can anything be more important than this!"

The idea of connecting the two sides of the Bosphorus with a bridge was generated by a railway contractor named Nuri Demirag in 1931. Nuri was given the surname Demirag (iron network) by Ataturk because, regardless of all the poverty and challenges facing the young Republic of Turkey, he managed to cover the country with a railway network. A project was prepared by experts brought from the United States who carried out a feasibility study, and designed a bridge including a railway, and presented it to the government of Ismet Inonu.

However, Demirag's project was rejected by the Minister for Public Works, Ali Cetinkaya, on the grounds that *"No, it will ruin the beauty of the city"*.

Nuri Demirag left the ministry in a state of devastation and said to those around him, *'This project will happen. Istanbul needs it. If I can't do it then I'll leave it to my child who can do it on my behalf. It is my legacy, let them hang a plate on the bridge which says 'Inonu will not pass this bridge and neither will Cetinkaya.' "*

Ara followed every step of the building of the Bosphorus Bridge from land and sea, from the 21-gun salute fired in Beylerbeyi during the laying of the foundation ceremony, the excavation works for the piers of the bridge in Ortakoy, and then in Beylerbeyi, the erection of the steel towers as well as the drawing of the two guide cables.

> "I walked along the pier of the bridge on the cable from one pier to the next. I am one of the three people to walk from Asia to Europe."

When the metal panels forming 60 bridge deck slabs, manufactured in Italy and the United Kingdom, had reached Istanbul by sea freight, this meant that it was only a matter of time before the two sides could be brought together.

> "There is only one place in the world that two continents are united, nowhere else do two continents connect with each other. This connection is available only in Istanbul."

When the final deck slab was mounted and the parts were welded, people walked over these metal panels for the first time from Asia to Europe. Once the rubber-alloyed asphalt was poured the bridge was ready to be inaugurated.

Ara, who was watching the ceremony in a state of excitement, was suffering about another issue. He had had one of the workers take a photograph of him on the bridge and noticed the discrepancy only when he was processing the photograph in his studio.

"I told the man to take a photograph which would show me as well as the Bosphorus Bridge. Look at this picture. How can I convince anyone that this has been taken on the Bosphorus Bridge!"

Psychic Surgery

In February 1978 Ara was in the Philippines with his colleague Orhan Tahsin. Incurable patients who had heard that various people with supernatural powers were operating patients with their bare fingers and restoring people to their health, were flocking to the Philippines. Flights called "Birds of hope" were carrying people to the country daily from all over the world. The owner of *Tercuman* newspaper, Kemal Ilicak, had commissioned Ara to prepare a feature about psychic surgeries which appeared frequently on the agenda of the world.

"When I went for the psychic surgery feature Guneri Civaoglu was the editor of *Tercuman*, but that was not my concern, I was dealing with Kemal. The big boss was my friend."

Before going to the Philippines, they memorized the book written by German Doctor Alfred Stelter on psychic healing, *Psi-Heilu*. They took a renowned psychiatrist in Turkey, Prof. Dr. Recep Doksat, with them.

As soon as they landed at Manila's airport they threw themselves into a taxi and sought the most well-known of the healers, Juan Blance, and they were very much impressed with the operations which were carried out in front of their eyes.

He tore people up.
First, he crumpled the white skin with his ten fingers and then he tore it. A bright red line progressed between his pinky and ring finger. The blood flowed like a tiny river looking for a bed on the body, found it and dribbled down. The ten fingers stretched the tear. Blood spurted. The ten fingers were covered in blood. Our blood froze. The tear under the patient's heart was bleeding, the surrounding area was congealing. The thumb and index finger entered the tear, a piece of flesh the size of 'a finger' (tumor) was removed, held in the air for a second and thrown into the rubbish bin at our feet.

"All three of us could not believe the surgeries. Our intention was to reveal the fraud committed by the healers and establish it with cameras. However, even if we were unable to comprehend, we were obliged to believe what we were watching and therefore could not catch any fraud."

It was very difficult to believe in the goings on in this filthy venue, which was used as a half church, half hospital, and served as a hotel at the same time. Their minds boggled.

Prof. Dr. Doksat who was on the team could not give any meaning to what he had witnessed and said that the events were way beyond medicine.

The feature was titled "*Mind Boggling Medicine*".

"While operating, Manila's famous healer Alex Orbito said to me 'do not bring your camera closer than thirty centimeters, otherwise the film will burn.

Ara believed in the words and the healing powers of the healers which had been declared superstition by positive science.

"Although various views consider that this is a hoax or fraud, these views are depicted by those who have not witnessed these operations as many times as I have or examined them as carefully as I have. I have been to the Philippines about six or seven times. These people do not operate with their own powers and say: 'I am a tool using God's power. My hands and brain are used by a superior force,' and they add that 'birds fly from continent to continent, do they have knowledge about geography?' All of them have faith, they are Catholic Christian people who take the miracles performed by Jesus with faith as their example. What we saw rendered us speechless."

The team spent quite a lot of money for the feature in the Philippines. Ara was left penniless and decided to visit his correspondent friend for Magnum in Hong Kong.

"I had a friend there, he was wealthy and worked for Magnum. I called him and failed to reach him. I thought he probably went home, his home was in New Zealand. I would do a stint from Hong Kong to New Zealand. Do you know how long it takes, 15 hours? I boarded a plane and went there. I disembarked, the man was not there I spent all this money getting there, now I had zero money."

He had spent his last money on the air ticket.

"My money was gone, I had 28 dollars in my pocket. I did not even have enough to spend the night. New Zealand is the end of the world. I had a return ticket so I went immediately to Lufthansa. 'I came here to find my friend but I could not find him'. The Lufthansa man looked familiar, he used to be in Istanbul. The man recognized me, that was luck. I said 'I need a hotel or room, someplace where I won't be put in hock, blah, blah.' 'Can you go immediately?' he asked. There was a flight that day, perhaps there was one every two or three days. Now there are hourly flights or three flights per day but not then. He put me on a plane immediately, 'Please send a message here,' I said and gave a number in Frankfurt. We were wearing shorts, it was summer; in Europe it was -7. I wanted an overcoat, it was winter otherwise I would freeze. On the flight I had a meal and filled my stomach."

It was tasking work what he did… No matter where he went in the world, it was hard to get there and harder to get out.

"Don't forget when you go on a job you go with 5-6 cameras. It was difficult to carry the film, there were so many challenges. You carry a suitcase of film. Once in Paris I said 'I am not boarding the plane'. He insisted that he had to check my belongings, I showed him my press card from *Paris-Match*, he sayid "I don't care if you bring 'General De Gaulle,' I can't let you board". If you curse then you go to jail. It happens every time."

Inside Wars

It was in the middle of 1978 that he went to Sudan to observe the Civil War in Eritrea. His mission was to photograph the armed conflict between Eritrea Liberation Front (ELF) and Eritrea Peoples' Liberaton Front (EPLF) forces.

"We were returning from an interview with Eritrea Liberation Guerillas. We arrived from Eritrea to Kesele town at the Sudan border with great difficulty. For ten days we had been drinking the filthiest and warmest brownish water on earth from a goatskin flask. For the first time in ten days we were drinking water which was equally filthy but at least it was not warm. The way out of this hellhole was to reach the capital of Sudan, Khartoum, which was still 900 kilometers away. We set off. The driver was an Eritrean guerila who had been wounded and was obliged to drive now. He was 21 or 23 years old at the most. He had a kind face, he was endearing, he smiled a lot. He was a good person. He fought actively for four years and when he was seriously wounded he was deputized as a driver. His current duties involved transporting ammunition, armament and weapons to the front. He took us to the Eritrea front on the same route. Now thinking retrospectively, it was a very dangerous journey.

Ammunition convoys were attacked regularly from the air. If we were hit there would be nothing left of us. At least we unloaded the material on arrival and we were returning empty."

On the endless journey back, Ara tried to communicate with the driver to pass the time.

"He knew twelve words in English in addition to yes and no. We could communicate as much as sign language could be. In sign language, I asked him 'how many people have you killed so far?' I was sitting in the car and drawing pictures with my finger in the dust, depicting the pulling of a trigger, getting shot. 'I am dead' I said. 'You? How many?' Finally, he understood. 'Hi!' he said and said something in his language, failed to find the English equivalent and squirmed. I wrote 15 with my finger in the dust, then 20. He looked and laughed. He wrote 80, 85, 100 in the dust with his finger... I looked at his face, 'Ya!' I said. He laughed, 'Ya,' he said. He was happy."

They got lost in the dark.

"As we were fearing the approach of the night and hoping for a moon, the truck tracks followed by our retired hero who had killed 100 people petered out. It was not as if we were in the Konya desert and sure to arrive somewhere. I thought of the map of Africa with Sudan in the center; after Sudan there was desert. Probably this desert was bigger than all of Turkey, it was endless. If we took a wrong turn we could have arrived in Erzurum instead of Istanbul."

Ara was seriously worried about their future in the pitch-black endless desert.

"Yes, we were stuck there, there was no road, no water, there would be morning, then there would be night. Buzzards would start to circle over our heads like those buzzards in the shapeless tree on the skirts of Kilimanjaro in Hemingway's story. Let's say we died, me and a hero. They would find us in three months. Dried up half consumed bodies or skeletons. Who are they? Nobody will know who I or the hero are...Let's say they found us, the hero and me, Ara Guler. I don't know about the hero but my symbolic body would be shipped to Istanbul. PM Ecevit would send one of the telegraphs that Ismet Pasha sent to my father's funeral."

This was not Ara's first experience with war, he had been tasked many times to the front.

"When I was young I went to four wars. Wars were different then. I remember the Palestine war. In the war in Israel a man was killed and fell on me, I held him but how long can you hold someone. See this white soil, it was like lime, mortar was shelled, whatever... If you got up to take a photograph you could not shoot anything except smoke. There was no point in risking your life. I have been to the Philippines, to Ethiopia. War is a very bad thing. I don't want to see a war setting again. I have taken enough pictures of war. This was enough... War is abhorrent. Very bad. Once you get immersed in it you can't get out. When I see war I want to return home immediately. But I can't ... if I were to go now I would probably die then and there."

He believed that photojournalists had a great responsibility in terms of war.

"Photojournalists are the historians of the 20th Century. Ever since photography was invented photojournalists have been writing history. For example, during Vietnam War there were 98 correspondents who witnessed the history. 96 were photojournalists and only two of them were writers. The other writers sat in their comfortable chairs in their homes, their places of work. We as photojournalists eternalize the historical moments that take place in our era. We capture these moments and transmit them to future generations. Imagine, nobody thought of taking photographs or filming during the Anatolian Operation. Nobody realized the importance of this work. Today nothing much has changed in Turkey, the Turkish press."

When His Mother Meets His Father

In May 1980 Ara lost his mother Verjin. As they were one way or another lived so close to eachother his mother was a dear to him.From time to time they lived in the same house or in the same building but they were never separated. When Ara left the house he would call out to his mother without failure and he would call out when he returned saying the only sentence he knew in Armenian: "*Maman, es ega, es vernam!*" (Mom, I'm home, I'm upstairs).

"My mother told me that I was born on the 16th of August 1928 at sixteen minutes past six o'clock. But she told me this when I was 30."

Verjin, who was the daughter of a very wealthy family, had never entered a kitchen in her life, had done no housework. She raised Ara with a nanny. According to her the kitchen was for servants and a lady had no business in the kitchen. *"Housework is service. It can be done by a woman who gets three thousand lira per month, the real trick is to be a lady,"* said Verjin whose housework was done by Mari and whose food was cooked by Madame Kornelya. Verjin would scold Mari who proudly announced that, *" I am a servant and proud of it,'* by saying *"Don't be ridiculous, a person can be proud to be a doctor, architect, engineer, but there is nothing to be proud about being a servant."*

Verjin was very devoted to taking care of herself, her make-up and dress, and she would not face anyone without washing her face and hands in the morning, brushing her teeth, brushing her hair and putting on lipstick. No one had ever seen her without lipstick, or without manicure. She would color her lips with grenadine red lipstick, apply red lacquer to her nails and dye her hair a coppery red.

"We knew Bedia Muvahhit intimately. She was a friend of my mother's. I photographed her until the end. She would always ask 'How is your mother?' and I would reply 'she is well' every time. Although my mother had passed away five years ago! They were the flashy women of the times, you know. Modern women of the time, they were like European women, the two of them."

Verjin made a living on the modest rent income from five flats in Guler Apartment in Galatasaray, and every time her son Ara wanted to raise the rents she would object and say,

"If we raise the rent the tenants will be gripped with sedition thinking what that old woman is going to do with so much money, let them pay less without begrudging it. See they all like me, respect me. In this world a person needs love and respect, not money. Furthermore, you are my only child, if I had had a few children every one would have said let the other one look after me and nobody would. But I am a smart woman, that is why I had only one child, since I don't have any other children you are obliged to look after me well, that is it!"

Verjin was religious in her own way and went to church as well as the mosque. She believed in God but did not accept any of the prophets. Ara's mother believed in entombed saints, saints, and hodjas. She would take packets of salt to the Tuzbaba Tomb in Besiktas at regular intervals and bring back the blessed salts. She believed that food cooked with blessed salt enhanced the benediction of a home.

Neither Ara nor his mother Verjin cared about materials-property, or money-securities.

When she received a recommendation to move to a house in Gumussuyu overlooking the Bosphorus she said, "I am accustomed to the noise, the fuss and revelry of Beyoglu, that place is like a fairground, this is too quiet, the water flows and the madman watches it flow. If you call this a sea view well I had the best possible sea view in my youth, which was spent in Adalar, and I do not call seeing the sea over rooftops a view of the sea, this is not for me".

Once when a neighbor's house was on fire and the fire department ordered the houses to be evacuated, Ara rushed into the street with his cameras and was worrying about his archive. He was astounded that his mother had exited the building without taking anything with her and said:

"Didn't you even take your handbag?"
"No but I took my identity card."
"Why didn't you take six passport photographs and some fiscal stamps while you are at it?"

Ara buried his mother Verjin who he had shared everything with for 52 years, in Sisli Armenian Cemetery next to his father Dacat, after the ceremony organized at the Balikpazari Uc Horan Church in Beyoglu.

In the Homeland of the Turks

In June 1980 dozens of people were killed on the streets on a daily basis because of the political and economic bottleneck in Turkey. The political system was deadlocked to the point that the presidential elections could not be carried out, and nightmare days passed as thousands of laborers working in hundreds of work places were on strike.

The President of CHP (The Republican People's Party), Bulent Ecevit, warned that, *"Civil war has started in various cities in Turkey,"* to which Prime Minister Suleyman Demirel replied, *"Ecevit continues to spout poison and speak like a provocateur".*

Ara thought that amidst this fighting it would be a good idea to go and display the Orkhon inscriptions which are the most ancient monuments to Turkish in the territories first inhabited by Turks. No journalist had gone to the region before.

His friend Oguz Akkan, who had established Cem Publishing house after leaving his job as editor for *Milliyet* newspaper, went frequently to the Soviet Union to meet with the writers published by his publishing house. Ara tagged along on one of those trips and found himself in Almaty.

"I was with Recep Bilginer and Oguz Akkan in a luxurious restaurant on top of a high hill at the invitation of the local Writers Union. The main thing I remember is that vodka was consumed like water. The Russian nation is accustomed to this drinking so they do not become inebriated. At dinner, a portly man with a bulging stomach, who was a renowned poet by the name of Olcay Suleymanov, was sitting opposite us. We were discussing Nazim etc. and then he started talking about his last trip. He had gone to Mongolia and talked about it. I wanted to go there since my youth; I have these images, visions of men shooting arrows, jumping on horses, hunting with falcons. As the man narrated his experiences I got an idea for an interview serial for *Hurriyet*."

When they returned to Moscow the narrations of Suleymanov remained in his mind. Oguz Akkan liked his interview idea.

"Oguz was friends with the writers here because he printed their books. For example, we were staying at Cengiz Aytmatov's house. I said, 'Damn Ara, don't be stupid. Since we were in Russia we needed to get permission from the government just to stay here. We couldn't even travel from one province to another. They wouldn't let you talk on the telephone. Even the writer Oguz Akkan was ready'. There was Vera, I said 'Vera, Oguz and I decided to go to Mongolia. Do you know the Ambassador of Mongolia?' 'I do but I have never asked for anything in my life, ' he said."

At Ara's insistence Vera called the Embassy of Mongolia to get an appointment.

"We went to talk to the man – we were speaking French – the man had been in Paris before coming to Russia. He kept saying 'Ah Paris is so wonderful, I want to go again'. He ordered coffee and when we had established a friendship I said 'Look nobody from our country has gone to Mongolia. There are historical ties between Mongolia and Turkey etc. and somebody will some day, so please help us and let us be the first journalists to visit.'"

Ara wanted to secure the deal so he did not refrain from threatening the Ambassador.

"I said 'We each have 1,000 dollars in our pockets and we can't spend money on hotels while we are waiting the processing of visas. If we can get our visas until Monday, fine, if not then it is too bad. If you don't do this I will prevent any journalists from Turkey to see you. So, ask whoever it is you need to ask in your government'; we got a 10-day visa."

They set off from Yakutsk, the coldest city in the dry cold of Siberia.

"It was spring but the temperature was below freezing. It was impossible to stick your head outside of the airport, anyway we were changing planes there. We flew over the deepest lake in the world, the Lake Baikal, to arrive in Ulan Batur. There were statues of Stalin everywhere, they had theaters and buildings which could not be found in Turkey. Buddhist temples was transformed into museums. They made statues depicting 20th Century civilization which had been tanks etc."

All movements of Ara and Oguz Akkan were under surveillance.

"We were under constant surveillance, the secret police were following us; you take a step, take a leak they report it. So be it, I didn't care."

They needed a vehicle to get to the places they want to see.

"We went into the city and needed a vehicle. Now if you have been invited by a government who pays for transportation, or they allocate a car, right? But they couldn't because the government of Mongolia had only nine cars."

When they checked into the hotel they were surprised to discover that all the windows were covered with wire mesh.

"It was the best hotel and the windows were covered by wire mesh as were the windows of all houses. The reason for this was that storms blew the sand from the Gobi desert into the rooms and it was impossible to survive, your mouth got filled with sand in five minutes."

Ara was surprised to see that a large part of the population still lived in tents.

"Most of them lived in tents called yurts. They were still living in the middle ages in the country. Bandits stopped busses on the way and robbed passengers. There were bandits on the roads! It was just like the Middle Ages. They had horse shepherds, horses' milk... We took a lot of photographs, the monuments of Kul Tigin, etc."

Finally, they were able to reach the Orkhun Monuments.

"The Orkhun Inscriptions were 70 kilometers from the city, there was no protection, just a fence had been erected around it. The rocks were the size of this car. We could not go anywhere else because they didn't provide a vehicle, only camels. Did you know that the camels there had two humps? I also photographed weddings, they had some very nice wedding ceremony venues, I had not seen anything like it in Europe."

Editor in Chief of *Hurriyet*, Nezih Demirkent, announced the feature on the first page of the newspaper for days before it started and wrote about it in his column.

"Ara Guler and Oguz Akkan flew all the way to Mongolia and are the first Turkish journalists to set foot on Mongolian territory. Soon you will be able to read about similar traits we share with Mongolia and the most intimate details of life in this large country in Asia."

Ara also took the feature titled "*In the Homeland of the Turks*" to *National Geographic* magazine.

"I took hundreds of photographs, made interviews. When I took my material to the magazine to hand it over to the photography editor, Bob Gilka, his first question was, 'how many days did you spend in Mongolia?'. When I said 10 days he said, 'don't show me the interview, I won't look at it'. 'But what are you doing! I took more than 1,500 photographs, I wrote material, does that not account for something? I said. His reply was, 'To know a country well first you have to capture its atmosphere, know the people. That cannot happen in less than three months. We only publish such interviews in our magazine."

Three months after the interview the military seized power in Turkey, This is the third military intervention he had witnessed.

"The 12th of September did not affect me because it remained local. At that time, I was working for external newspapers. They did not commission for such a task so I did not do one."

The coup of 12th September in the leadership of Chief of General Staff Gen. Kenan Evren, had put a stop to the civil war which killed dozens of people daily. But it had turned the country into an open air prison in which all political parties and associations were shut down, freedoms were eliminated and torture and executions became daily events.

"I wanted to take a picture of Kenan Evren. I used to work with the Presidency earlier anyway since Fahri Koruturk. When Evren came, they discharged all of us, only Ali Baransel remained. The personnel from the Ministry for Foreign Affairs protocol arranged for photographs to be taken in case they were needed. I took photographs of him in his office without anyone else present. He would ask me 'is Exacta a good camera'. It is not bad but not anything special either. He brought it and showed it to me. It was not a camera I am very familiar with. The entrance to the Presidency was different from what it is today. Everything changes very rapidly."

The Woman of His Life

Ara started to hang out at the Papirus Bar in Beyoglu, which was frequented by the apoliticized and passified intellectuals after 1980. He was impressed with the beauty, accumulation and sophistication of Suna Taskiran, whom he met often.

"One of the most beautiful women in Turkey. I had seen her years ago in the meetings in Ankara, at Ankara Palas. I admired her a lot."

Suna, who worked as an editor in Redhouse publishing house, had finished the Faculty of Archeology after Robert College and was the student of the legendary "Teacher of teachers Professor-in-ordinary Dr. Ekrem Akurgal". Suna's mother, Tezer Taskiran, was one of the first female MPs in Turkey and had written a book *Mantik (Logic)* which had been read and much liked by Ataturk himself. Her father, Nimet Taskiran, was one of the most prominent surgeons in Turkey. He had written numerous scientific articles and had had books written about him, for his contributions to Turkish medicine.

Her grandfather, Ahmet Agaoglu, was Azeri and occupied one of the close cadres in Ataturk's government and also the chairman of Anadolu Agency. The offspring of the Agaoglu family which had produced people with titles such as first female lawyer, first female pediatrician, first school principal. The family made an indeliable impression both in terms of the work they did as well as the education they had received in schools such as Oxford and Sorbonne.

"Suna comes from an important and sophisticated family. Her grandfather Ahmet Agaoglu is one of the founders of Kemalism. Like here we are talking, imagine I'm a sanitation employee next to her."

Suna's knowledge of the English language was very good so the relationship, which started when she helped Ara write his interviews, turned into love within time.

"I was falling in love with her bro. I didn't see anyone else!"

Suna had also been married before.

"Suna had children from her previous marriage. A girl and a boy. Ayse played the timpani in Ataturk Culture Center while Ahmet was the founder and guitarist in Kurtalan Ekspres band."

When they started to live together in Ara's house in Gumussuyu, Ara decided to set off on a world tour and asked Suna whether she would accompany him.

"I told Suna, 'OK' she said. We would start off at one end and exit from the other. I had no idea how long it would take. She resigned and took retirement from Redhouse. We set off on a world tour for 7-8 months. I made a deal with the newspapers to write on my return and we set off to Pakistan, Nepal, Thailand, India, Hong Kong, the Philippines, and New York. In Hong Kong we ran out of money; we waited for money from American Express. Then we went to Indonesia and finished the journey in Japan. It was -10 degrees. We spent New Year's Eve in Europe, went to London, Paris, prepared the ground for future interviews and contacts."

Ara, who was fed up with travelling alone for years, was very happy to be accompanied by Suna.

"One has to know everything. Suna deals with everything. She talks to people, collects documents, writes articles. That is why I took her everywhere when I was taking photographs. I was alone at night and bored anyway. I go to the strangest places after all! I stay in hotels with no waiters, nobody to cook. You can talk to your wife."

It was the promulgation of a divine connection that enabled their miraculous world tour on a limited budget.

"Redhouse is a member of the Society Bible community. Suna was on the executive board. Society Bible has venues all over the world – even in Burma. They did not let us pay five cents."

During the world tour which lasted eight months, Suna and Ara had the opportunity to get to know one another intimately and they decided never to part. In August, 1984, they got married. Their witnesses were Avni Arbas and Gultekin Cizgen.

"I was known for womanizing. The occupation is for womanizers. But that was all before marriage; after I got married I lived as an honest man. Marriage for me is sacred. It means observing and enjoying everything together."

Aragon

In the autumn of 1981, as Ara was walking the streets of Paris, he decided to put an end to the question *'why is Aragon not included among those whose pictures I have taken'*, which had plagued his thoughts.

"I got an appointment on the telephone for 4 p.m. It was the darkest day in the world. There was no light whatsover. There was a bar in Paris on Rue Danou near the opera. The Harris Bar. It was frequented by Hemingway etc. I always went there, it fits my mood… I had a beer, had a sandwich and waited for the clock to strike 4. Suddenly it occurred to me that tomorrow was a holiday, every place would be closed, I was returning so I should get something for the missus. I went and bought her a dress. It was in a nylon cover, I remember thinking that I should not lose it."

When the time for the appointment rolled around Ara came to the building inhabited by Aragon, with his shopping bags.

"I recall walking through a large foyer. I entered through a door with square windows. There was a reception area. I said I was visiting Louis Aragon. They said 'Take the elevator to the top floor'. 'Well what is this place?' I asked. 'It is a department of the Ministry of Culture,' they replied. So, Aragon occupied the top floor of the Ministry of Culture like its brain. Like the former Greek ladies, he had a Spanish servant. I passed into the salon with square windows and started to wait for Aragon."

Every place was covered with large and small photographs, designs pinned to the walls, paintings with and without frames. There were loads of letters and articles on the table.

"When Aragon entered, he said 'Hello,' to me and immediately started to point out the paintings on the walls. 'This is a Matisse,' he said, 'This is a Picasso, this is a Dufy, this is Lurchat's sun...' He explained non-stop. He paid no attention to my questions, he paced the room and talked about the paintings, the designs. I had been right. Louis Aragon was living in his past world. Aragon was still explaining. All his memoirs, pictures and the accumulation of his past. I kept taking photographs of Aragon and his past."

Subsequently Aragon took Ara to the rear section of the house.

This was the bedroom. The walls were covered full length in photographs pinned to the wall. There was a writing desk next to the bed. I made him sit there and took his pictures. He continued to ignore my questions and continued to talk. I remember at one point he said with great joy 'I saved Melina Mercury from the hands of the junta'. I completed the interview and took a lot of photographs but the man was so confused that no matter what you say he talked about the same things. It was impossible to free him of his obsession. He did whatever the servant told him to.

After two hours with Aragon Ara's heart sank. He steered towards the door thinking it was time to leave.

"I'm done, I'm going", just as I was leaving through the door I stretched to pick up the package I had for my wife. Aragon said, 'What are you taking? That is mine', 'No, it is mine, I put it there. It is my package. I bought my wife a dress,' I said. 'No, everybody who leaves this house takes something' he said. 'Right, I am sure that is correct but I did not take anything, it is my package' I replied.... But he insisted that it was not. How could I make him understand? Finally, the servant came and I explained the situation. The servant lady reprimanded him severely... Aragon sulked like a child as I took my package and left."

His Uncle's Separated Legs

At a time in the 1980s, when Ara was going through an active time involving exhibitions, he experienced an event which was comparable to the stories of Turkish Satirist Aziz Nesin.

"My mother's younger brother, uncle Adurjan, finished the British School. I was a student in high school. There were competitions held between schools, on the panel it said that A.Sahin was the champion for 100 meters, nobody could break his record. Then I found out that this was my uncle. I asked my uncle 'That A.Sahin, Adurjan Sahin, that is me' he said."

His uncle had developed the same disease as his mother had, familial Type 2 diabetes which was rampant in their family.

"He went through a lot of treatment, one of my uncle's legs had to be amputated. The champion was losing a leg. Some time passed by and they needed to amputate the other leg. I visited my uncle in Samatya Hospital. The top part of him was normal while below one leg was missing and now the other one would have to go. He was not afraid or anything. He had the operation and we went to see him in 2-3 days and then he came home."

Ara jumped out of bed when his telephone rang at midnight; it was a call from Samatya Hospital.

"I jumped into a taxi and went directly to the hospital. What is the matter? I asked and my uncle's wife said 'I am going to die'. He needed to pee but could not go to the toilet. They had wrapped the amputated leg in a piece of nylon and handed it to the wife; what could she do with it, she put it in the bathtub. He couldn't go into the bathroom at first because the leg was there and there was no other toilet, his nerves were already upside down so he fainted."

It was up to Ara to solve this traumatic situation.

"What should we have done with the leg? The man couldn't be buried as he was very much alive, we had to bury the leg. A burial permit was needed to bury the leg. I would look for such a document. I needed the document but how could I take the leg? I might have been searched on the way. A man was carrying a leg. You go to the police, first a doctor provides a document saying that we have submitted the leg. On the document the date was written, a description of the leg which was approved by the police. Then you take it to the cemetery for burial. You had it signed by the General Directorate of Cemeteries."

Ara had done every bureaucratic procedure to the letter to have the leg buried, but there was a *small* problem.

"Now my uncle's first leg was in the Balikli Armenian Cemetery in Zeytinburnu and the other one was in the Sisli Armenian Cemetery. When the end of the world comes and everyone is resurrected, my uncle will not be able to run even if he wanted to."

Exhibition at the CIA Venue

At the end of 1986, when the budget for the Grand National Assembly of Turkey was being discussed, Minister of Culture and Tourism, Mesut Yilmaz, declared that an exhibition featuring Sultan Suleyman the Lawmaker would be held in America. Prime Minister Turgut Ozal had launched a promotion to introduce Turkey abroad and asked that the cigarette company Philip Morris, operated by his former boss Sakip Sabanci in the 70s, covered the costs of the exhibition.

The exhibition was to be held in the most prestigious art showcase in the United States, being the National Gallery of Art in Washington, and the exhibition was going to display gold and silver coins from the Ottoman era, carpets, caftans and ceramics, in addition to photographs of Mimar Sinan's works photographed by Ara. There were plans to include the book published by the founder and Head of the History Department of Bogazici University, Prof. Dr. Aptullah Kuran, which included photographs of Mimar Sinan's works taken by Ara.

On a snowy day in January 1987, a large Turkish group, under the leadership of the Prime Minister's wife Semra Ozal, was in Washington. The first thing that Ara did when he came to the city, which was paralyzed in terms of transport due to unprecedented snowfall, was to call his friend and Washington representative of *Cumhuriyet* newspaper Tanju Akerson to tell him that he had arrived:

"Ara Guler has arrived in Washington."

Ara was furious as he barely made it to his hotel, because the transport workers had seized the opportunity given by the snowfall to go on strike, and the atmosphere was frantic.

"Even the toilets at the airport were closed. Ok the planes couln't fly. The personnel in information left. Nobody knew what anybody was doing. Like it was this snow, they had not seen snow."

He decided to leave the United States before the snow on his shoes melted.

"I have a man like Mimar Sinan and if these Americans do not recognize him and are going to know him with an exhibition of this scale then that is their shame. I cannot introduce my Sinan to them, they can come and be introduced to my Sinan!"

The second shock for Ara, who had been calmed down by the members of the delegation with difficulty, occurred when he saw the size of the hall of the Octagon House which had been chosen by the American Institute of Architecture (AIA), which had organized the Mimar Sinan exhibition, and was the size of a shop. This humble hall belonging to the American Foundation of Architecture (AAF) was 200 years old and was the place where the American intelligence organization, CIA, had been established. This small venue which had hosted even an American President perhaps carried a lot of weight for them, but Ara did not agree.

"It was a complete scandal. I found myself in an exhibition which did not feel Mimar Sinan, which visualized him only as a height of stone, an exhibition without any visual aesthetics. Is this the Sinan I wanted to present and in America of all places! Whether that building was historical or not, that hall was not fit for an exhibition, it could only be used to give lessons in architecture. Furthermore, I searched for Mimar Sinan among my photographs. Where was he? This exhibition was not my exhibition. The photographs might be mine but as long as this exhibition ran in America nobody was going to understand Mimar Sinan."

The Americans who toured the exhibition of Sultan Suleyman the Lawmaker, and the American media, were mesmerized. In a short time 393,000 people had visited the exhibition, and as result of popular demand the exhibition was extended and *The New York Times* wrote *"one of the magnificent and popular exhibitions opened to date"*.

Ara was bothered that his photographs had been presented in a low-ceiling venue, removed from the exhibition, which was the center of attention. It did not make him feel any better that subsequently the photographs of Mimar Sinan would be integrated with the Sultan Suleyman the Lawmaker exhibition and tour the other cities of America together.

"This exhibition could not be displayed with the Suleyman the Magnificent exhibition to be launched at the Metropolitan Museum in New York in its then present state. It had to be changed. A world had to be created for the presentation of Sinan, otherwise it would not do justice to Mimar Sinan. For such an exhibition, we had to establish the world of Mimar Sinan. Otherwise Mimar Sinan would tour the New World for nothing after 400 years."

The presentation of Mimar Sinan he had in his mind was very different.

"You can't collect and compress Mimar Sinan into one place. Mimar Sinan needed to be presented in his own space. Architecture is something within nature. The name of the exhibition must be 'Sinan within Sinan'. It had to be opened within Sinan, within the Suleymaniye. The music in the background should be composed by a composer who writes music from that era. The lighting should be special also. The room should be in complete dark and when a person comes in front of the piece, the painting should be lit . That is the way an exhibition should be."

While Semra Ozal was making the inaugurations, and making the participants giggle when she mispronounced the title of "Lawmaker" used for Sultan Suleyman as "Lovemaker", Ara was busy explaining Mimar Sinan to the visitors who gathered around him and bombarded him with questions:

"Sinan is a world within. Just like Leonardo da Vinci and Michelangelo, Sinan has a world of his own. All the worlds of these men coincide in the same century for some reason. What attracts me about Mimar Sinan is the way he used light. He filters the light so natural that it creates aesthetics and the venue accepts it. . Mimar Sinan is not an architect who builds a venue with stones, he gathers the world in it. The light seeping from his windows does not merely reflect beauty. The atmosphere created by the light provides the necessary divinity to mosques. When I look at Sinan's buildings from the outside I feel life in the stones. I unite him with birds, shadows made by trees, and take his picture. I want to listen to the music made by the wind seeping from the domes; architecture is a symphony that is what I find in Sinan..."

Bounty Hunters

In August of 1990, Editions Didier Millet, a publishing company renowned for its books introducing countries, took the best 45 photojournalists in the world to Malaysia and Indonesia for its new project. 350 photographs out of the 100,000 photographs taken throughout the tour were going to be made into an album introducing these countries. Ara was among those who had been invited. When Ara completed the seven day program, he realized that he had never been so close to his childhood dream that he had in years.

"Our job was finished and everyone left except me. When I travel to places on other peoples' money, I generally stay more to explore since I am there. When I was a child I saw an interview in the *National Geographic* when the magazine was still printed in black and white. The interview was titled 'Jungle Journeys in Sarawak'. I always wanted to go there in my mind: "Head Hunters"."

Kalimantan region in Indonesia was notorious for its headhunters.

"They are the most savage, the cannibals that is. I researched to find where they were located and one of the guides said 'Bro it is possible to go there only when the state is delivering aid, otherwise it is not possible, there is no road or anything. You have to go by canoe. It takes to go across rivers, there are alligators! If you fall in the water, they will eat you, you can't even put your leg out, if you rent a canoe I will take you,'" the man said. I said to Ian Berry 'I am planning to do a feature about this, do you want to come?' 'OK,' he said."

The team was ready to set off.

"There is me, Suna, Ian, a Chinese guide, a local canoe man, an armed man and we needed someone else to measure the depth. Such a person has to keep dropping stones in the water to understand whether the water is deep enough for the canoe because if it runs aground then the alligators will come. Such strange stories. One of the men, the Chinese one, got advance from me and went to buy a chainsaw operated with an accumulator. I asked him 'What do we need this for, why did you buy it? 'You don't know what can happen to us'. 'Alright,' I said 'take it then'. I found out later that tropical forests would consume each other, they would vie with one another and form networks that did not allow passage. That is why we cut the branches before they grew strong enough to block the passage. Here nature competes with itself and tries to wipe out each other."

The Chinese guide did not only get the electrical chainsaw but also lots of eggs, noodles, biscuits and water. He warned the team:

'They eat lizards, snakes, rats, alligators, monkey, woodworm. "
'They are very hospitable, they will offer you such foods but do not eat it. You should not consume anything except rice wine if it is offered. "

No matter how well they prepared themselves, their trip was dictated by the rules of wild nature.

"There were two hazards, one was that the forest might cover you and the second was the water might run low. Water running low brings two hazards, the alligators might appear and the canoe might brush the bottom and the men must carry the canoe to wherever the water is deep enough. Then you get in the canoe until you run low again and have to walk and then you have to beware the alligators. There were alligators in some places. There were no alligators where we had to walk but there were other creatures: there was 10 centimeters of water and wherever you stepped 20 species of snakes appeared. If you were bitten then you were dead because it would take at least three days to get out of there. The head hunter feature was launched amid such concerns."

Ara was 62 while his wife Suna was 57...

"At that time, my wife was very resilient. I got into the canoe but I had never boarded anything so wobbly; it wobbled even when I breathed so I couldn't breathe. I was a heavy smoker then, but never mind smoking I could not get the packet out of my pocket I was so scared. I couldn't take photographs either, the canoe was so wobbly, I was afraid but then I got used to it of course."

After a journey filled with fear of alligators, strong currents, waterfalls and gorges, they finally reached their destination.

"We had arrived. The cannibals lived in long houses. The houses measured 100-150 meters from one end to the other. They were sectioned inside and they were approximately 15 meters above the ground level. 168 people lived together. There were lots of animals below, lions, tigers, they lived on top of poles to protect themselves from them. They ate snakes' eyes. I was starving but there was nothing for me to eat. But most importantly if you get malaria from the water then nobody can save you. Luckily, we had brought our water with us."

When Ara entered the houses on poles, the first thing that attracted his attention were the skulls hanging from the ceiling. He counted exactly 29 skulls.

"I could not liken the first ones I saw to skulls because they were dusty and black. Most of them had been hung in reverse from the neck. I approached two elderly men who were sitting under hanging skulls in a corner. For a while we grinned at each other."

Ara was really bothered by the fact that he could not communicate with the locals.

"It was embarrassing that I did not know the cannibal language, how could I communicate with them. The Chinese guide could talk."

One of the elderly men pointed to a skull hanging from the ceiling and tried to say something, but Ara did not understand anything.

The Chinese guide rushed to his rescue:

"This is the skull of a British general. During their last battle with the British they had taken this elderly British general as a hostage and had kept him hidden in the forest for some time. Then he had been beheaded and the head had been brought to the village. They were considered heroes because they had beheaded so many people. The British had invaded their country and they had warred against the British and everybody would hang the British skulls on their walls as decorations. So, the head hunters don't eat skulls, they are patriots."

Ara warmed to the head hunters when he heard the anti-imperialist side of things...

"They are the best people in the world! If I were born again I would like to be a Massai warrior or a cannibal. The cannibals in the world have actually eaten how many people? A thousand, 10,000, 20,000, 1 million people. One Hitler comes along and destroys 40 million lives. So, which one is the real cannibal bro? Who is the enemy of humanity? Never mind films, they are made by the British, they always portray the other as cannibals. Cannibals are the most civilized community in the world. I prefer being a cannibal a thousand times over being an American."

Everything was very challenging and tiring during the feature.

"It was one of the most dangerous features I had made. I said to Suna 'If we get out of this alive perhaps it is time to quit journalism'. It was very difficult."

This was Ara's last feature in his 40-year career in journalism. He placed his old leather camera case, which had accompanied him throughout all his travels, next to his chair in his office never to be picked up again.

"But I was accustomed to viewing the world through a rectangular frame and that will always be like this."

The Crime of Desecrating a Film

Ara had started to a lead a quieter life, devoting his time to exhibitions and books, but he did not have very high opinions of publishers who he had to deal with personally.

"A pressman has to feel at least as much emotion as you feel. In order to make a reproduction of Picasso you have to be familiar with Picasso. In Europe, a pressman will have his wife and children dress up after breakfast on Sunday, get dressed himself, shave, and go to a museum to observe Rembrandt. It is the man's civilization, it is what he lives. If he is also slightly intelligent and loves his work he will make himself busy with it. Now our pressmen sit and watch a football game. A pressman in this country needs to be beaten for a week and then beaten again for one week during his apprenticeship."

Ara was infuriated by the lack of care shown regarding his negatives and photographs during printing:

"Did you see my note? I got angry and wrote it one day, it must be at least 20 years ago."

"Careful!"
Important note to editors, graphic designers, picture selectors, redaction supervisors and pressmen...

What you are holding in your hand is a photograph by Ara Guler...
While these photographs are being processed do not approach them with tea, coffee, soda,
Fanta and similar soft drinks!
Do not eat or drink around the photographs...
Do not place photographs on wet or hot surfaces, for example on ventilator or radiators...
Do not cough on them, hold them with wet or dirty hands, smoke near them or speak in a
loud voice!"

He could not stand to see how the photographs he had painstakingly taken throughout the years, as a result of hard work, were manhandled by unqualified personnel.

"I have made a lot of noise, I have sworn. People have lost their jobs because of me. When you are taking a photograph, you are imagining a composition, you are composing a sentence. If a photo frame is a sentence, the man is cutting off the beginning of your sentence. So, who is writing this sentence, is it me or him! Who is the boss here? I am the boss, I am involved in the event, I am the planner! Who are you? You are the technician, I am the signature. Most of the men doing layout have sick minds, they can't apply themselves elsewhere so they minimize you in the page layout. That way nobody is prominent, not them and not the photographer. That is disrespecting film."

As if that was not enough, he was obliged to battle with billion dollar hotels who would tear pictures from his books and frame and hang them on their walls, as well as renowned newspapers who used his photographs without permission.

"In Turkey photographs are not given much importance. 'Oh, so what,' says the man. He uses a photograph on the cover of a book. Never mind paying any royalties, he does not even print your name anywhere. If he does, you are lucky. I have fought a lot. *Milliyet* did it once. They failed to return the negatives that they took to publish a book called 'Photographs'. Then they printed postcards with them. I had no knowledge about it. Eventually I sued them, the litigation continued for four years. Finally, the court awarded one million lira. We split the money with the lawyer. What I mean is copyright is not something that is prioritized in Turkey by anyone. A British publisher will print your book, pay and send a copy. Turks print but they don't send anything, they don't even inform you. It is a matter of courtesy, a tradition. We have no respect for anything, for the past, so why there should be any respect for photographs. Everything is at the mercy of someone in this country. Which of them can you fight? "

A Market Vendor Punching Salgado

Ara was the permanent destination of those who visited Turkey for photography purposes, and in 1999 Ara's guest was Sebastiao Salgado. He was one of the few names who was Ara's junior and whose style he liked.

"Salgado was one of my favorite photographers. There is no one greater. He is a photographer of humanity. He does not shoot empty pictures, he shoots human drama. 'I always observed you,' he said to me, 'what camera you use, what diaphragm, what film. I used to write in magazines. Of course, he is much younger than me; Salgado was twenty-five years my junior."

Ara met Salgado through Magnum and they became friends. He helped Salgado with the feature '*Workers*' which created a major sensation in the world of photography.

"We were enjoying drinks in Paris and talking about work. At that time, he was interested in workers. I told him 'You can find the workers of all in Chittagong'. It is a city in Bangladesh at the tip of the Bay of Bengal. There is a tide because of the open sea and the water decreases and increases. Vessels to be dismantled enter the area and when the tide runs out they remain stuck in the mud. There are thousands of vessels which are being dismantled, the workers work up a sweat. I said 'It is a muddy place'. 'Tell me how to get there,' he said. The husband of Suna Kan (violinist) was there as the ambassador, Halit Guvener. We stayed at their house when we visited. Bangladesh is a chaotic country. This man was going there and do what? Whatever, we had an honorary consul there. He was the owner of Chittagong! The whole city, almost all the buildings belonged to this man. All the factories... He had a very large company in the United Kingdom and had facilities from weaving looms to shipyards... very wealthy. The wealthiest man I have known in my life. I decided to send Salgado to him. I called him but was unable to speak to him. I informed him through his brother with a letter that 'Ara Guler's friend is coming to see you, he will give you this letter, help him'. Salgado went and took photographs which later on became a book."

Salgado, who earned a lot of money for Magnum agency during the assassination attempt of US President Reagan, made a recommendation to Ara.

'I want a photograph from you' he said one day. 'I will give you one of mine and you give me one of yours, let's trade,' he said. 'I will give you as many photographs as you give me,' he said. Black and white. 'Choose fifteen pictures,' I said. 'Fifteen is not enough, I want more, like thirty,' he said. Thus, I gave him thirty black and white shots and he gave me thirty frames in return. I had just returned from India, I selected contact prints. He sent what I had selected and I sent his; but my prints were larger than his."

Salgado, who was photographing places with the most migration and the oppressed generated by this. He was beaten by the market vendors in the Istanbul phase of the major project.

"It was raining in the market place and the water accumulating in the canopy was flowing down. Salgado was waiting for the water to accumulate and flow. A market vendor said 'get away from there'. Of course, the vendor was speaking in Turkish which Salgado did not understand. He was waiting for the water to flow and it just did not happen. The vendor who had told him to leave punched Salgado because he did not go. Salgado had been to war, he fought back. Finally, he broke a bone in his foot. I was waiting for him at Pera Palas. He did not come, and I said, 'I have to go to his hotel'. I found him at the hotel lying in bed with his foot stretched in front of him. The next day he left for a hospital in Paris..."

Salgado was dragged in the streets by the market vendors and barely escaped with his life, and after being operated on in his country a few times, he was able to come again and finish his project, albeit with a delay of a few months.

Doctor of Photography

The Senate of Yildiz Technical University convened under the chairmanship of Rector Prof. Dr. Ayhan Alkis in mid April 2004. The fifth article on the agenda was 'granting the title of honorary PhD to photograph artist Ara Guler'. The idea was recommended by Prof. Mehmet Bayhan, Yildiz Technical University Art and Design Faculty Photograph and Video Program Executive. A petition explained why Ara Guler should be granted an honorary PhD, accompanied by a long list of his successes, exhibitions and books.

"I am presenting my proposal to grant the title of 'Honorary PhD' to art and culture person Ara Guler, a distinguished citizen of our country who humbly calls himself a photojournalist, our pride in the world of photography.

Ara Guler has continued his work for over 50 years.

With his remarkable talent, hard work, the power of observation, and rich culture, Ara is able to perform a comprehensive assessment that has brought fresh air to photography in our country. He rightfully becomes the owner of a name that has commanded respect and recognition for Turkish photography throughout the world.

He has a share in contributing to the perception of photography as an artistic and social-scientific discipline that is gaining value in our country. While he made our country popular through the works in albums and displayed at exhibitions opened in many countries, he has also contributed to world culture.

He is mentioned in anthologies and publications about the history of photography published in all countries. He has generated superior benefits in terms of introducing the cultural life of our country. Honoring our modest master of photography will emphasize the respectability of photography as a branch and mean that the name of our university is written in the history of culture."

After the articles were opened to discussion, the Senate unanimously decided to establish a commission. It was comprised of the Deacon of the Faculty of Architecture Prof. Dr. Emre Aysu, Head of Department of Architecture & Building Sciences Department Prof. Dr. Mujgan Serefhanoglu Sozen, and Deacon of the Art and Design Faculty Prof. Mehmet Bayhan. The Examination Commission completed its report in one month.

"The file attached to the proposal has been examined. As observed from the curriculum vitae of Ara Guler, he has had an intensive working life, achieved success nationally and internationally and earned respect (a summarized curriculum vitae is attached).

In parallel with the developments in photography and printing technologies, press photography started in 1925 and generated the inception of interview photography aiming at sociocultural studies after 1930. More and more newspapers and magazines started close cooperation with photographers to fulfill the increasing need for visual information. The term between the years 1920-70 is a period of exuberant social photography during which humanity transferred from verbal culture to visual culture in which social culture developed rapidly and perception and thought processes were greatly affected. During this 'period of exuberant social photography' some photographers, with their solid accumulation of culture-knowledge and distinguished personalities, transmitted their work as philosophers, sociologists, culture experts and historians rather than photographers. Ara Guler is a symbolic name of the generation of photographers emphasized above in Turkey and has won recognition, respect and been honored in all countries. We wish to indicate that we find the proposal appropriate."

When Ara heard that he was going to be awarded a PhD he rejoiced like a child and immediately informed his friends. Everyone from Henri Cartier-Bresson to James Fox, from French painter-sculptor Albert Bitran to Minister of Culture Erkan Mumcu, congratulated Ara with messages lauding his success. A message written in the handwriting of the legend of photography Henri Cartier-Bresson one month before his demise, said that he and his wife Marchine rejoiced with Ara for the happy news and said their hearts were with him.

In the beginning of June, Ara was listening to a music recital given in his honor in the wood paneled auditorium of Yildiz Technical University, accompanied by his wife Suna Guler and friends pharmacist and photographer Sakir Eczacibasi, writer Dogan Hizlan, musician Selmi Andak, author Hasan Senyuksel, journalist Recep Bilginer, painter Mehmet Guleryuz, and journalistVasfiye Ozkocak, as well as deacons and students.

As Ara was called to the stage to receive his Honorary PhD title and wear the dark blue robe, he pointed to the dozens of photojournalists who had collected in front of the stage to eternalize the moment with pride and said- *I am one of them.*

Finally, he had achieved the PhD title that his family, especially his mother Verjin, had desired so much. He was happy.

"It is important for me to be honored by the people of my own country, to be appreciated. Otherwise there is not much value in being awarded in France, Germany, Japan. I am sure those countries do not attach importance to awards given to foreigners. It makes me happy that the people in the country I live in like my work, give me titles."

5 Kilograms of Ara Guler Photos

If you were tasked with interviewing you how would you prepare yourself? Where would you start, what would you ask?

When I go for an interview I learn everything about the subject before I go. Like you. Because I see many people come to interview me and know nothing about me. I am not pompous which is why I don't tell people much so everything is sort of half-baked. You work systematically. I am taking you seriously, I have given you documentation which has not been given to anyone.

Thank you very much...

Then there is the story of me going on an interview. It is very difficult for me. For example, when a photojournalist goes somewhere it means he has to take at least 400-500 rolls of film with him. How much does that cost? That means your expenses for an interview amount to 10,000 dollars before you have your flight tickets or anything. Whereas it is easy for a writer to go for an interview, he sticks his hand in his pocket and off he goes.

The success of your photograph interview depends a lot on the relationship you have established with the subject previously, doesn't it?

I don't interview people I don't know anyway. I interview people who I can befriend or who I admire greatly, for example I can interview Bertrand Russell. The man is 90 years old, I am a kid next to him. I cannot be friends with him but I can show my admiration and he will feel it, he will open up to me...

So, it has to have a value...

Of course, otherwise why would I go? Some will say, 'can you take my picture', why should I? I am not Photo Sabah. If you want it so badly you can go kill someone and become a murderer. Then I will photograph you, otherwise you can't go on my record!

It is evident that you have a great gift for convincing people...

I have 'the luck of the devil'. These things develop fast.

Have you had interviews which you were challenged?

Nothing has actually been easy, but so be it. I always managed with my wits. In 1956, I started working for Time and I still continue. Then I became the Middle East Correspondent for Paris Match and I traveled a lot to Israel, Hong Kong, Tokyo, the Far East. Actually, I have traveled throughout the world.

Is there any place you have missed?

Yes, I never visited South America. Most recently I visited Acapulco – that is as far as I went in Mexico and then to Fiji Islands and down to Indonesia. I have been all over the world but for example Indonesia is comprised of 168,000 islands. If you wanted to visit one island per day your life would not last that long because there are places that can only be reached in 3-4 days.

If that famous bag of yours could talk...

That leather bag has traveled the world. It is filled with compartments. I have lined it with suede so the cameras don't scratch each other.

You have traveled extensively and you have had the opportunity to relocate but you never did, you stayed here.

Why would I? This is my country, the others are turncoats. They have not embraced the country. They say one can't live here, it is an underdeveloped country, what a blunder! Those who don't know what they are sitting on, have they ever developed the curiosity to see Topkapi Palace? A person belongs to the place he is born into. I am a man of the East. I feel it. When I go East I find something in the people around me.

Where in the world did you find it difficult to work?

The most difficult country is India. They really make it hard for you on the way to India.

Where did you get the best photographs?

The best pictures are also in India. It is impossible not to be affected by the setup. The compositions established and disrupted in peoples' lives starting with religion is so attractive... the population is so high, there are people everywhere. Somebody burns something, another one runs, something else is happening over there, there is massive chaos and activity. It is so crowded, so crowded, nobody understands what is going on. Whose hand is in whose pocket is not clear. You get confused about what to shoot.

You take a suitcase full of film when you go for interviews.

Let's say I am going to Indonesia for three months, 10 rolls per day, you do the math. How can you take it? The customs officer does not allow you to enter with a suitcase filled with rolls of film. The customs officer goes crazy when he sees what you are carrying, it does not seem reasonable to him. How can a regular customs officer think in terms of 10 rolls of film per day? He probably uses one roll of film per year. It depends on who you encounter, if you encounter an imbecile then there will be in trouble. For example he takes all the rolls and gives you just 10 rolls of film, what are you going to do? I sometimes finish 15 rolls of film a day, it is none of your business! The man wants guarantee that you will not sell it there.

In such a case what do you do?

What can I do, I provide a deposit.

Why don't you buy film where you go?

You can't buy film everywhere. If you buy film in India it will most definitely be over its shelf life because the weather is hot. I took 500 rolls of film and I finished it. Furthermore, they pass all films through the x-ray, but you have to reach an understanding, sometimes you get a good guy who won't insist that you pass the film through the x-ray but if the film passes through an x-ray four times then it is inevitable that the film is damaged. Now there are lead pouches available, you place the film in these pouches and it is protected.

To date many things have been photographed in many ways. There appears to be nothing left in the world to photograph. Do you have some place, some person in mind?

Actually, I have missed the best pictures, I have not been able to shoot them. Either I did not have a camera with me or something else was missing. I can never be wholly satisfied in this world because I am sure that there is still something to shoot. At least theoretically that is the case. You take a picture of a vehicle and it makes a certain shadow and there is a snail in the middle. That is an example of a composition. In five minutes, it will be different. In fifteen minutes, it will be something completely different.

Who has been the most compatible person you have worked with so far?

The best writer I worked with has been Nezihe Araz.

As a journalist which work of yours can you recall as your best?

I believe I have done three major works during my career as a journalist. I believe they serve the history of humanity. They are Noah's Ark, Nemrut Mountain, Afrodisias... Those are the most important features.

What do you think of our new generation of Turkish press photographers?

Is there such a thing?

How do you evaluate the use of photographs by newspapers, mainly their choices?

Now they have positions called picture editor. They are always selected from those who know nothing about photography. Furthermore, for some reason writers are important in our newspapers! Whereas I wholly disagree with that. They can get upset if they like, what can I do? For example, was it in Vietnam or Cambodia, 98 photojournalists were killed while two reporters were killed. The men run to their death but it has no value.

Have any of your photographs been censored? Do you have photographs that you have been unable to share due to various concerns?

Who? Who has such courage bro!

Well, have you auto-censored any of your photographs?

If you are a correspondent for Paris-Match you photograph an event here and send it to France. Somebody writes a caption there that will get you into trouble here. Whereas that is not the reason why you took the photograph in the first place or you had no ill intentions. You know what you shot but somebody writes something else underneath it. One has to be careful not to send such photographs.

Who was the first person to commission a portrait from you?

No. It was me who wanted to take a portrait shot. I thought why are we photographing all these men? Like Adnan Menderes disembarking from an aircraft or somebody is at some meeting, these men are not so important. They are here now but will be gone tomorrow. Whereas a Picasso will always exist for the world civilization same as a Chagall, a Salvador Dali. There are two kinds of men in the world, those who are temporarily prominent and those who are permanently known. I preferred the permanently famous ones, they are five thousand times more important than the others. Who after all is a politician?

You have always kept your distance to politics.

Never mind politics, who cares about politics...

Who comes to your mind as a politician?

Ozal loved cameras. He knew a lot about Leica, did you know that? He recognized all the models from a distance of 5 meters. Cameras and weapons. He would stay working in his office until all hours. I took some very good photographs of Suleyman Demirel for Life. I took pictures of Tansu Ciller, Erbakan. You know I did Ecevit's book. I took the best pictures of Kenan Evren, but I did not give them to him; perhaps I should have done that before he passed away.

Which of the statesmen you have photographed was the most photogenic, natural? Who did you workmost comfortably with?

Ecevit. Because we knew each other, we did not have a problem. He knew I was not going to do anything treacherous with the photograph. For example, he established a cabinet but there was no cabinet yet, there was a desk; the Council of Ministers chamber. I said; 'sit there'. The Prime Minister was there but there was no cabinet. It just occurred to me at that moment. In journalism first, the photograph is established in the mind and then it is eternalized with a camera. That is why I keep saying that the camera is not significant.

Which portrait challenged you the most?

The most challenging portrait was American Kenneth Galbraith. He was an economist, famous MIT professor. I went to interview him, he was a very distracted man, he was 2.5 meters tall, he stood in a strange way, in the wrong place, you couldn't really tell him what to do. I was very challenged with him. The situation was the same with Chagall. Chagall received me in his house but imagine there were no paintings on the walls, not a single one. You go to the house of one of the greatest painters in the world and the walls are blank. Never mind pictures, there was no sign of nails on the walls, the walls were absolutely white, there was one flowerpot and nothing else. What could I do?, I took the man outside and put him on the stairs to photograph him, I showed you.

There are no photographs on the walls of your home either...

Photographs are not important enough to be hung on walls.

What photographs did you fail to take during your career... what frames are missing in your accumulation of photography in your opinion?

There are people I have wanted to photograph and failed to do so for example Charlie Chaplin. Charlie Chaplin established my world, gave me vision, taught me to look at life.

But you tried hard.

Yes, I did but it did not happen. I could not shoot Jean Paul Sartre either.

I believe you had a problem with his secretary?

He had a man named Rosif who was his secretary, he did not understand. He did not recognize me for who I was. He thought to himself, 'A Turkish journalist has come, never mind him.' It happens all the time, you go to a country everybody passes through passport control, when they see a Turkish passport they hold you.

After all these years, you are at the head of a magazine. What do you do at *Iz* magazine?

The task of Iz magazine is to teach the nation about photographs because they are not informed about photography. Various individuals, even historians confuse many issues. Like Abdullah Frères images are not photographs. A photograph is something else. A photograph is witticism. A photograph is a piece of life that will remain for future generations. I believe it is valuable because it has meaning. For example, this Abdullah Frères; the Sultan commissioned him to take photographs of the palace, the mansions and it is a good thing that he did because they are also necessary but people think these are photographs. He has taken some faces, people with national costumes and prepared a book. But these have no place or meaning in the art of photography because during the same era we have the Robertsons, the Berg-grens. The photographs taken by them have composition and meaning, the ones taken by our photographers have just been taken.

When you compare yourself with Henri Cartier-Bresson do you find you are less or more alike in some ways?

You pronounce a name which has been an idol for me.

That is why I am asking.

Of course, we all follow his path. Cartier-Bresson is immortal because we exist. Cartier-Bresson used to be the one, now there are 80 Cartier-Bressons. 100 perhaps 1000.

You are Turkey's representative...

There are others in addition to myself, I am not the only one who knows Cartier-Bresson. I am his friend, the others perhaps find him intimidating.

Who are your favorite photograph artists, who do you like?

To tell you the truth I don't very much care for others than myself.

What is the profile of the followers of photography in Turkey?

Turkey has to be reborn three times to understand photography. It has to pass away three times, be born again and then perhaps it will understand.

You tried your hand in the theater, cinema, writing and finally chose photojournalism; why is that?

I guess I am dumb, that is why. It is easier. The other works require a lot, they are more challenging. Imagine when you are a painter and paint a face, you have to spend fifty hours adjusting the colors and what not. With a camera, you just push a button.

Now don't make it sound so easy...

What can I do, I am a footsoldier of photography, I am a slave.

Your usual modesty... theater has had a major influence on your photographs.

If you observe carefully you will see the impact the theater has on me. The feeling of composition in my photographs is the décor in those plays. If there is a success in all my photo-

graphs – which I doubt – it is because I look from that perspective. They all have a composition. In the theater, the face is very important, gestures. I observed the faces of the actors very carefully. Every day a composition is established in front of you and subsequently it is destroyed.

What about the cinema?

In the meantime, I am interested in the cinema. I go behind the camera. When they do montage, synchronicity, I am there. I view the world through the cinema. All this has had a great impact on photography because I learned planning particularly from the cinema. I am not just saying this to chat. These are accumulations without which there would be no one by the name of Ara Guler. My involvement with the cinema and theater developed into photography. When I look at a tree I don't see wood, I see the green of the tree, I smell it, I feel its life.

In your youth, it is rumored that you used to say 'I plan to exhibit the similarities between crows and humans'.

I was probably letting it fly, who knows!

Do you know how many slides you have in your archive?

It is a lot. I don't know the exact number, perhaps 800,000 or 1 million. But my archive is orderly. I have organized it according to years, venues, people. Sometimes I find photographs that I don't even remember taking. I have a lot of photographs because I have been shooting continuously. I still do.

Have you been able to collect the photographs you took for the newspapers you worked for?

I don't take everything, just the ones I like. I take some negatives for my archive in case I ever need them for anything. I took very few negatives from Yeni Istanbul, likewise with Hurriyet.

You left them there?

One day I received news that Yeni Istanbul was demolished and I went there to take pictures. Anarchy prevailed, youth were demolishing the newspaper and I took their pictures with a Rolleicord camera. I might have been shooting the demolition of my own archive, there were negatives on the ground, among the rocks and soil.

What will happen to your archive, do you have any plans for it, who will get it? What do you want done with it?

The archive should go to a foundation, I don't know. Actually this archive business is a serious business, I really don't know what to do. There is no such foundation in our country, even if it was established it would be transformed into something else after a while. In Turkey, an organization does not necessarily remain the same. For example, my wife's family collected all the books of her grandfather Ahmet Agaoglu and a library was established. Years passed and one day I passed the library – opposite Kariye Mosque, perhaps we went there together. I went inside to ask the manager and he did not know what library he was managing.

When I take pictures of Topkapi Palace a fireman accompanies me to prevent any fires. This is all a lot of rubbish. 'Look kid' I said 'I am here now, if a fire starts what are you going to do?' The fireman in uniform replies, 'I shall report the fire'. 'Who will you report it to?', 'The manager' and then... he has nothing to fight the fire with. Half of the place will have burned by the time the fire department gets there.

I guess you are slightly relieved after seeing Cartier-Bresson's archive...

That is different. He is the founder of Magnum. His position is different, Magnum is the biggest agency in the world that does not earn money.

Why did you get angry with *Time*?

If you recall one or two years ago Time prepared a special edition to commemorate the twelve thousand anniversary of mankind's history and put Einstein on the cover. In the preparation phase, they requested information from me about some historical subjects and great men who grew up in the region. So, I did research. I studied about Sultan Suleyman the Lawmaker, Genghis Khan, went to Topkapi Palace for months. I sent them photographs but they did not use any of them. That is perhaps not so important but when they did not pay me I was upset.

They did not pay you?

I had spent a lot out of my pocket, commissioned special studies. Anyway, when I called to ask what is going on they said I had been late. They said that the commission that had been established for that job had been dissolved. So, there was no responsible counterpart. This time I called the editor and said 'you and your magazine... you are disgrace to the press. Shut the magazine down why don't you! God's curse on you!' and hung up.

Did it do any good?

A few days later they sent me a package. I saw it was a present and no less than a Rolex watch. Of course, I did not respond. Then they telephoned from the office in Rome, I cursed again, 'I don't want to work with you,' I said but they could not afford to lose me, we still continue like that. It is easy to say but I have been with Time for 50 years. Don't think that they pay a lot. It is just pompous. But we aware that if Time wants to destroy or boost a state it can do it. Shall I be completely truthful? I don't worry about anybody. Why should I? For example, if I was offered the position of manager at Time I would not accept it.

Initially you took a stance against digital photography which has subsequently mellowed.

That is a normal reaction. It is like you get used to an old shoe and the new shoe rubs your foot the wrong way. At first I can say I was a bit contrary but I did not really harshly object...

No, you were really adamant in your convictions...

Well, OK, so I was, but then I thought this is a technical evolution that is bound to happen. Imagine a color film can maintain its colors only for 12 years after which it turns bright red. Whereas on digital record everything remains forever, keep their colors. So, which is more important in terms of history? The objective of art is to transmit painters, photographers, musicians of the era they live in to the present with their paintings, photographs and songs respectively with cameras, literature, paintings. This is transmitted to the future generations through art. For example, where do you know the Hittites from, you know them through architecture. Why there are no Ottoman buildings from the 14th Century available in Istanbul, because they are made of wood. Wood like film is perishable while digital is forever. We shall leave a more reliable material in history.

Were you concerned that digital can be manipulated?

Of course, digital also paved the way for forged photography. You take a venue anywhere you want, whereas that is not the true situation.

Well was this practice not carried out by some in the dark room in your time?

I don't consider them photographers anyway, they are the microbes of photography.

Let's get this clear, lots of youth are taking digital photographs. They have this image in their minds that Ara Guler opposes digital.

That is not true.

What is your opinion on Photoshop?

Photoshop is good, it helped me to correct the picture, you take off the spots and whatever. To that extension it can be alright but they take your photograph and make you walk in New York. There used to be Daguerreotype which was followed by shooting on record film. It is a similar evolution. What used to be done with chemical is now done with electronics.

To what extent does the brand and the quality of the camera contribute to photography?
In my opinion the camera does not carry much weight. Of course, a good camera makes the job easier but don't forget that it is only a recording machine.

To date you have taken tens of thousands of photographs but you only share a limited number of photographs, say 2 out of 36 frames...

Not even that much.

Sometimes you use none of them. What is your criteria for sharing photographs with the public?

The criteria is mine. Actually, not all photographs are artistic photographs. Just because it was taken by Ara Guler does not make it an artistic photograph. An artistic photograph has a scale, a measure, when it tells me something, when it adds something to your future it becomes an artistic photograph; otherwise it remains as an interview photograph. That is why I have taken so many photographs, I go to India and take a few thousand photographs. None of them really matter. Those places have already been photographed by thousands of people.

What is the "sine qua non" for Ara Guler when selecting a photograph? What do you look for initially in a photograph that you have taken?

Now look, you don't take just one picture, they all resemble one another. One of them has captured the composition, it reflects the object perfectly, I say perfectly but it can always be better. You choose the best one. You put the photograph you have chosen on the lighting table and reject the others (into a box). Then something else comes along, you need to select 200-300 frames for a feature. I am talking about long term features, not small scale newspaper features. When you have the photographs lined up you actually do not need most of them so you discard them. Actually, the master in this subject is our editor at Magnum by the name of Jimmy Fox. He calculates everything, how a hand is supposed to be and he is very good at this, he is a picture editor. Here a picture editor is appointed who has seen four pictures in his life. Forget about seeing a book. He selects a picture without justification and this is considered important by others, what can I say?

You have received a lot of criticism for failing to tutor anyone. Why don't you share your experiences and why have you made no effort to gain new people into the profession of photojournalism?

Photojournalism is not something that can be learned. Can I transform you into an artist? Can a Picasso be created?

Do you think this is the absolute truth?
If only it could be done, but it can't. Why not?

Have you ever tried?

What do you mean have I tried? I have not, why should I, let somebody else try. Why should I try and lose time!

All right, I totally respect that there cannot be any obligation in this. On the other hand, the knowledge, the experience you have, this expertise, will you be taking it to the grave?

My bro, if you knew everything what would you actually know? Perhaps it is not that important.

It goes without saying that as Ara Guler you have a certain accumulation.

Yes, there is an Ara Guler, it has accumulated on its own. I am not filling my head like a jar with anything, if it has accumulated on its own then so be it, what can I do!

Who are you tutoring, teaching the profession?

There are a few people.

You are secretive in this matter, why is that?

What do you mean by secretive?

Like you don't want to talk about having people around you, teaching them…

Bro this is an individual profession. For example, a novel is not written by five people. That is the way a photojournalist operates. Does Salgado work with somebody, or Josef Koudelka… it is not a collective effort. Whereas cinema and theater are collective efforts, they are realized with more people. Somebody comes and says 'our boy has grown, he is interested in photography, tutor him why don't you'… come and let me tutor you. Whereas the man knows nothing about the job. If a man is writing a book you have to let him write it alone, leave him free so he can find his way.

What do you think of youth?

I look at present day youth who think they know everything after three days… whereas I did all kinds of jobs in film studios to get to where I am today. You have to start from the beginning. That is valid also for photographers. A man takes a camera and shoots three films and opens an exhibition the next day. That cannot be possible.

It is rumored that once upon a time you recommended youth to 'stay away from photography, it is a virus'.

Of course, it is like a disease, a cancer. You can't get rid of it. And then you suffer.

174

Speaking of this, there are numerous young photographers in Turkey taking photographs of landscapes, portraits and abstract photographs without much meaning. Who is going to tell them to 'stop, what you are shooting is not photography'. How will these people learn what photography is?

Where did I learn from bro?

Do they have to experience what you did?

For one thing, it is a matter of culture. Photography, the art events in the world are all cultural events. Our people do not deal with that side of the matter at all.

What is the infrastructure required for a photograph?

Like I say, it is a matter of culture. But what is culture? The man does not have a life system. For instance, enjoy life, do everything in life and generate a meaning from it. Reading books, going to the cinema; all this is happening but what is the resulting accumulation in your mind?
Actually, you visualize something, for instance something passes by here but if you can't find a composition there then you can't plan a composition. The composition has to be appropriate. The composition can only be appropriate if you have seen the relevant pictures, if you are able to compose, etc.

In other words, it does not happen only by the pressing of the button...

The moment you press the button is the time you have record it. The photograph is prepared in your mind and you press the button not to lose it. The camera steps in which means nothing. If I get you the best typewriter on the market will you write the best novel with it? In that case monsieur Kodak would have been the best photographer in the world because he manufactures all the cameras. Well, is it so? No, it is not, the best photographer is Eugene Smith, Cartier-Bresson but not Monsieur Kodak, not monsieur Ilford.

Do you believe in education in terms of photography?

Everything can be learned with education but is every academy graduate a painter bro? How on earth can it be! A thousand people graduate from the academy and perhaps five become artists. Or rather they think of themselves as artists and convince others.

Have you applied to teach anywhere?

I get frustrated, I cannot...

Have you ever tried to do so?

No. They made me a teacher at an academy, I went there and told them to fire me imme-diately. That was at Mimar Sinan University...

Have you adjusted to the New World Order?

As you know the world applies the build, operate, transfer system, 'use and discard' they say and the wheel of economy rotates, the systems are established accordingly. Whereas a Ger-man-made Leica was bought to use for a lifetime, in that case let everybody divorce their wives and get new wives. Can you discard your good mother? Your mother will always be your mother, this is fake and impossible. A person likes something, a tool, a painting and becomes attached to it. I have millionaire friends living in Europe, etc. When they stay at hotels they take 2-3 of their favorite paintings with them, have them insured and hang them on the hotel room walls; these are Renoirs, Cézannes.

You found out your birth date at the age of 30, isn't that very late?

The 16th of August. Until that date, I knew I had been born, but I did not know the date.

What is your sign?

Leo. About this being born business; I went to a fortune teller in India with Suna. I told the fortune teller the date. The man looked at some books, calculated stars and gave me a map: a map of life. I keep it. One day I will have it read by somebody. Be informed that such a map exists but I can't find it now.

How do you see yourself from the outside? People have the impression that you are main-ly cantankerous, why do you think that is?

Stupidity drives me crazy is why. Somebody asks something stupid and I admonish them and it makes me a cantankerous man.

You do not appear very fastidious, like you wanted luxury... you don't mind where you lay your head.

I will sleep anywhere bro. Years ago when we went up Agri Mountain for the first time, we stayed at a hotel in Dogubayazit, there were donkeys in the lower floor of the hotel and a balcony above. I saw the same arrangement in Pakistan. I reserved three rooms and took the one in the middle and told him not to put anyone in the rooms next to me. There were 3 beds in the room, at midnight somebody came in and lay down because they rented the beds instead of rooms. The animals tied downstairs make the place warm, their heat floats up.

How do you spend your day?, What is your routine starting from the morning?, What do you do?

I get up in the morning but not very early. I don't shave, I shave once a week if that. I might not shave for a long time, I enjoy myself if I am not meeting anyone of course. Then I go to the coffee shop and see what's going on. When I had lots of assignments, I didn't have minutes to spare but I am more relaxed now. I am correspondent for Paris-Match, Stern, Life, I look at Sunday Times, there are fax messages to see even if can't read them all, and there are questions asked that need answering etc.

Does this situation make you happy? That you have more time for life that is.

I have this accumulation. This accumulation is in the form of an archive... now I need to make a book out of it. Don't forget that I took pictures of Afrodisias 50 years ago and there is also other material to be prepared...

It made you happy, didn't it?

Well, yes it did but what is the result going to be now? For example, you write this massive book but the money will be inconsequential. How much will you get for this book? People act in commercials – various rubbish actors and do you have an idea of what they are paid?

I do indeed. Incredible figures.

Well so? What kind of a country is this!

Did you earn from journalism?

You make plans before you leave. If I plan to go to Pakistan, from there to Afghanistan, then Nepal and Thailand etc. You are still in Galatasaray Tosbaga Street and you have already paid 10,000, 20,000 lira before setting off without going anywhere. How can you go? I never really earned money anyway. The newspaper pays me 2,000 dollars where I spend 5,000 dollars just for film. Then there are hotel bills, food to pay, travel costs plus the aggravation that is included. A freelance journalist never earns money. If they did, I would have, I am telling you.

You don't seem to care for money anyway, your photographs sell up to 700,000 dollars but you did not want 5 cents.

The daughter-in-law of Koc Family, Caroline Koc, is a friend of mine. They have a society, the Family Planning and Health in Turkey, they collect money for the indigent, etc. She came to see me in a café and she said 'Bro help me. Give me your pictures so I can sell and get revenue for the society'. 'How many do you want?' '15 would be nice'. I gave them to her. They hold open auctions at the Koc Museum, they invited all the millionaires; they invited me also. You have to pay 250 dollars per person to enter. I could not attend because I had a Signature Day in Antalya. Plus, I don't like occasions like that, so I was saved. Auctioneer Rafi Portakal was selling 15 Ara Guler photographs, nothing else was on sale. So many people got together to buy Ara Guler's photographs. Do you know for how much the first and least expensive photograph was sold? 40,000 liras. The photograph depicting handing over a picture of a letter from the porthole was sold for 85,000 lira. After that time one day I needed an Apple laptop, the Apple distributor in Turkey was Koc, and they sent me one. That is the way it is.

Do you think that you could have done this profession without the economic means of your family?

Well it is like this, if you have noticed, all French photographers come from wealthy families; for example, Cartier-Bresson, Marc Riboud. Let's say that photography is the toy of rich kids. That is because your father does not send you to work, you go to school and take photographs in your spare time or not. If they were not wealthy they would not send you to school but to a factory to earn money. Gultekin Cizgen came to me and said 'I am going to be a photographer'... I asked him 'tell me, are your parents wealthy or not?'. That was the first sentence because this is something rich kids play with.

Where did you get the opportunity to act in a commercial, and then regretted it?

For years, I have taken photographs of people with ease. The worst thing that could happen to a photojournalist happened to me after I got part at the commercial,, I became famous. Even the sanitation workers recognized me. I went to buy gasoline for the car and the attendant said 'say the "GSM company name" and I will give you the gasoline'. I met my match of course. Furthermore, there are many film makers who shoot commercials. Nowadays every tom, dick and harry become film makers, is it so easy to be a film maker! How can it be, who makes them film makers?

But you have acted in films.

Yes, I have. They came and begged me to participate. I never got any money.

So you have acted a lot!

Yes, I am in every one of Yesim's films. She is a great director.

Who do you see, which ones of your former friends are still around?

There are a few, there have not been so many losses.

What do you do in the evenings, how do you spend your time?

I go home around seven thirty, eightish, and watch television.

What do you watch?

I must listen to the news, I am curious anyway. I like debating programs, when I say like I mean we get to see ourselves as we are. Then there are some very good documentaries.

I know you don't care about football, you don't support any team but I am sure you favored some team in your youth?

My school team would have been my favorite, Galatasaray. But not any more. If I were the prime minister, I would shut down all football teams.

When did you learn English?

I learned English doing journalism but all my writings are done by my wife in English of course.

You used to do stained glass works at one time.

I tried to do stained glass on one of the windows of my house and cut myself. One window was done by my artist friend Mustafa Pilevneli and I did another one.

Can you cook?

I haven't got a clue about kitchen works. I can't even boil an egg.

You mean you have never cooked?

No, never. I go to a restaurant to eat. I can make tea because my wife has already put the water in the pot, I light it and use tea bag.

How do you get along with alcohol?

I have always consumed alcohol. Yesterday I had four glasses of wine (in Koudelka Istanbul).

What are you most afraid of?

I fear earthquakes. It is a disaster without redemption. I see, take photographs, I have become an expert on earthquakes. I have witnessed so many…

Then you have been rather restless recently…

Of course. I went to Adapazari after the earthquake, I went to Gediz, I have been to many locations after the earthquakes. When I went to Varto, the earth was still shaking, there was water spurting like geysers in the earthquake in Varto. Erzurum was like that, too.

You used to smoke a lot...

I had a lot of interviews going on, more than I can remember. It is not easy, there is a terrible stress that is why I started smoking. The work carries a lot of responsibility. You have to meet the deadlines, you worry what is going to be written as captions, you worry about mishaps.

When did you stop?

I stopped smoking 10 years ago.

Your father was a heavy smoker too, how much were you smoking?

Four packs per day. I was a chain smoker. I was so full of smoke that if somebody had attached a propeller in my butt I would have travelled to the islands...

Cigarettes appear to be your signature. There are no photographs of you without a cigarette...

Yes, that is right. But no more. I did not smoke anything else such as pot, pipe. Once I tried smoking a pipe but it made me sick so I threw it away. I have enjoyed a hookah in Emirgan, took a few breaths...

Do you have any other addictions?

Addiction is bad. I can't remember now but perhaps I am addicted to something.

How is your health? You recently had a check up.

I am fine for now.

You had an ulcer at one point?

It is gone bro.

Where did the fear of flying come from?

I never had this fear before but for the past year I started having this fear of flying. I'm ok in a helicopter but on a large passenger plane I am scared. It feels contradictory to me. Do you know how much an aircraft weights, 300 tons. 300 tons flies in the air and I am supposed to sit in it. No way. Imagine iron is flying at 10,000 meters and you are inside, then there is gravity, and the engines carry it?

You save every newspaper clipping, every invitation.

I just started such a collection, I did not have one before. I keep things to remember important events.

What kind of music do you listen to?

Jazz, classical music, Turkish music.

Do you remember the first time you were interviewed?

The first interview with me was about the exhibition.

You appear attached to brown, beige, cream colors...

Yes, yellow, khaki, military colors. Never mind that my current shirt is blue. Nikos sent it, it is thick and keeps me warm, I am not wearing it because of its color.

Who gave you a raw deal in life?

I never thought about that, if something comes to my mind, I will tell you. All newspaper bosses are the same. For example, Sevket Rado gave me a raw deal. He was my boss. They made us workhard for little money because we did not need money; they took advantage of us by making rich kids interested in journalism.

You have printed photographs of persons you have photographed and sent them to the people.

It is a gesture, after all they posed for me so I might just as well send them a copy.

You have even kept your uniform from military service...

I can't fit in it anymore and then it has been eaten by moths. There is only the cap left, Fatih found it and put it in a box to protect it from moths.

Do you go shopping?

I hate shopping. I have this thing, for example, if I need a tweed jacket I buy it in the United Kingdom, I also buy shoes from the UK. I have not shopped here for anything.

Do you shop yourself or does your wife help you?

I shop by myself. I can't be bothered to ask for someone else's opinion, I go in, like it and buy it. I would go crazy if I had to tour shops.

I ask these obnoxious questions so that people can get to know Ara Guler; is there any feature about you that you would rather not have?

I am volatile and use foul language.

In what situations?

Well, actually I am a shitty man.

I am sure that is not true...

I saw some nice vignettes that you had drawn once upon a time. Why did you stop drawing?

I didn't stop because I never started, everybody doodles some. Just because I drew two pictures does not mean anything...

I noticed an interesting style and balance in them.

Well after all, I have taken so many photographs of paintings. I have so many artist friends, something is bound to rub off.

Your favorite food?

Not food but I like lakerda (salted bonito) a lot. But when it is well done. The reason why I can't live anywhere else than in Turkey is because the lakerda is good. If it were not for the lakerda then I would live elsewhere bro.

Do you read newspapers?

I read a newspaper every morning. I read all newspapers including the obituaries. However, I skip news that does not interest me for example, stupid economy news, crisis is here, crisis is over, who said what about a crisis, who cares what somebody says!

Your favorite author?

There are so many bro.

Which work affected you the most?

Ahmet Kutsi Tecer's "Kosebasi" and Haldun Taner's "Fazilet Eczanesi" affected me immensely.

Painters...

As a Turkish painter I give you Orhan Peker. These are men I believe to be painters. Maybe a couple of others.

Can you name any photographers?

From time to time various people make something, take very good photographs. Recently, I was on a jury and I said to myself 'If I took a picture like that I would never take any more pictures, I have not taken such a picture in my life'. It was somebody local, I don't know who. During another jury task, there were pictures of laborers, they were lovely. They received awards and I said we should use them in Iz and we used three or four of them.

This generates hope.

So, there are interesting things. However, what happens is this; a person might take wonderful photographs and you say what a wonderful guy, compare him to James Nachtwey. The next day he takes a picture of his sister which is rubbish. There is no consistency, no integrity. Actually, it takes around 20 years to understand that a photographer is a real photographer. There is an art historian called Marchinez – you wrote about him. For 15 years, he did not print me in any magazine, he kept me waiting. Most people use journalism, photojournalism as a stepping stone into public relations manager position in a bank. When you stay in the profession for 20 years, that means you equal the task, you are a foot soldier of the job.

Which is your favorite photograph, The Fishermen or Tramway?

I can't say. I like Tramway more; Marc Riboud and Cartier-Bresson preferred this one. As you know there is no negative.

Fishermen from Kumkapi is actually not bad in terms of composition...

You are right but some good photographs have only one frame, can you imagine?

You took it with a Rolleicord right?

It is a coincidence that all my good pictures have been taken with a Rolleicord, what luck.

So, it does not have to be a Leica.

The camera is not important, what is important are the men behind the cameras. A good photographer can take a picture with a sewing machine. A good camera does not make you a good photographer, getting a good typewriter does not make you a great writer.

Yes, but in your heart don't you say to yourself 'I think this is the best?'

I love them all actually. Every one of them has a meaning.

You perceive them as your children.

They are like my children. Actually, no photographers remain with 5,000 pictures. Guy de Maupassant wrote 480 stories. He was poor, if he did not write for the newspaper continuously, he would be starving. That is why he wrote every day, he wrote stories every day, he lived on that income. So, is everything written by Guy de Maupassant important? At most you are familiar with 10 of them. I keep telling Yasar Kemal, 'keep your shirt on, you will be remembered with two novels in the world.'

Is there any photograph that was published but that you did not like? In other words, a photograph that was liked by the public but you wished you had not taken?

Lots.

For example?

I can find such pictures, there are many. If you remember my book, Old Istanbul Memories, that was published seven times. The seventh edition is being printed now. When the most recent edition was being made, I changed 17 or 19 pictures. The book is not about Ara Guler's beautiful photographs, it is about beautiful photographs that describe Istanbul. There are a lot of unnecessary photographs of boats and the Bosphorus, pictures which are nothing special, not great in any way.

Which one is the people's favorite among your photographs?

Their favorite picture is the one with two chairs and a ship in the background. People are romantic, they force themselves to be romantic. They want to fall in love but they cannot, it is difficult. They wait for Godot hoping he will come.

Why is the ideal Leica size 24x36?

Bro, I don't know how they figured it out. It is a perfect size.

Is it very well balanced?

It is a great invention. You can describe a lot with it. A person who has stayed with Rolleiflex means that he has not taken a photograph yet. For example, the 6x9 is also a good form. The camera used by old times for example is 6x9 Linof.

Do you prefer black and white or color photographs?

It depends, some subjects appear better in color but black and white photographs are solid photographs. Perhaps it is because that is the way we have familiarized ourselves. We have black and white in our genes.

For example, black and white would have difficulty in depicting India, right? That chaos needs color...

Of course, think of the colors, the shadows, yellow, India is yellow.

Apparently, you keep films in the refrigerator.

Where else would you keep them!

When did you shoot your last roll of film, it has probably been a while?

Yes, it has.

Who processed it?

I did it myself. I have a very good laboratory. However, the final process is given to the laboratory.

Were your last shots taken 10 years ago?

I can't remember exactly, something might have happened which I shot, I have shot perhaps 6x6 or I just had that camera with me.

Now I am coming to the most controversial issue, you do not consider photography an art form...

No, I don't, I want to but it is not. No matter what you do.

You believe that art is generated out of lies, it tells lies, it depicts the world as a falsification.

But I don't say that.

Oscar Wilde says in "*The Decay of Lying*" that art cannot be done without lies...

Imagine a director. The difference between me and a director is that I walk around, see beautiful compositions, and wait for a man to move over there. When he moves where I want I shoot and I present you with reality. That is a photograph. OK? Now let's look at the film maker, it is a cowboy film. This man has to shoot that man but how. A train is coming, a man jumps off a horse and shoots the man. A director plans this scene. There is an acting artist, the locomotive is a lie, everything is a lie, the man does not really die, you just think he has. Hamlet dies every night; how many Hamlets are there! Art is really generated from lies. Which painting made by Picasso depicts the truth, woman with massive ass, a headless man, are they the truth?

Although your paths and styles differ immensely, you and Sahin Kaygun have an understanding.

He was a good kid. Sahin Kaygun is one of the few whose photography is an art. He actually mixed things in his photography. His work is more artistic.

Actually, you want distinct art photographs like those made by photographer Sahin Kaygun, not works that combine elements...

What we do is closest to art, it cannot be argued that it is art in the full meaning of the words. For example, you know Marchinez – in his opinion Dali is not a painter but an illustrationist. Abidin is an illustrationist. Illustration is not an art, neither is caricature. In the world, Turkey and African states have rubbish in terms of art.

Your voicemail in the office says 'you have reached the press telephone of photojournalist Ara Guler'.

That is because I am a photojournalist. I consider myself to be a photojournalist instead of a photograph artist.

When we went to Bursa and said "I am a photojournalist" a lady on the jury panel replied 'Come on, you are too modest'.

Actually, she was right. In our circles photojournalists are the least sophisticated. She believed photojournalism was something unsavory.

You consider yourself a photojournalist.

Of course. I am a photojournalist, not a photographer; I certainly am not an artist. I shoot what I see. I don't do art. I transmit what is natural, what I see to people. That is called photojournalism.

What separates a photojournalist from a photographer?

A photographer is very different from a photojournalist.

I am asking what that difference is.

Look, a photojournalist is the man who runs to the scene when an explosive detonates. Whereas a photographer runs away from the scene, runs to his wife; whereas the other rushes towards death, throws himself in danger, that is the difference. For me a photographer is non-existent, there is only the photojournalist. A photojournalist records history with his camera. Some call themselves photojournalists. Photojournalism is a different setup. A journalist can become a photojournalist.

You are ascribing a lot on photojournalists.

Naturally, it is not the photojournalist's only task to monitor the development of events, he is also tasked with transmitting the life of the era, its arts, traditions and customs, what people are involved in, their joys, their sorrows to the future eras.

You have been the man who runs towards the explosion all your life.

Yes, I have been but everyone does not know that, do you know where they recognize me from? They recognize me from my photographs. I am a photographer not a photography artist, who says that I am an artist. Beethoven is an artist or Mozart. For example, in the Sirkeci incident a bomb went off and where did I go? I went to the place where the detonation took place. I took photographs which were printed on the newspapers. I had a writer with me, the editor of Cumhuriyet but he did not come because he said 'Bro I can't see blood'. That is the difference between writers and photojournalists.

That is your choice but does everybody holding a camera have to be a photojournalist?

No.

One can run towards the bomb as well as away from it...

He should, he should save his life, is he stupid? I am a fool! He should run and kiss his girl on a street corner...

Is the perception of photojournalism different between your era and the current era?

In my time photojournalists were considered of equal importance as writers. That is not the case now.

In other words, photojournalism has undergone a transformation since your time...

Photojournalism has declined actually. Now everyone is an artist for nothing and that is only possible with photography. Everybody takes photographs. You press a button and become an artist. God sent this and it is a good thing or the world would have perished. It is so important I am afraid to walk the streets for fear of bumping one of these important men.

Is photojournalism considered a man's job?

In my opinion it is a branch of journalism. A female journalist can't go into a war zone, if she did she would die. She can't run for long, she does not know how to take cover, she will get hurt, die. In other words, a woman will not be dispatched anyway. They dispatch batchelors because if they send a married man and he dies then the compensation will be a lot.

In your opinion what is the fundamental difference between a Turkish photojournalist and a foreign photojournalist?

There is an abyss in terms of education for one thing. However, there is another issue, the persistence that Turks have. Now if a task is given to a British photojournalist to photograph something in Dolmabahce Palace, Topkapi Palace or Buckingham Palace, he will go there dressed appropriately. If the man at the gate says that we do not allow journalists, the British photojournalist will respect that, give up and return to his office and their paper won't print any pictures. Whereas if you give this task to a Turkish photojournalist, he will get that photograph from between a rock and a hard place. If you repel him from the door, he will enter through a window. Once he has been tasked, he is a Turk, he will not be distracted. Turkish photojournalist might not be high quality but they are predatory, persistent and they will do the job. He will enter through a window, take a shot which might be blurry but he will get it. He delivers a photograph, it is poor but so what, but the other one? It is better than bringing nothing bro. Therefore, a Turkish journalist is better although he might die for it.

About permission, should permission be asked when taking a photograph?

No permission necessary. Actually, a photographer does not ask anyone for permission and then gets violent, shouts and intimidates. When photographers such as Cartier-Bresson or Eugene Smith take photographs, the moment will be spoiled if permission is asked. Imagine two people are playing a game and you want to shoot the moment, if you interrupt to ask whether you can take a picture or not the game will become crippled, its naturality will be ruined. There is such a law now, four United Nations lawyers take decisions about human rights etc. In that case, all the photographs the greatest photographer on earth Cartier-Bresson has taken have been taken without notice. In that case must we photograph a world without humans? We can't keep asking for permission from everyone! Just because two lawyers from the United Nations say so, do photojournalists have to take their orders? They should give up lawyering, photojournalism is more important.

What is needed to be a good photojournalist? I am not asking about tools and equipment.

He must know how to see. He has to see, understand and assess and then say 'let me take this picture' and press the button. Taking a photograph is more than pressing a button. But which of these people are aware of this. Talk to them and see it for yourself.

Do you continue your storytelling with your photographs?

Even when I was writing stories I was actually taking photographs – you have probably read my short stories. It happens and why? It means my mind leaks somewhere. Even when I write stories I actually write about a photograph. I describe a landscape or create a world or prepare a décor and place the subject in it.

The most important element in your photographs is the human being...

Of course, it is! Without humans, there is nothing. A person who is not fond of people cannot be a photographer. Why does a photojournalist go into a war zone to take photographs? These men endanger their lives to tell others that there is a disaster going on, don't join them, I love you esteemed humanity, please do not get involved.
I get injured for you, I die. Look at this photograph and don't do it again.

Was the human element initially present in your photographer's mind?

Of course. There is nothing without humans. An aircraft is manufactured for humans, roads are built for humans. The wheels of vehicles turn to take humans somewhere. Everything is for humans. Why are temples, mosques built, for humans.

You have been to many places in Turkey, in your opinion which venue has generated the best photographs?

That depends on the climate, the light. For example, this street that you showed a while back has a different composition now. The magic that enhances our world is nature, the cosmos itself, when light is spread it is beautiful, when the light is gathered it becomes dark, something else. Therefore, the magic paint will always be present. This is light, everything starts with light. Like the holy books say, God said let there be light, light appeared and people started to see. Then people started to draw pictures onto the walls of caves so they would not forget what they had seen, like first hunting trips which generated into art.

There is an opinion that photographs can be taken only during a certain time of day...

Because that beautiful light is not available. Early hours of the morning are good up to 9:30-10. Then after 5 is good. However, it also depends on the weather. For example, in summer 4 o'clock has raw light which gets better at 6. During other seasons 4 o'clock can be pitch black. Light is important. Light is everything. Art always starts with light.

You have said "me and my photographs are slightly romantic".

If you think about what my photographs could be called; I could be a romantic realist, right? If you add romanticism to reality then you could be considered a social romantic...

What makes a photograph valuable? I mean, what makes a photograph stand out among others? Is it clarity for example?

No, it is not a technical matter. Does a picture take you somewhere? Why do you read a book by Thomas Mann? Why do you look at a painting by Picasso? You have to look at a photograph like he does. When I say art, I mean a photograph, not an interview photograph. Does it transport you into another world, does it give you a taste of something else? Does it generate thoughts in your mind? Does it teach you how to observe a horizon?

Those are the photographs I am talking about. They add something to you. Clarity is a minor issue, perhaps they can even be blurry.

You say "a good photograph should say something". Lots of people take pictures which say a lot in their opinion...

They think that what they have photographed says something. The person who has taken the shot, has attributed the picture a meaning. They assume that everybody sees it. Most of them survive, but are they shooting water in a well or shooting pictures that are not clear. Perhaps they are shooting pain.

How many cameras do you have?

I don't know, I have not counted but I believe around 40-50.

Have you sold or traded any of them?

I had one camera stolen in Ankara. That is the only camera I lost.

In your frames, you mostly use a wide-angle lens. Is that so that you can capture everything?

I want to gather the whole world into a photograph, that feeling. With a wide angle, you lose composition but my hand is accustomed to it as is my eye, I take good pictures with a wide angle.

First you take the photograph in your mind and then transfer it onto your camera.

That is what I have been saying from the beginning, first you plan the composition in your mind and then you use the camera not to lose it.

How many times have you pressed the button since you first held a camera?

I have pressed a lot.

Give a ballpark figure.

I have 1 million Photographs. I have taken 1 million more which means that I have pressed the button 2-3 million times.

What era in the history of humanity would you have liked to photograph the most?

I have thought about that many times, in which century I would have wanted to be a photographer and if I was the only one. For instance, I would have liked to be around in the time of Sultan Mehmet the Conqueror, in the era of the Lawmaker. Imagine that you are living in the same era as Jesus and you take his pictures. Could anything be greater!

You used to carry a camera everywhere, now you are not bothered?

Well what can I do, I am fed up.

Is there nothing left to shoot in Istanbul?

It was never about venue what I shot. I shot pieces of life.

Eyup appeals to you a bit.

Eyup is one of the old places.

In your mind is that where Istanbul lives?

There is some of the old life left, there are other places like Sutluce. There used to be Mevlevi lodges, those old places have been run down, dirty.

With what you know today what profession would you prefer?

I would like to be an architect. An architect is somebody who adds something to the crust of the earth. Making a wall means making a lot of things. Why do you draw a wall? One side is yours and the other side is mine. That is where separation starts, ownership, the reason for wars. An architect does that. Have you ever thought about that? I bet you have not. The story starts with the building of that wall. Cain and Abel fought within walls. I would have liked to be the man that made that wall.

Why did you reject UNESCO's offer of being a diplomat?

They wanted to engage me, I even filled the forms. In other words, I almost became a diplomat, I was going to start at UNESCO but at that time I was getting marryed to Perihan so I did not accept.

Is it because Perihan did not know any foreign language?

Who told you that?

Is it true?

It is true. She did not know any language, it would have been difficult.

Now that you are exactly 80 years old, is there something you wish you would have done, any regrets?

I am sure there are but I can't think of anything right now. I wish I could have photographed Charlot, Sartre. I wish I could have photographed Einstein.

I was asking more about life and not photography.

No, not for now anyway, if I think about it I am sure to come up with something.

Why did you not have children?

I really don't know.

Would you have liked to have children?

It would have been nice. Now it emerges, if there was a child, he would inherit something. What is anyone going to do with that inheritance, perhaps sell all the photographs in kilograms? Imagine somebody buys 5 kilograms of Ara Guler photographs, they are weighed on scales.

Have you given up the idea of opening a museum with your photographs and archives?

No.

Is there a bureaucratic obstacle...

I have a two storey museum but a private museum for me.
If I open up to the public what is the point?

What percentage of your work have people seen?

Not even one percent.

It is evident that when writing dissertations about you, academicians have been unable to place you into any mould, but your approach to photography does not please the artist brothers who practice photography as a form of art. They want to speak the same language with you but you have no such pattern.

My bro, I live for myself, I look at the world for myself, I take photographs for myself, if they are of use to mankind that makes it even better. All good and well and thank you but I take photographs for myself. I also take photographs for journalism. My concern is not who will look at the photographs and their opinions.

In your opinion can a personal style be reflected in photography?

Of course, style is personal anyway.

When you say "Photography in Turkey started with us" who do you mean?

Actually, what we have here is the continuation of what exists in the world. When I say it started with us, I mean photojournalism started with this but there is also the predate. There are a few. German agencies, newspapers which have printed photographs of war. Photographs did not exist before. When photographs were unavailable, draftsmen would draw pictures. That is how stencil was invented. This was followed by the generation of the halftone. With the generation of the halftone it became possible to print photographs, otherwise stencils could only draw.

What has Othmar contributed to you and Turkish photography?

Othmar brought a nice romantic atmosphere. He ran after beauty, he took beautiful romantic photographs. Sunlight etc., he calculated the light.

Well did he affect you personally?

I did know Othmar. His shop was here.

You must have been about 3 years old when Othmar opened his shop in Beyoglu.

I have a photograph where me and my nephew play the cinema. My father took the photograph; my father took the picture and gave it to Othmar. Othmar corrected it, made a reproduction, that is the photograph.

How did you feel when you received awards such as the Légion d'Honneur, the Presitdency Grand Award for Culture?

Not much. I get a lot of awards. Of course, although I did not get excited I did enjoy getting the Presidency and Légion d'Honneur awards because they are hard to get. The Légion d'Honneur is something given to me by a foreigner. For me it is more important to be awarded by one of my own. The Presidency award is more important to me than the Légion d'Honneur because it represents the appreciation of my nation, a foreigner's appreciation is not so important for me.

What is your association with Ara Cafe?

Ara Cafe is like my tenant. That building was left by my father.

Everybody thinks it is yours...

People can think what they please...

A major part of your day is spent there...

That is because I don't want to go up five floors and prefer to sit there.

Does the interest of people bother you? When they ask for your signature, they want to take photographs together...

I enjoy it although it is a drudgery bro.

But it is not something bad.

No, it is not bad. Perhaps I might even get upset if nobody comes around for a few days.

How should people contact you?

They can come and find me at Ara Cafe. I have a telephone, they can call.

(As we pass Sisli Armenian Cemetery)

See this is my next address. Our family grave is here, I can give an appointment here in 25 years, come if you like.

We shall meet there in the end.

But ours is the Armenian Cemetery.

We might enter through different doors but we shall end up in the same place...

Awards and Honors (1961-2008)

"Master of Leica", Germany 1961.

British Journal of Photography Year Book, United Kingdom 1961.

Association of Journalists first prize for Photography, Istanbul 1979.

Prime Ministry Directorate General of Press and Information Press distinguished Services Plaque, Ankara 1981.

Prime Ministry Directorate General of Press and Information Honorable mention for 'Contribution to Promoting Turkey Abroad', Ankara 1991.

IFSAK "Photographer of the Year Award", Istanbul 1995.

Istanbul University Faculty of Communication "Successful Communicators Award for 1995", 1995.

World Book Award, Istanbul 1995.

World Fellowship Award Call for Peace and Universal Brotherhood

World Brotherhood Union Mevlana Supreme Foundation, Istanbul 1997.

Marmara University Faculty of Communication "Honor award for those at the top", Istanbul 1999.

Aydin Dogan Foundation "Visual Arts Grand Award", Istanbul 1999.

Turkey Journalists' Society, 50 years in the Profession Press Service Award, Istanbul 1999.

Photographer of the Century in Turkey, Istanbul 2000.

Armenian Patriarchate Order of Merit, Istanbul 2000.

"Légion d'Honneur; Officier Des Arts et Des Lettres" Medal, Istanbul 2000.

Truva Culture and Art Awards Photograph Award, Istanbul 2002.

Republic of Turkey Ministry of Foreign Affairs, 2003 Turkey in Japan Special Award, Tokyo 2003.

Photographic Art Society, Honorary Award for Fifty Years in Photography, Ankara 2003.

Yildiz Technical University title of Honorary PhD, Istanbul 2004

Republic of Turkey Grand Presidential Culture and Art award, Ankara 2005.

Republic of Turkey Ministry of Culture and Tourism, Culture and the Arts Service Award, Ankara 2008.

Books (1960-2008)

Oster om Eufrat, Tidens Forlag, Isvec, 1960.

Nazim Hikmet: In Quest'anno 1941, Milano, 1961.

Young Turkey, Mariana Noris, Mead & Company, New York, 1964

Topkapi Palace-Portraits of Sultans, Dogan Kardes Publications, Istanbul, 1967.

Can Pazari, Vay Kurban, Fikret Otyam, Dogan Publications, 1968.

Turkei, Terra Magica, Munich, 1970.

Hagia Sophia, Lord Kinross, Newsweek Books, New York, 1972

Creative Americans, Ara Guler, American News Center, 1975.

The Splendour of Islamic Calligraphy, Thames & Hudson, London, 1976.

Harems, Chene & Hachette, Paris, 1980.

Fikret Mualla, Abidin Dino, Cem Publications, Istanbul, 1980.

Photographs, Ara Guler, Karacan Publications, Istanbul, 1980.

Mevlana Celaleddin Rumi and the Whirling Dervishes, Talat SaitHalman-Metin and Dost Publications, 1983.

Bedri Rahmi, Turan Erol, Cem Publications, Istanbul, 1984.

Mimar Sinan, Prof. Aptullah Kuran, Hurriyet Vakfi Publications, Istanbul, 1986.

Istanbul Sarkisi, Celik Gulersoy, Istanbul Kitapligi, 1987.

Mimar Sinan, Prof. Aptullah Kuran, Institute of Turkish Studies, Washington DC, 1987.

Ara Guler's Film Makers, Hill Publications, Istanbul, 1989.

The Sixth Continent, Fisherman of Halicarnassus, Ministry of foreign Affairs Department of
        Culture, Ankara, 1991.

Sinan: Architect of Suleyman The Magnificent and the Ottoman Golden Age, A. Romano Burelli-John Freely; Thames & Hudson, London and New York, 1992, Edition Artheau Paris,
        1992.

Living in Turkey, Stephanos Yerasimos, Thames & Hudson, London and New York, 1992.

Demeures Ottomans de Turquie, Stephanos Yerasimos, Albin Michel, Paris, 1992.

Turkish Style, Stephanos Yerasimos, Archipelago Press, Singapore, 1992.

Living in Turkey, Thames and Hudson, Paris, London, New York, Singapore, 1993.

A Photographical Sketch on Lost Istanbul, Ara Guler, Istanbul, 1994

Old Istanbul Memories, Ara Guler, Dunya Sirketler Grubu, Istanbul, 1994.

Bir Devir Boyle Gecti Kalanlara Selam Olsun, Ara Guler, Ana Yayincilik, Istanbul, 1994.

Yitirilmis Renkler, Ara Guler, Dunya Sirketler Grubu, Istanbul, 1995.

Vanished Colours, Ara Guler, Dunya Sirketler Grubu, Istanbul, 1995.

Yuzlerinde Yeryuzu, Ana Yayincilik, Istanbul, 1995.

Babil'den Sonra Yasayacagiz, Ara Guler, Aras Publications, Istanbul, 1996.

The Ends of the Earth, Robert D. Kaplan, Vintage, 1997.

Rethinking Modernity and National Identity in Turkey, Sibel Bozdogan-Resat Kasaba,
        University of Washington Press, 1997.

Contemporary Turkish Writers, Louis Mitler, Routledge Curzon, 1997.

Ara Guler'e Saygi, Ilker Maga, YGS Publications, Istanbul, 1998.

Turkish Coast, Metin Demirsar, Insight Guide, 1998.

Selections from Ara Guler's Collection: "to my dear friend Ara", Kitap ve Sergi Katologu, YKY,
        Istanbul, 2000.

The Rough Guide to Turkey, Rosie Ayliffe-Marc Dubin, Rough Guides Ltd, 2000.

Pakistan, Tony Holliday, Insight Guide, 2000.

Istanbul Boy Middle School Years: The Autobiography of Aziz Nesin, 2000.

Joseph S. Jacobson, Southmoor Studios, 2000. *Turkey Unveiled*, Hugh Pope-Nicole Pope, The Overlook Press, 2000.

Turkey Today, Marvine Howe, Westview Press, 2000.

Turkey Handbook, Dominic Whiting, Footprint Handbooks, 2000.

Architecture and Identity, Chris Abel, Avon Books, 2000.

See Once Upon a Time: from an Empire to a Republic Istanbul, National Geographic, 2000.

Istanbul Des Djinns, Edition Fata Morgana, Montpellier, France, 2001.

Paper Before Print, Jonathan Bloom, Yale University Press, 2001.

Istanbul Des Djinns, Enis Batur, Lukseation, Edition Fata Morgana, France, 2002.

Screen World, John Willis-Tom Lynch, Applause Books, 2002.

The Last Poet in Istanbul Ara Guler, Enis Batur, YKY, Istanbul, 2002.

Seven Signs on Earth, YKY, Istanbul, 2002.

100 faces-Portraits of Turkish Authors, YKY, Istanbul, 2002.

Our Companion the Horse, Kudret Emiroglu-Ahmet Yuksel, YKY, Istanbul, 2003.

Western Humanities, Roy Matthews-Dewitt Platt, McGraw-Hill, 2003.

Demir Yol Tren Cagi: Iron Track Age of the Train, YKY, 2003.

Retrospective–50 years of Photojournalism, YGS Publications, Istanbul, Bremen, 2004.

From Trout to Gar Fish, the fish of Turkey, Ali Pasiner, YKY, 2004.

The Western Shores of Turkey, John Freely, Tauris Parke Paperbacks, 2004.

Time Out Film Guide, John Pym, Time Out Guides, 2005.

Ara Guler, Antartist Publications, Istanbul, 2005.

Bali and Lombok, Francis Dorai, Insight Guides, 2006.

Ara'dan Yetmisyedi Yil Gecti, Photographevi Publications, Istanbul, 2006.

Tales from the Expat Harem, Anastasia M. Ashman, Seal Pres, 2006.

The Man with the White Pidgeon, Photographevi, Istanbul 2007.

Turkey, Verity Campbell, Lonely Planet Publications, 2007.

Istanbul-Eyewitness Travel Guides, DK Publishing, 2007.

Rick Steves' Istanbul, Rick Steves-Lale Surmen, Avalon Travel Publishing, 2007.

Osman's Dream the History of the Ottoman Empire, Caroline Finkel, Basic Books, 2007.

Imperial Istanbul, Jane Taylor, Tauris Publishers, 2007.

Notebooks, Tennessee Williams, Yale University Press, 2007.

Les Grands Photographes de Magnum, Hachette, 2007.

Istanbul, Virginia Maxwell, Lonely Planet, 2008.

Call of Aphrodisias, Ara Guler, YKY, December, 2008.

Afrodisias Cigligi, Ara Guler, YKY, December, 2008.

Exhibitions (1965-2008)

Turkey through the eyes of three photographers, Ara Guler-Fikret Otyam-Ozan Sagdic, R.T. Ministry for Foreign Affairs Organization, Germany, December 1964; Italy, February 1965; France, April 1965.

1. Solo Exhibition, Robert Koleji Exhibition Hall, May 1966.

Sheldon Art Gallery, Continuous Exhibition Participation, Nebraska University Collection, Nebraska, 1966.

Osaka World Fair – Turkey Pavillion, Ara Guler, Architect Ragip Buluc and Orhan Peker, Osaka, March 1970.

2. Solo Exhibition, American News Center, Istanbul, 1972.

3. Solo Exhibition: "Photographs", American News Center, Istanbul and Ankara, 1972.

4. Solo Exhibition, American Cultural Center, Ankara, October 1972.

5. Solo Exhibition: "Mimar Sinan", R.T. Ministry for Foreign Affairs Organization, Arab Countries, Europe and Africa, 1972-1973.

6. Solo Exhibition, Istanbul, October 1973.

Ara Guler - Kamil Sukun Exhibition, Drugstore, Istanbul, 1974.

7. Solo Exhibition, Applied Fine Arts School, Istanbul, 1974 .

8. Solo Exhibition: "Creative Americans", American News Center, Istanbul, Ankara, Izmir, 1975.

Creative Americans, The American Center Lahor, February 1977, Karachi, March 1977.

10. Solo Exhibition: "From the world of Humans", Yapi Kredi Exhibition Hall, September 1977.

11. Solo Exhibition, Artizan Sanat Galerisi, Ankara, April 1978.

12. Solo Exhibition, Kunstgalerie Turkei, Stuttgart, February 1980.

La Religion dans le Bassin Mediterraneen, 6emes Journees internationals de la Photo et de L'Audiovisuel, Salle des Rencontres, Hotel de Ville, Montpellier, May 1985.

13. Solo Exhibition, Akbank Art Gallery, Istanbul 1985.

Tskuba World Fair, Tokio, March 1985.

Eye Gallery, Ara Guler - Sharon Guynap - Sarkis Baharoglu, San Francisco, June 1986.

14. Solo Exhibition: "Mimar Sinan", American Architectural Foundation & Turkish Studies Institute organization, American Chamber of Architects, Washington D.C., January 1987.

Bu Dunya Boyle Dunya, Ara Guler - Coskun Aral, Press Museum, Istanbul, May 1988.

Sadan Arl Verden, Ara Guler - Coskun Aral, Odense and Copenhagen, October – November 1988.

Sadan Arl Verden, Ara Guler - Coskun Aral, Amos Andersen Gallery, Helsinki, April 1989.

15. Solo Exhibition: "Ara Guler's film makers", 8. International Film Festival, Istanbul, April 1989.

16. Solo Exhibition: "Classical Era, 1950–1971", Press Museum, Istanbul, June 1989.

Ara Guler's filmmakers, Galeri Kare, Istanbul, 1989.

"Mimar Sinan", R.T. Culture Center, Ankara, 1990.

17. Solo Exhibition, Ayse Taki Galerisi, Istanbul, February 1990.

Ara Guler's filmmakers, Palais Rohan, Strasbourg, February 1990.

18. Solo Exhibition, British Culture Center, 1990.

19. Solo Exhibition, Bursa, December 1990.

20. Solo Exhibition: "Strasbourg through the Eyes of Ara Guler", Strasbourg Municipality October 1991.

21. Solo Exhibition: "Mimar Sinan", The Marmara Hotel Exhibition Hall, Istanbul, September 1992.

Mimar Sinan, Expo-1992, Sevilla, 1992.

Ara Guler's Film Makers, Ankara International Film Festival, Ankara, March 1993.

22. Solo Exhibition: "Unending Interview Istanbul", History foundation organization, Sandoz Gallery, Istanbul, April 1993.

23. Solo Exhibition: French Culture Center, Ankara 1993. 24. Solo Exhibition: "Image de Tuquie", Bibliotheque E. Triolet-Aragon Hall, Argenteuil, 1993.

25. Solo Exhibition, Landesmuseum, Dusseldorf, April 1995.

Bu Dunya Boyle Dunya, Ara Guler - Coskun Aral, Milli Reasurans Galerisi, Istanbul, 1996.

26. Solo Exhibition: "Ara Guler, a Look at Istanbul 1950-1990", Una Volta Culture Center Bastia, Corsica, December 1997.

Jacques Prevert Galerie de I'nstitut Francaises, Istanbul, April 1997.

Exhibition in Thessaloniki, August 1997.

27. Solo Exhibition: "Ara Guler's Classics", Pamukbank Photograph Gallery, Istanbul, February 1998.

28. Solo Exhibition: "Ara Guler Halic Exhibition", Worpswede, Germany, March 1999.

29. Solo Exhibition: "Ara Guler, Photographs of Old Istanbul", Umag (Ugur Mumcu Art Gallery) Investigative Journalism Foundation, Ankara, December 1999.

30. Solo Exhibition: "Vienna Landscapes", Interkult Theater, January 2000.

31. Solo Exhibition: "Ara Guler's Photographs", Hanesburg, Germany, February 2000.

Group Exhibition: "Les Villes Chantees", Biaritz, France, May 2000.

Selections from Ara Guler's Collection: "To My Dear Friend Ara",, YKB, Galatasaray, Istanbul, January 2001.

32. Solo Exhibition: "Master Portraits from Ara Guler", Galerist Gallery, Istanbul, January 2001.

33. Solo Exhibition, Izmir-Turkish American Association, Izmir, January 2001.

34. Solo Exhibition: "Ara Guler's Nostalgia", Tropeninstitut Galerie, Amsterdam, Hollanda, April 2001.

35. Solo Exhibition: "Ara Guler's Istanbul", Huckleberry Gallery, London, September 2001.

36. Solo Exhibition, Galerie de Chateau D'eau, Toulouse Feurier, France, 2002.

Ara Guler Photograph Exhibition, Uludag University, Bursa, June 2002.

37. Solo Exhibition: "100 Faces Artist Portraits Exhibition", Yapi Kredi Art Gallery Sermet Cifter Kutuphane Hall, Istanbul, November 2002.

'100 faces' Exhibition, Yapi Kredi Culture Center, Istanbul, December 2002.

38. Solo Exhibition: "Ara Guler Classics", Istanbul Photograph Center, Istanbul, April 2003.

39. Solo Exhibition: "Ara Guler Classics", Diyarbakir Sanat Center, Diyarbakir, 2003.

Group Exhibition: "Three Photographers Exhibition", Ara Guler, Jeny Schatzberg, Sakir Eczacibasi, Derimod Art Gallery, April 2003.

40. Solo Exhibition: "Ara Guler Fotografien Von 1950 -1994", Fotografie Forum International, Frankfurt, Germany, June 2003.

Sebastiao Salgado-Ara Guler, Yapi Kredi Culture Center, Istanbul, February 2004.

Zaman Diaphragm-50 Years of Photojournalism, Bremen Sehir Gallery, Bremen, February 2004.

2005 Collection Exhibition, Istanbul Photograph Center, May 2005.

Greece Photographer Association Exhibition, Athens, June 2005.

Seventyseven Years Have Rassed, Fotografevi, Istanbul, August 2005.

Once in a While 10, Ara Kafe, Istanbul, October 2005.

Selections from Ara, Bursa Metropolitan Municipality 16. Photograph Days, Bursa, November 2006.

Seventyseven years have passed, Russia Federation National PhotographCenter, St. Petersburg, March 2006.

Istanbul Photographs Exhibition, European Commission Charlemagne Building, Brussels, October 2006.

41. Solo Exhibition, Ege University Art Gallery, Izmir, April 2007.

Ara Guler Classics, Edirne Photograph Art Association, Edirne, October 2007.

Magnum Photographs and Turkey, Istanbul Modern Photograph Gallery, May 2007.

Open Your Eyes to Light, Ege University Campus Culture Center Art Gallery, Izmir, May 2007.

Faces, Turkish-Greek Friendship Festival, Antalya, June 2007.

Ara Guler in the Historical Olive Oil Factory, 18. Burhaniye-Oren Tourism, Culture and Art Festival, Balikesir, July 2007.

Selections from Ara, Gaziantep 2. International Culture and Art Festival, Gaziantep, September 2007.

L'Altra Istanbul, Ara Guler, Erdal Yazici, Kutup Dalgakiran, Coskun Asar and Ercan Arslan, Ara Pacis-Fotografevi Exhibition, Roma, November 2007.

Alinteri, Zafer Carsisi, Ankara, December 2007.

42. Solo Exhibition, American University, Cairo Egypt, April 2008.

Istanbullu, Mac Art Gallery, Istanbul, April 2008.

AFSAD 7. Photograph Symposium-Documentary Photograph Rendezvous, Cankaya Municipality Cagdas Sanat Merkezi, Ankara May 2008.

Istanbul'da Alin Teri, Taksim Metrosu, Istanbul April 2008.

Dissertations (1984-1999)

- Photograph and Ara Guler, Prepared by: Hakan Mahmut Negis, Suleyman Demirel University G.S.F, Graphic Department, Seminar works, Isparta, 1999.
- Ara Guler, Prepared by: Rosa Bucher, Munich University, Germany, The fundamentals of Documentary and News Photographs in the World and in Turkey, 1999.
- Case Study: Ara Guler, Prepared by: Seyda Sever, Ankara University, Institute of Social Sciences, Radio Television Cinema Department, Ankara, 1998.
- Development of Photography and Ara Guler, Prepared by: Ibrahim Ogretmen, 9 Eylul University G.S.F. Department of Stage and Visual arts, Izmir, 1984.

Bibliography

Interviews with Ara Guler
19 October 2007
8 December 2007
17 December 2007
18 December 2007
25 December 2007
22 January 2008
28 January 2008
29 January 2008
30 January 2008
4 April 2008
5 April 2008
23 April 2008
5 June 2008
9 August 2008
30 August 2008
11 October 2008
12 October 2008
17 October 2008
22 October 2008
17 November 2008
25 December 2008
26 December 2008
27 December 2008
17 January 2009
30 January 2009
4 April 2009
11 April 2009
16 May 2009

Archive
Yeni Istanbul, Gunaydin, Son Havadis, Yeni Ortam, Tercuman, Cumhuriyet, Milliyet, Hurriyet, Hayat, BYEGM Ayin Tarihi (1947-2009).

Encyclopedias
AnaBritannica
Compton's General Culture Encyclopedia
Republican Era Turkey Encyclopedia
Meydan Larousse-Great Dictionary and Encyclopedia
Encyclopedia of Turkish and International Celebrities
Turkey Authors Encyclopedia
Homeland Encyclopedia

Books-Dissertations-Articles-News

(1915-1916)' on a book", *Ataturk Research Center Magazine*, No.: 53, Volume: XVIII, July 2002.
"46 lensmen all set for seven-day assignment", *New Sunday Times*, 26 August 1990.
"A correspondent who writes visual history with photographs: Ara Guler", *Gunes* newspaper, 6 May 1990.
"A photograph does not lie", *Cumhuriyet* newspaper, 6 January 1990.
"A photographer is an artist, a photograph is art", *Yeni Ortam*, 11 May 1973.
"A real artist: Ara Guler", *Tercuman* newspaper, 27 July 1981.
"A world scale success by Ara Guler", *Yeni Istanbul*, 19 November 1960.
"After 400 years Mimar Sinan will tour the New World for nothing", *Cumhuriyet* newspaper, 8 May 1987.
"An unending interview with a photographer from Istanbul", *Cumhuriyet* newspaper, 26 April 1993.
"And there was a Koruturk", *Gunes* newspaper, 18 October 1987.
"Another masterpiece from Ara Guler", *Dunya-Kitap*, 7 July 1995.
"Ara Guler accepted by international exhibition", *Hurriyet* newspaper, 21 September 1966.
"Ara Guler and Coskun Aral joint photograph Exhibition", *Vizyon*, February 1996.
"Ara Guler and man", *Meydan* magazine, No: 69, 10 May 1966.
"Ara Guler in Indonesia", *Ekonomik Bulten*, August 1990.
"Ara Guler in Istanbul and Bremen", *Agos* newspaper, 13 February 2004.
"Ara Guler launches his first Exhibition", *Yeni Ortam*, 11 September 1972.
"Ara Guler Prominent Photographer", *The Armenian Reporter*, 13 June 1974.
"Ara Guler's Creative Americans", Exhibition Brochure, Istanbul, April 1975.
"Ara Guler's Creative Americans", *Hurriyet Gosteri*, February 1989.
"Ara Guler's Exhibition", *Cumhuriyet* newspaper, 6 May 1966.
"Ara Guler's first 10", *Yeni Yuzyil*, 12 March 1995.
"Ara Guler's Istanbul depicted in magnificent vanished Colours", *Turkish Daily News*, 2 Agustos 1995.
"Ara Guler's Istanbul", *ONEP Saglik ve Estetik* magazine, May 2000.
"Ara Guler's new work", *Aksam* newspaper, 29 July 1970.
"Ara Guler's Photograph Days Opening Statement", *Hurriyet Gosteri*, December 1988.
"Ara Guler's Photograph Exhibition", *Sesimiz*, No: 40, December 1972.
"Ara Guler's Salgadolari", *Finansal Forum* newspaper, 1 January 2004.
"Cantankerous Photojournalist Ara Guler", *Indeks Icerik-Iletisim Danismanlik*, 2003.
"Central Intelligence Agency-CIA, Noah's Ark and Mt. Ararat", *FOIA Declassified Documents*, 2 July 1994.
"Comedian Bob Hope dies", *BBC News*, 29 July 2003.
"Confession 44 years late", *Star* newspaper, 10 August 2008.
"Cumhuriyet's Family Albums", History Foundation Publications, Istanbul 1998.
"Dali Dolu Salvador", *Tempo* magazine, 14 August 1988.
"De l'autre cote du miroir", *Contreplongee*, February 1990.
"Discourse with Ara Guler", *IFSAK* magazine, November 1990.
"Discourse with Picasso", *Yeditepe* magazine, May 1973.
"Don Romeo de la fotografia", *Liberation*, 28 November 1990.
"During the last days", *Vizon* magazine, January 1987.
"Eisentrager Exhibit at Sheldon", *Lincoln Journal Star*, 11 September 1966.
"Falling in love with a venue", *Elele* magazine, December 1988.
"Fifteen is not enough, more photographs", *Cumhuriyet* newspaper, 12 February 2004.
"Florya Mansion", *Skylife*, November 2004.
"From a legal perspective, the events in 1915 do not qualify as genocide", *Istanbul University News Agency Bulletin*, 15 March 2006.
"Golden Shutter Release Ara Guler", *Cosmopolitan*, No: 11, 1990.
"Guler shot 2160 frames of film", *Cumhuriyet* newspaper, 22 January 1996.
"Half a century of memoirs", *Milliyet* newspaper, 26 February 2006.
"He even informed on Charlie Chaplin", *Aksam* newspaper, 30 September 2003.
"I am 77 years old and still hanker for life", *Sabah* newspaper, 14 August 2005.
"I am a photojournalist", *Gokkusagi* magazine, December 1987.
"I am observing the world from within a frame", *Hurriyet Kelebek*, 29 November 1988.
"I am one of the men who gets closest to life", *Elele*, November 1990.

"Irwin's fraud", *Hurriyet* newspaper, 14 August 1984.

"It beneficial for everything, it is good for nothing", *Sik Gazete*, 15 November 1971.

"Legacy of the Fish Master", *Milliyet* newspaper, 26 February 2004.

"Les stars de Ara Guler", *Dernières Nouvelles d'Alsace*, 23 February 1990

"Nihat Akyunak's autobiography", *Sanat Cervesi* magazine, No.: 39, January 1982.

"Once upon a time Istanbul", *Hurriyet* newspaper, 3 August 1997.

"One Man's Day", *The Guide*, No.: 20, January-February 1995.

"One Master 25 Masters", *Milliyet* newspaper, 24 January 2001.

"One of the 7 stars in the World is a Turk", *Milliyet*, 3 March 1962.

"Photography Open Session", *Gercek Sinema* magazine, No.: 1 October 1973.

"Portrait of Ara Guler, Master of Portraits", *Arkitekt* magazine, No.: 6 1993.

"Restoration of Elia Kazan's honor", *Radikal* newspaper, 18 January 1999.

"Sadan er verden", *Politiken*, 12 November 1988.

"Secret plot to catch out Nazi spy", *BBC News*, 1 April 2005.

"Silhouettes of a Vanishing City", *Time* magazine, 17 October 1994.

"Sinan in Brussels", *Toplum* magazine, No.: 9, 2 June 1972.

"Sinan", *Focus* magazine, February 1996.

"Soeharto to receive 45 leading photographers", *The Jakarta Post*, 28 August 1989.

"The adventure of engraving in Turkey", *Gazete Kadikoy*, 26 January 2008.

"The changing colors of Istanbul", *Hurriyet* newspaper, 23 March 2006.

"The communists have burnt AKM", *Radikal* newspaper, 28 March 2007.

"The first photograph taken 27 years ago", *Hurriyet* newspaper, 28 August 1984.

"The first Turkish artist to be accepted by Picasso", *Cumhuriyet* newspaper, 15 May 1971.

"The Grand Master of Documentary Photography: Ara Guler", *Genc Boyut*, No: 3, May 1993.

"The important thing is to find and expose the story", *Cumhuriyet* newspaper, 16 July 1995.

"The Istanbul in Memories: Arnavutkoy, Fatih, Gaziosmanpasa, Moda", History Foundation, 30 March 2006.

"The Master's photographs worthy of a museum", *Cumhuriyet* newspaper, 30 January 1990.

"The Name of a photographer from Turkey has been written in the History of World Photography", *Tercuman*, 25 February 1973.

"The photograph artists debated about the problems of the art of photography in a panel", *Cumhuriyet* newspaper, 20 August 1977.

"The publishing of the Art Book is still in a bottleneck", *Cumhuriyet* newspaper, 15 January 1977.

"The voice of Anatolia", *BYEGM*, No: 166, May 2000.

"Their's is in a museum, ours' became razor blades", *Tempo* magazine, 14 January 2003.

"They are not shooting photographs, they are suffering", *Nokta* magazine, 6 October 1991.

"This World is another World", *Gunes* newspaper, 19 November 1988.

"This World is such a World", *Skylife*, February 1996.

"Those looking for Noah's Ark on Agri mountain", *Evrensel* newspaper, 12 September 2006

"Truth itself", *Iletim Istanbul University Press Publication Academy Magazine*, November 1989.

"Turkey is losing its Turkishness", *TURSAB Tourism Magazine*, June 1989.

"Turkey is represented by Ara Guler in an exhibition of famous photographers",

"Turkish Armenian Photographer Featured in Istanbul Exhibit", *The Armenian Reporter*, 5 October 1972.

"Ara Guler, the great name in Turkish photography", *Adam Sanat* magazine, December 1975.

"Two Masters Ara Guler-Sahin Kaygun 'Discussed photography", *Hurriyet Gosteri*, September 1984.

"We are very late in taking ownership of Fikret Mualla", *Milliyet* newspaper, 19 January 1972.

"We are writing visual history in the world", *Dunya* newspaper, 6 January 1989.

"Writer of a visual history", *Nokta* magazine, 12 June 1988.

6-7 September Events Photographs -Documents; Fahri Coker Archive, Tarih Vakfi Yurt Publications, Istanbul, September 2005.

Ababay, Rifat, "My father's ban made me a photographer", *Sey* magazine, 10 August 1982.

Acar, Bedir, "I am writing visual history", *Milli Gazete*, 23 January 1995.

Adil, Fikret, "Ara Guler", *Son Havadis*, 29 March 1962.

Agaoglu, Adalet, "Being oneself", *Milliyet Art*, No: 378, 15 February 1996.

Ak, Seyit Ali, "A lifetime of passion for photography", *Hurriyet* newspaper, 13 May 1988.

Ak, Seyit Ali, "Around the world with Ara Guler", *Hurriyet Gosteri*, May 1984.

Ak, Seyit Ali, "Our photograph Exhibition Billboards", *IFSAK Sinema Fotograf Magazine*, January 1987.

Ak, Seyit Ali, "Questions for Ara Guler", *Art Cevresi*, September 1983.

Ak, Seyit Ali, "This world is such a world", *Gosteri*, July 1988.

Aka, Mehmet, "Guler: Photography is not Art", *Seyhan* newspaper, 1-15 June 1993.

Akagunduz, Ulku Ozel, "I have proved that photography is not fun", *Zaman* newspaper, 1 January 2005.

Akerson, Tanju, "Americans meet Mimar Sinan", *Cumhuriyet* newspaper,29 January 1987.

Akin, Bedii Faik, Printed Press, Dogan Kitapcilik, May 2001.

Akin, Sunay, "Believing in continuous peace", *Milliyet Art*, No: 378, 15 February 1996.

Akin, Sunay, "Photographs in poetry", *Milliyet Art*, No: 311, 15 February 1993.

Akkusak, Osman, "Sevket Rado-Turkan Rado", *Yeni Safak* newspaper, 11 March 2007.

Akogul, Merih, "Catching the moment", *Genis Aci* magazine, September-October 2000.

Aksoy, Fahir, "A photograph artist: Ara Guler", *Yeditepe* magazine, July 1960.

Aktas, Suna, "He knows about Noah", *Radikal* newspaper, 30 July 2001.

Aktunc, Hulki, "Ara Baba's Outlook", *Aydinlik* magazine, 13 May 1993.

Albayrak, Cahid, "A great gap will be filled", *Balikesir Birlik* newspaper, 9 October 1976.

Alkan, M. Ethem, "Is photography a minor Art?", *Yeni Ortam* newspaper, 27 May 1973.

Alkaya, Orhan, "Let's keep the present cleaner", *Radikal* newspaper, 1 April 2007.

Alpman, Cengiz, "an amnesty for shanties, early elections are here", *Kenthaber*, 6 December 2005. Altan, Cetin, "Ara Guler, Coskun, Komet", *Sabah* newspaper, 6 July 1995.

Andac, Sukru, "I object to digital", *Milliyet Business*, 16 January 2005.

Andak, Selmi, "Ara Guler and his Photographs", *Cumhuriyet* newspaper, 25 September 1972.

Andak, Selmi, "Ara Guler's New Exhibition Subject Creative Americans", *Cumhuriyet*, 19 April 1975.

Andakyali, Abdurrahman, "Ara Guler Interview", *Fotomuhabiri*, 12 November 2005.

April 2005. Basar, Rahati, "Our man in Ankara was playing the piano while the Turkish butle was stealing files", *Hurriyet*, 23 May 2003.

Aras, Vahit, "The Devil took it", *Nokta* magazine, 7 May 1989.

Arkan, Joan Kem, "A lifelong Love Affair", *Hilton Turkey Magazine*, No.X 105, 1996.

Armaoglu, Fahir, *20. Century History of Politics*, Turkiye Is Bankasi Kultur Publications, 1987.

Arolat, Osman S., "These are our people", *Dunya*, 22 February 1996.

Aroyan, Armen, "Eight Hundred thousand slides", *Armenian International Magazine*, No.: 9, November 1993.

Arzik, Nimet, "Mister Shah", *Ankara* magazine, July 1971.

Aslan, Sema, "Witness to 50 years", *Milliyet* newspaper, 10 July 2001.

Assouline, Pierre, *Eye of the Century: Henri Cartier-Bresson*, YGS Publications, October 2007.

Ataov, Turkkaya (Prof. Dr.), "Turkish foreign policy during the 2nd World War years", *Turk Solu*, 17 December 2007.

Ataturk ve Spor, Genclik ve Spor Genel Mudurlugu, 2006.

Atmaca, Efnan, "Elia Kazan from Kayseri completed the 94-year film", *Aksam* newspaper, 30 September 2003.

Aubozian, Zmrouthe, "Ara Guler, chroniqueur visuel de notre epoque", *FranceArmenie*, October 2003.

Avci, Zeynep, "Discourse with Ara Guler", *Yeni Dusun* magazine, May 1988.

Aydin, Murat, "Gallows clamped by EU-APO", *Aksiyon* magazine No.: 389, 20 May 2002.

Aydogan, Metin, *Notes on Turkey 1923-2005*, Umay Publications, July 2005.

Ayman, Oya, "Ara Guler's Film makers", *Gunes* newspaper, 30 November 1989.

Ayman, Oya, "Photography is a sub-specialty of science", *Gunes* newspaper, 16 December 1986.

Aytas, Giyasettin, "Ahmet Kutsi Tecer and his contribution to Drama", *G.U. Gazi Egitim Fakultesi Magazine*, Cilt 23, No.2, 2003.

Bagci, Ozlem, "Together with Ozan Sagdic", *Fotografya* magazine, No. 10.

Bagdat, Tarik, "49th anniversary of the Uskudar ferry", *Kocaeli* newspaper, 2 March 2007.

Bahadir, Mehmet, *Massacres in Cyprus*, Rustem Yayinevi, Nicosia, 2001.

Bardakci, Murat, "The Russians were going to kidnap Huseyin's father from Ortakoy", *Hurriyet*, 7 February 1999.

Barlas, Mehmet, "A Sunday with Ara Guler", *Sabah* newspaper, 8

Barlas, Mehmet-Guler, Ara, "The Forsaken", *Cumhuriyet* newspaper, 20 December 1973.

Basarir, Mert Ali, "A Photograph does not lie", *Aktuel* magazine No. 213, 3-9 August 1995.

Baslangic, Celal, "77 years of Ara", *Radikal* newspaper, 15 August 2005.

Batur, Enis, "anti-cliché film from Ara Guler; Yavuz", *Cumhuriyet* Newspaper, 3 June 2001.

Baydur, Memet, "Hard bitten Memory", *Dunya Aktuel*, 23 April 1995.

Baydur, Memet, "What is it good for", *Cumhuriyet* newspaper, 14 January 1996.

Bayhan, Mehmet, "Once upon a time Istanbul from Ara Guler", *Milliyet Art* magazine, 15 April 1993.

Baysan, Mine, "Old photographs make no impact", *Sabah* newspaper, 8 July 2000.

Bek, Kemal, "Here, this is Istanbul", *Yazko Edebiyat*, September 1981.

Benmayor, Gila, "The daily lease rate for the famous yacht of Onassis was 100 thousand Euro", *Hurriyet*, 24 October 2004.

Bezna, Elyesa, "German Spy Cicero in War, Dies", *New York Times*, 25 December 1970.

Bezna, Elyesa, *Ankara Spy Cicero*, Karizma Yayinevi, Istanbul 2000.

Bezna, Elyesa, *I Was Cicero*, Harper & Row, New York 1962.

Bicer, Yilmaz, "Once upon a time O Istanbul", *Aynali Pazar*, 15 December 2004.

Bildirici, Faruk-Demirkan, Suleyman, "Farewell to the silent general of 12 September", *Hurriyet*, 6 October 2005.

Birsel, Salah, "People", *Cumhuriyet Dergi*, 13 November 1988.

Boran, Yasemin, "Spiritual surgery", *Hurriyet* newspaper, 13 April 1998.

Bortacina, Azer, "Mister Shutter release", *Milliyet* newspaper, 31 October 2000.

Bortacina, Azer, "Passionate writers /a tough journalist", *Milliyet* newspaper, 27 June 2000.

Bostancioglu, Adnan, "Istanbul's Memory: Ara Guler", *Skylife*, October 1995.

Boysan, Aydin, "Nurtured press", *Aksam* newspaper, 28 October 2001.

Burak, Durdu Mehmet (Assoc.Prof. Dr.), "British J.R. Pilling: the struggle to seize the Ottoman Railway Concession", *Ankara University Ottoman History Research and Application Center Magazine-OTAM*, No:17, 2005.

Caglayan, Tamer, "A life dedicated to Photography: Ara Guler", *Yazin* magazine, May 2003.

Cakici, Fatma, "All good photographers in the world are journalists", *Yanki* magazine, 14-20 September 1987.

Cansu, A. Sami, "Uskudar disaster", *Milliyet* blog, 6 March 2007.

Capin, Halit, "The king of the agoras", *Takvim* newspaper, 10 July 2004.

Celebi, Bunyamin, "An Angry Man: Ara Guler", *Istanbul* magazine, No. 32, January 2000.

Celikel, Pinar, *Sebastiao Salgado, Ara Guler Collection*, YKY, Istanbul, February 2004.

Cerrahoglu, Nilgun, "Those within the mirror: Ara Guler", *Milliyet* newspaper, 16 May 1999.

Cirim, Cengiz, *IInd World War*, Hacettepe University, Department of History, Seminar Series, 2004.

Cizgen, Gultekin, "a trail team cadre of photographers albeit a few has been raised in Turkey", *Milliyet Art*, 2 November 1973.

Cizgen, Gultekin, "Josef Koudelka in Istanbul", *Cumhuriyet* newspaper, 17 September 1985. Cizgen, Gultekin, "Thoughts on 15 black-white Turkish photographs", *Art Olayi*, December 1981.

Cizgen, Gultekin, "Reviewing the photographs of foreign cadres", *Art Olayi*, October 1987.

Cizmeli, Sevket, *Menderes, A star of Democracy?* Arkadas Yayinevi, September 2007.

Clogg, Richard, *Politics and the Academy: Arnold Toynbee and the Koraes Chair*, King's College (University of London), Centre of Contemporary Greek Studies, Routledge, 1986.

Cobankent, Yesim-Karakurt, Sebati, "Greetings to Master Ara", *Hurriyet* newspaper, 13 January 2001.

Cobanoglu, Haluk, "What does a photograph by Ara Guler tell?" *Bilisim* magazine, June-September 2004.

Cokyigit, Coskun, "Istanbul was a Planet", *Dunden Bugune Tercuman*, 11 July 2003.

Coskun, Alev, "27th of May and Youth", *Cumhuriyet* newspaper, 27 May 2004.

Cumhuriyet newspaper, 13 August 1964.

Cunbur, Mujgan, "Female Education in the Ataturk Era", *Ataturk Research Center Magazine*, No: 23, Volume: VIII, March 1992.

Curry, Natasha, "Capturing Turkey", *Turkish Times*, 19 February 1990.

Dag, Haluk, "Ara Guler's half a century journey in photojournalism", *Art Dunyamiz*, Bahar 2005.

Dag, Haluk, "I wrote a poem about the sad story of Yavuz", *Aksamlik*, 4 April 2003.

Demirel, Muammer, *Armenian Operations around Erzurum and its Vicinity during the First World War (1914-1918)*, Ankara 1996.

Demirkan, Oge, "Life closed for the second time", *Sabah* newspaper, 7 May 2000.

Devletoglu, Jan, "The Pope Earthquake in '67", *Vatan* newspaper, 28 November 2006.

Devlin, A. J.-Tischler, N.M., *The Selected Letters of Tennessee Williams*, New Directions Publishing Corporation, November 2004.

Devrim, Hakki, "A neighborhood coffee house in Ankara", *Radikal* newspaper, 20 March 2002.

Dino, Abidin, "a monument-book worthy of Mimar Sinan", *Cumhuriyet* newspaper, 10 August 1992.

Dino, Abidin-Guler, Ara, *Fikret Mualla*, Cem Publications, Istanbul 1980.

Dogan, I.-Dilek, N., "Paul the 6th prayed in Hagia Sophia', *Aksiyon* magazine, No.: 625, 27 November 2006.

Dokumaci, Muserref, *Yavuz and Midilli Cruisers*, Canakkale Onsekiz Mart University Faculty of Science–Literature, Canakkale, January 2003.

Durbas, Refik, "Excitement does not become a Journalist", *Yeni Yuzyil*, 13 October 1996.

Duru, Orhan, "Ara Guler's run of bad luck", *Milliyet* newspaper, 21 August 1971.

Duru, Orhan, "Ara Guler", *Milliyet Art* magazine, 7 February 1975.

Duru, Orhan, "The Photographer who took his own picture", *Yeni Yuzyil*, 26 October 1995.

Durukan, M. Yasar, "He steered magazines in the 1960s", *Aksiyon* magazine, No: 500, 5 July 2004.

Durukan, M. Yasar, "Leicas saved two cities from bombardment", *Turkuaz*, No: 148, 13 February 2005.

Durukan, M. Yasar, "The Story of that photographer", *Aksiyon* magazine No: 492, May 2004.

Ede, Nadir, "Discourse with Ara Guler", *Fotograf* magazine, No: 49, June-July 2003.

Edgu, Ferit, "Ara Guler", *Vizon Gazete*, May 1980.

Elekdag, Sukru M., "'Blue Book' and the Turkish-Armenian issue", *Radikal* newspaper, 8 December 2006.

Elkatip, Demet, "This is our World", *Milliyet Art*, No: 378, 15 February 1996.

Erduran, Leyla, "Dustin Hoffman", *Milliyet* newspaper, 6 June 1976.

Erduran, Refik, *Demons, Saints, Women; the Memoirs of a Strange Man*, Dunya Publications, April 2005.

Ergir, Yalcin, *Doctor Dream -4*, Cinar Publications, September 2004.

Eroglu, Nadir (Assoc.Prof. Dr.), "The development of economy policies in Turkey /1923-2003', *a paper presented at the '80th anniversary Republic of Turkey Symposium' organized by Marmara University Ataturk Principles and Reform History Research and Application Center'nin during 29-31 October 2003 in Istanbul.*

Esatoglu, Mehmet, "Those who write history with a shutter release", *Evrensel* newspaper, 21 February 1996.

Evren, Burcak, "Discourse with Ara Guler", *Yeni Ortam* newspaper, 2 May 1975.

Evren, Burcak, "Photograph Exhibition in April", *Yeni Ortam* newspaper, 25 April 1975.

Evren, Burcak, "The reasons for the underdevelopment of Turkish photography art", *Yeni Ortam* newspaper, 4 October 1974. "Exhibition", *The Sun*, 24 February 1977.

Fakir, Cem, "Documentary about the Uskudar Ferry", NTV, April 2002.

French, Amelia-Toptap, Atilla, "Photographer Guler in search of obscure", *Dateline*, 18 November 1989.

Fuat, Memet, "earth on their faces", *Cumhuriyet* newspaper, 3 January 1996.

Fuat, Memet, *Anthology of Modern Turkish Poetry*, Adam Publications, 1997.

Fuat, Memet, *Dictionary of Intellectuals*, Adam Publications, Istanbul 2001.

Gage, Nicholas, *Greek Fire: The Story of Maria Callas and Aristotle Onassis*, Knopf, October 2000.

Gezer, Taner, "See and understand the world's situation", *Cumhuriyet* newspaper, 14 February 1996.

Gezgin, Ahmet Oner (Prof. Dr.), "Photography from the Republic to Date", *Fotografya*, No: 4, December 1995.

Giritli, Ismet (Prof. Dr.), "Alphabet Reform and Ataturk", *Ataturk Research Center Magazine*, No: 13, Volume V, November 1988.

Gruber, L. Fritz, "Ara Guler Exhibition Opening Speech", 14 March 1995, Dusseldorf.

Guer, Ara, *We shall live after Babylon*, Aras Publications, Istanbul 1996.

Guler, Ara, "A photograph should not exceed reality", *Hurriyet Gosteri*, May 1989.

Guler, Ara, "An Indian riddle", *Milliyet* newspaper, 1 November 1984.

Guler, Ara, "Bertrand Russell has passed away", *Hurriyet* newspaper, 5 February 1970.

Guler, Ara, "Bladeless Surgery", *Gunes* newspaper, 6 December 1987.

Guler, Ara, "Head hunters", *Sabah* newspaper, 21 October 1990.

Guler, Ara, "I lost my creative American", *Gosteri* magazine, August 1981.

Guler, Ara, "Potatoes, Leeks and photographs", *Gosteri* magazine, 27 July 1991.

Guler, Ara, "Thoughts raised by the Sahin Kaygun Exhibition", *Hurriyet* newspaper, 14 March 1984.

Guler, Ara, *Kim* magazine, 5 December 1960.

Guler, Ara, *Orkestra* magazine, 1973.

Guler, Ara, *Yanki* magazine, 7 June 1971.

Guler, Ara, *Yeditepe* magazine, No: 162, October 1969.

Guler, Ara-Akdogan, Lutfu-Tahsin, Orhan, "African Horn", *Tercuman* Newspaper, 6 August 1978.

Guler, Ara-Akkan, Oguz, "In the Homeland of the Turks", *Hurriyet* newspaper, 20 June 1980.

Guler, Ara-Dora, Aysegul, "Commando girls in the Palestinian Army", *Gunaydin* newspaper, 28 July 1970.

Guler, Ara-Dora, Aysegul-Kuturman, Perihan, "15 Days in the Palace in Iran", *Hurriyet* Newspaper, 12 January 1969.

Guler, Ara-Tahsin, Orhan, "Bladeless Surgery", *Tercuman* newspaper, 13 February 1978.

Guler, Ara-Tahsin, Orhan, "Hot Asia", *Tercuman* newspaper, 12 April 1978.

Gunaydin Pazar, No. 25, 25 May 1969.

Gunaydin, 20 September 1969.

Gundem, Mehmet, "Non-muslim homeland martyrs", *Milliyet* newspaper, 2 March 2005.

Gungormus, Nilufer-Citak, Manuel, "Armenians", *Gunes* newspaper, 10 December 1990.

Gunsolley, Bob, "Smile You May Be on Distinguished Visitor's Film", *The Sioux City Journal*, 1 July 1974.

Gunumuz Turkiyesinde Kim Kimdir (Who's Who in Turkey) 1989, Profesyonel Iletisim Organizasyon, Istanbul 1989.

Gureli, Nail, "from DP to AKP, from the press to the media", *Milliyet* newspaper, 21 February 2007.

Gurlek, Dursun, "The Cinar (sycamore) incidents in Istanbul", *Turk Edebiyati* magazine, March 2004.

Gursel, Idil, "18 year censorship of the Fisherman of Halicarnassus", *Cumhuriyet* newspaper, 13 November 1989.

Guven, Dilek, *6-7 September Events; in terms of Republican Era Minority Policies*, Tarih Vakfi Yurt Publications, Istanbul August 2005.

Guven, Kayihan, "Vakit: a newspaper competing with Zaman", *Cumhuriyet* newspaper, 11 January 1992. Guven, Zeynep, "Photography is a profession of womanizers", *Hurriyet* newspaper, 22 February 1998.

Guzel, M. Sehmus (Prof. Dr.), "Abidin Dino and Fikret Mualla", *Art Criticism*, 8 September 2008.

Hamdy Bey and Osgan Efendi, *Le Tumulus de Nemroud-Dagh: Voyage, Description, Inscriptions avec Plans et Photographes*, Imp. F. Lceffler, Constantinople, 1883.

Hekimoglu, Muserref, "Capital Days", *Cumhuriyet* newspaper, 29 November 1988.

Hekimoglu, Muserref, "Greetings to all", *Cumhuriyet Dergi*, 19 February 1995.

Hekimoglu, Muserref, "The esthetics of the non-esthetic", *Cumhuriyet* newspaper, 3 February 1995.

Hikmet, Nazim, *In Quest'anno 1941*, Lerici Editori, Milano 1961.

Hizlan, Dogan, "A book about the days I want to forget: 6-7 September Events", *Hurriyet*, 10 September 2005.

Hizlan, Dogan, "A name recommended for Tosbaga Street", *Hurriyet* newspaper, 25 June 2000.

Hizlan, Dogan, "Beyoglu resembles a mad palace resident", *Hurriyet* newspaper, 14 January 1991.

Hizlan, Dogan, "I have never gone to see slides", *Cumhuriyet* newspaper, 7 April 1972.

Hizlan, Dogan, "Istanbul's Past", *Hurriyet* newspaper, 26 July 1995.

Hizlan, Dogan, "Sinan in Photographs", *Hurriyet* newspaper, 10 August 1992.

Hizlan, Dogan, "They drove even Ara crazy", *Hurriyet* newspaper, 12 November 2003.

Hizlan, Dogan, *Prose Separator*, YKY, July 2001.

Ince, Ozdemir, "Demir Ozlu's letter and history without mirrors", *Hurriyet* newspaper, 20 November 2007.

Inceoz, Semih, "Greed for power burnt bridges", *Aksiyon* magazine, No: 117, 1 March 1997.

Ipek, Murat, "Art is fraud", *Dunya* newspaper, 8 August 1992.

Irler, Von Klaus, "Was bleibt nach einem Kunstlerleben?", *Die Tageszeitung*, 15 February 2004.

Isli, Emin Nedret, "Fire of 1954", *Kapalicarsi* magazine, No. 2, 2002.

Iyem, Nuri, "Ara Guler's new trend in photography", *Yeditepe* magazine, 16-30 June 1962.

Iyem, Nuri, "Photograph exhibitions", *Yeditepe* magazine, No. 127, November 1966.

K., Tarik Dursun, "I gave Ara Guler to my grandchild!", *Yeni Yuzyil* newspaper, 16 May 1995.

Kabacali, Alpay, "The visual narrative of history", *Cumhuriyet* newspaper, 4 June 1990.

Kabacali, Alpay, *Press Censorship in Turkey from the past to the present*, Gazeteciler Cemiyeti Publications, Istanbul, 1990.

Kabas, Sedef, *Those who brought time to heal*, Dogan Kitapcilik, June 2005.

Kabas, Sedef, *Those who think aloud*, Dogan Kitapcilik, June 2003.

Kalay, Aramis, "We are historians, we write visual history", *Dekorasyon* magazine, No. 70, May 1995.

Karabat, Ayse, "Middle East's war of fate", *NTV-MSNBC*, 5 June 2002.

Karabuda, Gunes, *Portraits from the Garden of Time*, YKY, 2001.

Karacizmeli, Ca€atay, "about film makers with Ara Guler", *Hurriyet Gosteri*, February 1990.

Karakus, Harun, "Cinema is the most serious business in the world", *Beyazperde* magazine, 4 February 1990.

Karaman, Nilay, "Slam book Ara Guler", *Cumhuriyet Dergi*, 20 August 1989.

Karatas, Aslihan A., "They came with a dream to unite churches", *Yeni Safak* newspaper, 28 November 2006.

Kaya, Dogan (Dr.), *Asik Veyse's Lifei-Art-Poems-Songs*, Istanbul, 2000.

Kayabal, Asli, "Istanbul is a poisonous jar", *Tempo* magazine, 21 April 1993.

Kayserilioglu, R. Sertac, "A tramway for Istanbul from Dersaadet", IETT History Series, Istanbul 1998.

Kemal, Mehmed, "Ara Guler and Picasso", *Gosteri* magazine, April 1981, Kemal, Yasar, "Ara's Anatolian Epic", *Adam Sanat*, No: 119, October 1995 Kemal, Yasar, "Children are people", *Cumhuriyet* newspaper, 9 September 1975.

Kemanci, Dogan, "The Grand Master of Realistic Turkish Photography Ara Guler", *Ufuklar* magazine, 6 April 1981.

Keshishian, Levon, "Armenian World", *The Armenian Observer*, 12 June 1974.

Keskin, Adnan-Kivanc, Ahmet, "amnesty to the embezzler is the legacy of Ozal", *Radikal* newspaper, 17 June 2004.

Kilimci, Sibel, "Picture of the world", *Aktuel* magazine, February 1996.

Kislali, M. Ali, "A businessman in politics", *Radikal* newspaper, 15 May 2001.

Kislali, M. Ali, "People", *Yanki* magazine, 2-8 October 1972.

Kocoglu, Sevilay, "Photograph doctor Ara Guler", *Cumhuriyet* newspaper, 8 June 2004.

Kohen, Sami, "What is expected of the Pope", *Milliyet* newspaper, 28 November 2006.

Kongar, Emre (Prof. Dr.), "The Morality of Underdevelopment (immorality)", *Cumhuriyet* newspaper, 9 July 2007.

Kongar, Emre, *From an Empire to the present day social structure in Turkey*, Remzi Kitabevi, Istanbul 1995.

Koni, Hasan (Prof. Dr.), "On the importance of the Alphabet Reform", *Ataturk Arastirma Center Magazine*, No: 21, Volume: VII, July 1991.

Korkmaz, Zeynep (Prof. Dr.), "Alphabet Reform", the text of speech made on the occasion of the 70th anniversary of the Language Revolution in Dolmabahce Palace on the 26th of September 1998.

Kucukkurt, Fatma-Yaylagul, Levent, "The Secret Heroes of Cinema:

Kuran, Aptullah (Prof. Dr.), *Mimar Sinan*, Hurriyet Vakfi Publications, Istanbul 1986.

Kurkcuoglu, S. Sabri, *The Photographer of the Century in Turkey: Ara Guler*, May 2002.

Kurtoglu, Akin, "Boshorus Bridge and IETT", *Wow Turkey*, 2 March 2005

Kutlar, Onat, "Ara Guler's Photographs", *Yeni Ortam* newspaper, 10 October 1972.

Kutlar, Onat, "Modern Marco Polo", *Cumhuriyet* newspaper, 13 June 1993.

Kutlar, Onat, "The thoughts generated by Ara and Sinan", *Milliyet Art* magazine, 1 October 1992.

Lampien, Rainer K., "Ihmisia eleman nayttamolla", *Kamera*, 11 March 1989.

Maga, Ilker, *Ara Guler/There are no memoirs without people*, YGS Publications, Istanbul 2005

Metinsoy, Murat, *Turkey in the Second World War*, Homer Kitabevi, Istanbul 2007.

Modiano, Alberto, "Istanbul, the city of vanishing colors from Ara Guler", *Tiryaki* magazine, November-December 1995.

Modiano, Alberto, "Publishing of Photographs in Turkey", *Cumhuriyet Kitap*, 23 May 1995.

Monceau, Nicolas, "Ara Guler", *Qantara*, No.: 48, Summer 2003.

Morrison, Hedda, "Jungle Journeys in Sarawak", *National Geographic Magazine*, May 1956.

Mumcu, Ugur, "Dikmener", *Cumhuriyet* newspaper, 29 April 1979.

National Intelligency Organization's History, MIT Undersecretariat, Ankara, January 2002.

Nezir, Seyit, "Ara Guler: I am writing the visual history of our revolution", *Broy*, February 1990.

Nezir, Seyyit, "While a photograph displays the world it also leaves your mark" *Hedef Saglik*, May 2000.

Nihan, Sevilay, "I am taking photographs", *EuroClub* magazine, No.: 11, September 1988.

Oktu, Leyla, "A Master: Ara Guler", *Podyum* magazine, 15 April-15 May 1993.

Okur, Hulya, "The man who opened Turkey to the world: Ara Guler", *Gaziantep Olay Haber*, 6 November 2007.

Okur, Meliha, "THY should use the Pope opportunity well", *Sabah* newspaper, 28 November 2006.

Ondes, Osman, Who ruined welfare? Denizler Kitabevi, 2006.

Ordu, Senay, "The death of Princess Leyla is no surprise", *Hurriyet* newspaper, 17 June 2001.

Otyam, Fikret, "A critique published in the French press", *Cumhuriyet* newspaper, 23 June 1972.

Otyam, Fikret, "My Child Ara", *Antalya* newspaper, 19 August 1995.

Otyam, Fikret-Guler, Ara-Peker, Orhan, "Matter of life and death", *Cumhuriyet* newspaper, 13 October 1968.

Oymen, Altan, "This event should not be forgotten", *Radikal* newspaper, 7 September 2006.

Oymen, Altan, *The Years of Change*, Dogan Kitapcilik, Istanbul, 2004.

Ozatay, Dalida, "The black andwhite witness of history", *Aksam* newspaper, 26 September 2004.

Ozden, Tuba, "Today I looked at you from the past oh Istanbul", *Aksiyon* magazine, No: 534, 28 February 2007.

Ozdogan, B. -Oguz, A., *Cinema Discourse 2006*, Bogazici University Publications, Istanbul 2007.

Ozedincik, Sinan, "A Lens opening to the World", *Fiesta* magazine, 6 March 1994.

Ozel, Tayfun, "There would be no Magnum if Capa had not lost gambling", *Ifsak Photograph and Cinema Magazine*, No: 1, May 1986.

Ozel, Zuhal (Dr.), *The presentation of reality within photograph trends*, Ege University Faculty of Communication Photography and Graphics Department, 2005.

Ozendes, Engin, "An Era has gone by like this", *Yeni Yuzyil* newspaper, 20 February 1995.

Ozendes, Engin, "Earth on their faces", *Yeni Yuzyil* newspaper, 1 February 1996.

Ozendes, Engin, "The Madman of Photography", *Yeni Yuzyil* newspaper, 15 June 1995.

Ozenen, Cigdem, "First photographs", *Kapris* magazine, June 1990.

Ozgenturk, Nebil, "50 years have gone by like this", *Sabah Pazar*, 16 July 1995.

Ozgenuturk, Nebil, *A Human being -5 Ara Guler*, Boyut Yayin Grubu.

Ozgiray, Ahmet (Prof. Dr.), "'Treatment of the Armenians in the Ottoman Empire prepared by Arnold J. Toynbee and James Bryce

Ozgurel, Avni, "Autumn and years of destruction", *Radikal* newspaper, 29 August 2004.

Ozgurel, Avni, "The death of a warrior", *Radikal* newspaper, 3 June 2001.

Ozguven, Fatih, "The Turk's test with Hollywood", *Radikal* newspaper, 30 May 2002.

Ozkaya, Sukran, *Step by Step 27th of May*, Ileri Publications, 2005.

Ozuer, Cigdem, "Celebrity photographs", *Cumhuriyet* newspaper, 13 April 1989.

Ozyurt, Ahmet, "Ara Guler", *Refo Fotograf Sanati* magazine, June 1989.

Ozyurt, Olkan, "Ara's censorized film", *Radikal* newspaper, 6 August 2001.

Ozyurt, Olkan, "Is it possible to put a price on Ara Guler?", *Radikal* newspaper, 23 March 2004.

Ozyurt, Olkan, "There are more important things than art", *Radikal* newspaper, 22 January 2001.

Peksen, Yalcin, "Guler's Creative Americans", *Cumhuriyet* newspaper, 19 April 1975.

Perincek, Kiraz, "Frames from great humanity", *Aydinlik* magazine, 22 February 2004.

Pulur, Hasan, "'although there is no magical ancestorship there is a race related ancestorship", *Milliyet* newspaper, 22 November 2007.

Pulur, Hasan, "we lived through 6-7 September", *Milliyet* newspaper 7-8 September 2005.

Ramazanoglu, Gulseren, "Aphrodisias", *Hilton Turkey Magazine*, No: 105, 1996.

Redfern, Nick, *Strange Secrets: Real Government Files on the Unknown*, Paraview Pocket Books, May 2003.

Rifat, Samih, "Ara Guler and 'Allah'", *Yeni Dusun* magazine, July 1988.

Rifat, Samih, "Do you know Ara Guler well?", *Cumhuriyet* newspaper, 20 February 1990.

Rifat, Samih, "The mountain of Nemrut's Gods", *Turizmde Focus*, January 1986.

Rifat, Samih, Between Black and White, YKY, September 2002.

Rifat, Samih, *To my beloved friend Ara*, YKY, December 2000.

Roman, Gul Azer, "I see the world as a rectangle", *Milliyet* newspaper, 30 January 1986.

Russel, John, "Art: 'The Age of Sultan Suleyman', *The New York Times*, 26 January 1987.

Sahin, Onder, "The Great Turkish Entrepreneur Nuri Demirag", *UTED* magazine, August 2006.

Saka, Fusun, "Photographs are formed by frozen moments of life", *Ekonomik Bulten*, July 1990.

Sandys, Celia, *Chasing Churchill: The Travels of Winston Churchill*, Carroll & Graf, September 2004.

Sarioz, Perihan, *Istanbul Paris Istanbul*, Dogan Kitapcilik, Istanbul 2000. Saris, Mayda, "The story of half a century", *Agos* newspaper, 7 January 2005.

Saris, Mayda, *Your memories leave a mark*, Aras Yayincilik, Istanbul October 2007.

Sazak, Derya, "This man", *Milliyet* newspaper, 15 April 2006.

Scognamillo, Giovanni, *Cinema in adde-i Kebir*, Metis Publications, July 1991.

Senden, Fatma, "Undestanding Boz Mehmet", *Urun* magazine, No. 7, September-October 2000.

Sener, Nedim, *Uzanlar: The dissolution of an empire of fear*, Guncel Yayincilik, Istanbul, March 2004.

Seni, Nora, *If I forget you Istanbul*, Kitap Yayinevi, February 2008.

Senturk, Ozlem, "Stage experience in the audience seat", *Hurriyet* newspaper, 21 February 1999.

Sezer, Sennur, "Literature is the work of a handful of beautiful people", *Evrensel* newspaper, 11 June 1995.

Sezer, Sennur, "The lens and human drama", *Cumhuriyet* newspaper, 10 October 1972.

Sharma, Shiv, "Photos tinged with bring artist fame", *Saudi Gazete*, 30 May 1976.

Silivri, Kerim (Prof. Dr.), "About the Academy fire of 1 April 1948", *SanatCevresi*, No.: 53, March 1983.

Simon, Mark, "Ara Guler: Reality, History and Lost Istanbul", *Photo District News*, August 1995.

Sipahioglu, Goksin, "The first Turkish journalist in Picasso's house", *Yeni Gazete*, 20 June 1971.

Smith, Helena, "Passionate and previously unseen love letter among mementoes of golden Greek", *The Guardian*, 6 October 2006.

Sol Gunluk Siyasi Gazete, 9 October 2006.

Sonar, Suavi, "The last nudes in Cannes", *Hayat* magazine, 7 June 1957, No.: 35.

Sonmez, Tekin, "Suleyman the Lawmaker's Era in America", *Gosteri* magazine, June 1987.

Sonok, Hakan, "Ara Guler's film makers", *Video Haber*, May 1989.

Sora, Steven, *Relics from Noah's Ark to the Shroud of Turin*, Wiley, January 2005.

Soysal, Mumtaz, "Puzzle", *Milliyet* newspaper, 9 May 1984.

Suter, Sakir, "Discount for Raki", *Aksam* newspaper, 27 October 2003.

Tahiroglu, Gulcin, "Man of the next century Ishak Alaton", *Platin* magazine, February 2007.

Tahsin, Orhan-Guler, Ara, "Bladeless Surgery", *Tercuman* newspaper, 13 February 1978.

Tahsin, Orhan-Guler, Ara, "Hot Asia", *Tercuman* newspaper, 12 April 1978.

Tamer, Ulku, "He projected his youth into his magazine", *Sabah* newspaper, 7 May 2007.

Taner, Haldun, *Fazilet Pharmacy*, Bilgi Yayinevi, October 1994.

Tanju, Sadun, "Let us love life", *Cumhuriyet* newspaper, 21 April 1975.

Tanju, Sadun, "The death of a hero", *Cumhuriyet* newspaper, 12 July 1975.

Tanju, Sadun-Guler, Ara, "A man like Miho", *Hurriyet* newspaper, 1 October 1978.

Tansug, Sezer, "The 150th anniversary of photography", *Vizon* magazine, May 1989.

Tasdemirci, Ersoy, "Minority School and Foreign Schools in the History of Turkish Education", *Erciyes University Social Sciences* magazine, No.: 10, 2001.

Taskent, Kazim, *The days of my life*, Binbirdirek Matbaacilik, Istanbul 1980.

Taspinar, Suat, "Live like Vera, die likeVera", *Radikal* newspaper, 10 June 2003.

Tayanc, Turkan, "Master of Lecia", *Dateline Turkey*, 6 October 1984.

The Projectionists", *New Trends in Turkish Film Studies, Paper presented at Conference*, Bahcesehir University,

1 June 2003.

Tolgay, Ahmet, "The truth about EOKA", *Kibris* newspaper, 1 April 2006.

Topuz, Hifzi, *Fikret Mualla Memoirs, Pictures, Letters*, Everest Publications, Istanbul 2005.

Toynbee, Arnold Joseph, "Turkey: A Past and a Future", *Hodder & Stoughton*, 1917.

Tuna, Nimet, "...and man created photography", *Somut*, 8 April 1983.

Tuncer, Baran, "we sent Osman Okyar off", *Radikal* newspaper, 21 April 2002.

Turgut, Seda, "Doyen of documentary photographs", *Aksam* newspaper, 25 January 2004.

Turker, Suat, "The art of photography in Turkey", *Milliyet Sanat* magazine, 6 October 1972.

Turkoz, Meltem, "Harvesting images accumulating history", *Turkish Daily News*, 7 August 1992.

Tweedie, Neil-Day, Peter, "Envoy's singing valet was Nazi spy", *The Daily Telegraph*, 22 May 2003.

Ucok, Yildiz, "A Festival of News photographs", *Cumhuriyet* newspaper, 13 December 1988.

Uluc, Dogan, "Ara Guler's film Yavuz on US TV", *Hurriyet* newspaper, 16 November 1981.

Uluc, Dogan, "The search for Ataturk", *Hurriyet* newspaper, 27 July 1998.

Unlu, Cemal, In time *-phonograph-Gramophone-gramophone records*, Pan Yayincilik, Istanbul 2004.

Unsal, Artun, *Talking about Beyoglu in Beyoglu, Tuesday Meetings 2000- 2001*, YKY, Istanbul 2002.

Ural, Murat, "The second bullet is for the journalist", *Cumhuriyet Dergi*, 25 February 1996.

Uras, Gungor, "Taskent, Sahenk, Karamehmet and now the 'Koc's'", *Milliyet* newspaper, 10 May 2005.

Usman, Erkin, "Turkey's Cankaya Pains", *Yeni Asir* newspaper, 25 October 2006.

Ustun, Nevzat, "6 questions for Ara Guler", *Sozcu* magazine, 23 December 1960.

Uyanik, M. Mesut, *80 Year Chronology of the Republic of Turkey*, Anadolu Agency Publications, Ankara 2003.

Whitman, Alden, "Henry R. Luce, Creator of Time-Life Magazine Empire", *The New York Times*, 1 March 1967.

Williams, Tennessee, *Notebooks*, Yale University Press, January 2007.

Wires, Richard, *The Cicero Spy Affair*, Praeger, Connecticut 1999.

Yalcin, Selahattin, "The Promoters of Turkey", *Peron Magazin*, March 1988.

Yalcin, Soner, "An extra-ordinary life which ended in a poorhouse in France", *Hurriyet*, 22 July 2007.

Yanki magazine, 23 May 1976.

Yazan, Nihal, "a photograph does not lie", *VIP* magazine, No.: 3, 2003.

Yazgan, Ercan, "I look at everything from a rectangle", *Cumhuriyet* Newspaper, 6 October 1988.

Yeditepe magazine, No.: 15, 6-31 December 1959.

Yegen, Mehmet Rifat, "taking a saw to the only live witness of the Platanus incident", *Zaman-Pazar*, No.: 56, 23 December 2007.

Yetkin, Cetin, *Political Power against Art*, Bilgi Yayinevi, 1970.

Yilmaz, Ihsan, "100 faces of our literature from the lens of the master", *Hurriyet* newspaper, 29 November 2002.

Yilmaz, Serpil, "Ara Guler won from Bentley", *Milliyet* newspaper, 1 January 2004.

Yuksek, Derya, "We write visual history", *Buyuk Kulup* magazine, May-June 2004.

Yurdalan, Ozcan, *Documentary Photograph and Photo-interview*, Agora Kitapligi, 2007.

Zaim, Kazim, "Discourse with master Ara Guler", *Gosteri* magazine, December 1994.

Index

Abasiyanik, Sait Faik 32, 33
Aciksoz, Isfendiyar 54
Adams, Ansel 10, 131
Adil, Fikret 30, 31, 42, 61, 113
Adivar, Halide Edip 45
Agaoglu, Ahmet 151, 171
Ailey, Alvin 131
Akcan, Nihat 30
Akdogan, Lutfu 70,
Akerson, Tanju 154
Akin, Necdet 141
Akinli, Hamit 26
Akkan, Oguz 63, 148-150
Aksoy, Orhan 24
Akurgal, Ekrem 113, 151
Akyol, Mete 101
Albayrak, Cahit 42
Albee, Edward 131
Alkis, Ayhan 160
Altan, Cetin 104-105
Amiryan, Hacik Bedros 27
Andak, Selmi 162
Anday, Melih Cevdet 30
Angles, Fernande 62
Anli, Hakli 61
Arad, Agop 34, 39
Arafat, Yaser 110
Aragon, Louis 152-153
Araz, Nezihe 44-45,166
Arbas, Avni 61, 152
Arit, Fikret 57, 82
Artemel, Talat 25
Askin, Firuz 37, 55
Askin, Samim 37
Atalay, Sahap 70
Ataturk, Mustafa Kemal 13, 17
Atay, Falih Rifki 30
Ay, Ismet 26, 141
Aybar, Mehmet Ali 100
Aygun, Ali Ihsan 27
Ayla, Safiye 14, 23
Aysu, Emre 161

Aytac, Kadri 54
Aytmatov, Cengiz 149
Ayyildiz, Mehmet 92
Babey, Maurice 115,
Barutcuoglu, Arslan 47
Batur, Sabahattin 113
Bayar, Celal 48
Bayhan, Mehmet 160-161
Bazna, Ilyas (Cicero) 87-89
Bedii Faik 35
Bener, Vus'at O. 27
Benk, Adnan 30
Berk, Nurullah 122
Berman, Ahmet 54
Berry, Ian 156
Beukert, Gunther 60
Beyatli, Yahya Kemal 44
Bilginer, Recep 35,148, 162
Biro, Pierre 58
Birsel, Salah 30, 142
Bitran, Albert 161
Blance, Juan 144
Bondarchuk, Sergey 103,
Bozok, Husamettin 30- 31, 33-34,
42, 113
Brown, Lester 131
Buñuel, Luis 124
Butak, Behzat 25, 89
Butto, Zulfikar Ali 136
Buyrukcu, Muzaffer 30
Buyukalp, Orhan 64
Caglayangil, Ihsan Sabri 94,109
Calapala, Rakim 44
Callas, Maria 74
Camli, Ibrahim 79, 80, 136
Cansever, Edip 30
Capa, Robert 31, 86, 87,
CartieBresson, Henri 87, 133, 161-
162, 169, 178,
Cayligil, Sadan 67
Cem, Ismail 21
Cemal Pasa, Ahmed 40, 82

Cemal, Hasan 40
Cemal, Kamran 47
Cemal, Mehmet 40, 46-47, 64
Cetinkaya, Ali 143, 154
Chagall, Bella 119,121-122,125
Chagall, Marc 122
Chaplin, Charlie 107, 168,167-168
Chaplin, Oona 107
Churchill, Winston 74,
Ciller, Tansu 167
Cimcoz, Adalet 23, 49
Civaoglu, Guneri 144
Cizgen, Gultekin 152, 178
Cocteau, Jean 52
Copland, Aaron 131
Cosar, Omer Sami 64
Cumali, Necati 113
Cunningham, Imogen 131, 134
Da Vinci, Leonardo 156
Daglarca, Fazil Husnu 142
Dali, Gala 122,124
Dali, Salvador 122-127, 167
Dalli, Erol 77
De Maupassant, Guy 184
De Sica, Vittorio 52
Demir, Nurettin 37
Demirag, Nuri 143
Demirel, Suleyman 148, 154-155, 167, 171
Demirkent, Nezih 150
Derderyan, Maryam 13
Derderyan, Migirdic 13, 15-16
Dino, Abidin 39, 61,114
Dirimlili, Basri 54
Doksat, Recep 114
Dora, Aysegul 109-110
Doyuran, Rustem 67
Dufy, Raoul 153
Durupinar, Ilhan 71
Ecevit, Bulent 90,101,146,148,167
Economopoulos, Nikos 181
Eczacibasi, Nejat 48
Eczacibasi, Sakir 162
Eczacibasi, Suleyman Ferit 13, 16
Eden, Anthony 46

Einstein, Albert 107-108, 171, 192
Emeksiz, Turan 79
Ercins, Ergun 54
Erduran, Refik 39
Ergin, Melih 113
Erhat, Azra 30
Erim, Kenan 67
Erkilic, Veysel 56
Ertan, Mustafa 54
Ertegun, Ahmet 142
Ertugrul, Muhsin 21, 25-26
Eryavuz, Ihsan 140
Es, Hikmet Feridun 44-46, 72, 82-83
Esendal, Memduh Sevket 27
Eser, Bedri 37
Evliyagil, Sevket 35
Evren, Kenan 150, 167
Eyuboglu, Bedri Rahmi 61
Eyuboglu, Sabahattin 27, 31, 32, 56, 58, 85
Fatih Sultan Mehmet 94, 191
Faulkner, William 138
Fazli, Berc 26
Feonova, Vera Borisovna 128
Feray, Ayfer 42
Fikret Mualla 61-63
Filmerides, Joachim 23
Fonda, Jane 135
Fox, James A. 10, 161
Franco, Fernando 21
Frères, Abdullah 168
Galbraith, John Kenneth 131,
Gandhi, Mahatma 85
Garbo, Greta 74
Gardner, John 131
Geghetsik, Ara 13
Gelenbevi, Baha 39
Genghis Khan 171
Geseryan, Aram 24
Gezmis, Deniz 111
Gherbrandt, Alain 53, 56
Gicirli, Ali 37
Gilka, Bob 150
Ginsberg, Irwin Allen 135

Giz, Bulent 44
Giz, Selahattin 31
Gluck, Felix 98
Goebbels, Joseph 17, 18
Gogus, Ali Ihsan 101
Gokay, Fahrettin Kerim 45
Gokce, Enver 39
Gorgus, Namik 31
Goya, Francisco 26
Grantz, Norman 117
Griffiths, Philip Jones 69
Guler, Dacat 21, 97
Guler, Suna (Taskiran) 162, 1
Guler, Verjin 14-15, 31, 139, 147-148, 162
Guleryuz, Mehmet 162
Gulsum, Ummu 23
Gumuspala, Ragip 72
Guner, Semsi 141
Guney, Eflatun Cem 30
Guntekin, Resat Nuri 25
Gunver, Semih 112
Gunyol, Vedat 45
Gurmen, Huseyin Kemal 25,
Gursel, Cemal 82
Gurzap, Resit 25
Guvemli, Zahir 30
Guvener, Halit 160
Haas, Ernst 86
Hall, Norman 69
Hancerlioglu, Orhan 27
Hansoy, Ferit 83
Has, Mehmet Ali 54
Hekimoglu, Muserref 44
Hemingway, Ernest 138, 152
Hilelson, John 69
Hill, George Roy 131
Hitchcock, Alfred 131
Hitler, Adolf 17-19, 88,158
Hizlan, Dogan 162
Hoffer, Eric 131-132
Hoffman, Dustin 131
Hope, Bob 131, 133
Ilhan, Attila 113
Ilhan, Nihat 90

Ilicak, Kemal 98, 144
Ilicak, Nazli 98
Inonu, Ismet
19, 26,79,81,83,101,141,143,146
Ionesco, Eugene 40
Ipekci, Abdi 53, 80, 97
Ipekci, Ihsan 21, 27, 39
Isin, Cemal 37
Johnson, Lyndon B. 90
Kabaagacli, Cevat Sakir 112-113
Kan, Suna 160
Kanik, Orhan Veli 27, 32-34, 43,
Karabuda, Gunes 73, 103,
Karaca, Cem 23
Karaca, Mehmet 23
Karaca, Muammer 25
Karaca, Osman 30
Karakas, Fethi 34
Karakurt, Ali 64-65
Karaosmanoglu, Yakup Kadri 34, 35
Karasu, Bilge 70
Karay, Refik Halid 27, 30
Kaygun, Sahin 140, 186
Kazan, Elia 89-90, 107
Keen, Peter 73
Kemal Tahir 37-38
Kennedy, John Fitzgerald 49, 74, 108
Kenter, Yildiz 24
Kertesz, Andre 131
Khachaturian, Aram Ilyich 127-128
Khalid, Leyla 110
King Hussein 78
Kiray, Mubeccel 42
Kisakurek, Necip Fazil 25
Klein, William 69
Knatchbull-Hugessen, Hudge 88
Koc, Caroline 177
Koc, Vehbi 23
Kocagoz, Samim 27, 30, 42, 113
Kocunyan, Ara 29
Kocyigit, Samet 40
Kohen, Ginesta 123,
Kologlu, Dogan 43
Kologlu, Orhan 47 111

Kondakciyan, Henry 110
Korur, Ahmet Salih 45
Koruturk, Emel 63
Koruturk, Fahri 63, 142 150
Koudelka, Joseph 87, 174, 179
Kucukandonyadis, Lefter 54
Kucuksorgunlu, Nejat 54
Kuran, Aptullah 154
Kurkciyan, Karabat 15
Kuturman, Perihan 90, 109, 131, 134
Lakaz, Andrea 53
Langlois, Henry 141
Lattuada, Alberto 52, 74
Libi, John 70-71, 76
London, Jack 26
Loren, Sophia 73-74
Luce, Claire Booth 49
Luce, Henry 49, 51, 86
Lumet, Sidney, 131
Lupino, Ida 131
Lurchat, Jean 153
Mahmut Ekrem 26
Mankiewicz, Joseph 88
Mann, Herbie 131
Mann, Thomas 189
Marais, Jean 52
Marchinez, Jacqueline 105
Marchinez, Romeo 83, 85, 106, 135
Mason, James 87
Massora, Giovanni 69
Matisse, Henri 161
McCarthy, Joseph Raymond 39, 89, 107, 111
Mehmed Kemal 34, 64
Menderes, Adnan 36, 43, 45, 48, 51, 72, 79, 82, 167
Mercury, Melina 153
Michelangelo 156
Miller, Arthur 111, 131
Mimar Sinan 154-156, 176,
Mimaroglu, Ilhan 141
Minnelli, Liza 135
Minnelli, Vincente 131, 135

Miricanyan, Sinork Migirdic Amira 13
Monroe, Marilyn 74
Montanes, Mariano Miguel 116, 118
Monti, Paolo 105
Moore, John Peter 123,
Morali, Mahmut 23
Moravia, Alberto 52
Moyzisch, Ludwig Carl 87
Mumcu, Erkan 161
Mumcu, Ugur 10
Muvahhit, Bedia 25, 147
Nachtwey, James 183
Nannen, Henry 60
Nayir, Yasar Nabi 30
Nazim Hikmet 25, 27, 37, 39, 83, 128
Nesin, Aziz 48, 63, 153
Nevelson, Louise 131
Neville, Bob 49, 50, 88
Niépce, Janine 69
O'Neill, Eugene 26, 107
Ofluoglu, Mucap 26
Okmen, Necdet 27
Oktay, Metin, 54
Okyar, Fethi 109
Okyar, Osman 101
Olgac, Meftun 40, 68
Olson, Lennart 69
Onar, Siddik Sami 37
Onassis, (Kennedy) Jacqueline 105, 108
Onassis, Aristotle 74,
Orberk, Teoman 41
Orbito, Alex 144
Orhan, Kemal (Ogutcu, Mehmet Rasit) 27, 30, 34-35, 46,
Osman, Hamdi 26, 57
Otyam, Fikret 101-103, 137
Ozal, Semra 154-155,
Ozal, Turgut 114 154,
Ozbayrak, Cetin 139
Ozbayrak, Nazan 139
Ozel, Mehmet 63
Ozer, Kemal 30

Ozgen, Abdulkadir 29
Ozkocak, Vasfiye 37, 162
Oztekin, Mukadder 93
Ozyalciner, Adnan 30
Parmelin, Helene 114
Passos, John Dos 138
Patton, George S. 131
Pehlevi, Farah 110
Pehlevi, Leyla 110
Pehlevi, Shah Riza 109,
Peker, Orhan 101, 103, 182
Pferschy, Othmar 193
Picasso, Claude 115
Picasso, Pablo 107
Pignon, Edouard 114,
Pilevneli, Mustafa 179
Pirinccioglu, Inci 108
Polda, Yilmaz 53
Ponti, Carlo 73
Pope VI. Paul 93-94
Portakal, Rafi 177
Queen Zeyn 78
Rado, Sevket 44, 45, 51, 59, 67, 71,
82, 83,181
Ray, Man 105
Read, Herbert 67
Reagan, Ronald 160
Regu, Sukru Enis 44
Rembrandt 158
Renoir, Pierre Auguste 117
Riboud, Marc 69, 85, 92, 178, 183
Rifat, Oktay 30
Robertson, James 169
Rodger, George 87
Rodgers, Richard 131
Roiter, Fulvio 105
Ruspoli, Mario 115
Russell, Bertrand 98-101, 164
Sabanci, Sakip 154
Sadak, Necmettin 30
Sahenk, Hilmi 44
Sahin, Adurjan 14, 153
Sahin, Ozkan 44
Sahiyan, Araksi 14
Sahiyan, Kirkor 14

Sahiyan, Mayda 24
Sahiyan, Sona 16, 24
Salgado, Sebastiao 87, 159
Salk, Jonas 131
Salti, Judas 28
Samuelson, Paul 131
Santi, Rafaello 26
Sarioz, Perihan (Guler) 129-130
Saroyan, William 134, 137-138
Sartre, Jean Paul 168,
Satiroglu, Veysel (Âsik) 56 -57
Schlesinger, Arthur 131, 132
Senyuksel, Hasan 11, 86, 162
Serefhanoglu Sozen, Mujgan 161
Seren, Turgay 54
Seymour, David 87
Sezgin, Mukadder 63, 112
Simavi, Sedat 30, 35, 37
Sipahioglu, Goksin 46, 95, 108
Siyavusgil, Sabri Esat 30
Skira, Albert 115-116
Smith, Eugene 175, 188
Sogomanyan, Gomidas 13, 95
Sonar, Suavi 30, 44, 52
Sonku, Cahide 23
Spock, Benjamin 131
Stalin, Josef 149
Stark, Freya 105
Steinbeck, John 26, 138
Steinem, Gloria 131
Stelter, Alfred 144
Stephanopoulos, Stephanos 46
Stevens, George 131
Stieglitz, Alfred 10
Stockler, Heinich 84
Stone, Edward Durell 131
Strand, Paul 10
Su, Ruhi 39, 43
Suleymanov, Olcay 148
Sulker, Kemal 34
Sultan Suleyman 154, 155, 171
Sunay, Cevdet 94
Surenkok, Mehmet 45
Sureya, Cemal 30
Sururi, Gulriz 26

Tabanlioglu, Hayati 111
Tahsin, Orhan 75, 76,144
Talal, Emir 78
Taner, Haldun 182
Tanpinar, Ahmet Hamdi 27
Tansel, Irfan 90
Tarus, Ilhan 30
Taskent, Dogan 23, 43, 47
Taskent, Kazim 43-45, 51, 82
Taskiran, Nimet 151
Taskiran, Suna 151
Taskiran, Tezer 151
Tayfur, Ferdi 23
Tecer, Ahmet Kutsi 182,205
Tedu, Suavi 30, 42
Topel, Cengiz 90
Tor, Vedat Nedim 25, 30, 43, 44, 69
Torehan, Habip Edip 35, 35, 63
Tornatore, Giuseppe 23
Toynbee, Arnold 8,101,206
Tozan, Salih 34
Tuglaci, Pars 38
Tunc, Yalman 30
Turan, Selim 61
Turkali, Vedat 39
Turkes, Alparslan 79
Uluc, Dogan 89
Ulunay, Refii Cevat 30
Umar, Leyla 132

Updike, John 131
Ustaoglu, Yesim 178
Ustun, Nevzat 30, 42, 49, 97
Utrillo, Maurice 117
Vala Nurettin 30
Van Beethoven, Ludwig 187
Vandivert, William 87
Varjabedyan, Nerses 21
Vehbi, Yusuf 23
Velazquez, Diego 26
Venturi, Lauro 119
Von Braun, Verhner 131
Von Papen, Franz 19
Wayne, John 74
Welles, Orson 52, 141
Weston, Edward 10
Wilde, Oscar 185
Wilkins, Roy 131,
Williams, Tennessee 41-43,133-134
Wise, Robert 131
Wissenbach, Walter 69
Wolgang Amadeus, Mozart 187
Wyeth, Andrew 131
Yakup Cemil 68
Yalcin, Huseyin Cahit 30, 34
Yamasaki, Minoru 131
Yasar Kemal 30, 137, 139, 184
Yesari, Afif 44

Printed in Poland
by Amazon Fulfillment
Poland Sp. z o.o., Wrocław

35790141R00125